STARS AND SHADOWS

STARS AND SHADOWS

*THE POLITICS OF INTERRACIAL
FRIENDSHIP FROM JEFFERSON
TO OBAMA*

SALADIN AMBAR

OXFORD
UNIVERSITY PRESS

Oxford University Press is a department of the University of Oxford. It furthers
the University's objective of excellence in research, scholarship, and education
by publishing worldwide. Oxford is a registered trade mark of Oxford University
Press in the UK and certain other countries.

Published in the United States of America by Oxford University Press
198 Madison Avenue, New York, NY 10016, United States of America.

CIP data is on file at the Library of Congress

ISBN 978–0–19–762199–8

DOI: 10.1093/oso/9780197621998.001.0001

1 3 5 7 9 8 6 4 2

Printed by LSC Communications, United States of America

For my friends.

We put out the camp fire at the cavern the first thing, and didn't show a candle outside after that.

I took the canoe out from shore a little piece and took a look, but if there was a boat around I couldn't see it, for stars and shadows ain't good to see by.
—MARK TWAIN, *The Adventures of Huckleberry Finn*

CONTENTS

Introduction

Tea and Cigars: The Case for Friendship

———

IN THE SUMMER of 1998, I moved from Astoria, Queens, to Plainsboro, New Jersey. It was my first time living in anything approaching a suburb. All of the apartment complexes were named with great intentionality, lest I forget that was the case: Fox Run, Deer Creek, Quail Ridge, Hunters Glen. I remember going out for a run in a nearby trail and nearly having a heart attack after what I thought was a rat had crossed my path. It was a rabbit.

It was that kind of place. My neighbors would talk to me in passing, and I got to know a few of them in the most superficial way. There was the Indian couple next door. The friendly, cute girl who would catch a smoke on her second-floor balcony. A tall, lanky, former professional basketball player, who, for the sake of anonymity, I will call Paul. Paul was an older black man who grew up in the South and was now working at one of the nearby high schools. He had two Cadillacs, neither of which ever worked at the same time. He was always outside in the lot, two cars, two hoods up, figuring out what to do.

I noticed that Paul had a friend, an older white guy I'd see him hanging with—they'd stand there talking, laughing. This fellow—I'll call him Peter—was always in a Mercedes, with the top down, golf clubs in the back. He was retired. I seem to remember a blonde woman with him on occasion. He liked to wear hats.

One Saturday morning—I think I was in a stupor from overeating and watching college football—I heard a knock on my door. It was Paul.

"Hey, Din, can you help out, man, you busy?"

"Sure, Paul, what's up?"

"It's Peter, man. He's tried to hurt himself. He's upstairs."

"Sure, give me a second."

I had no idea what to make of what was going on, but I threw on some sweatpants and walked upstairs behind Paul, who was in quite a hurry. I remember being led into the apartment and to a bedroom in the back. Sure enough, there was Peter, sitting upright in bed, wearing a white tee shirt. He looked alert and just as calm as you might expect of someone at home on a Saturday. Then I looked more carefully.

There was a black object protruding from Peter's chest. And that black object was surrounded by what was a perfect circle of red blood. I looked again, and could see that the object was a kitchen knife, the small kind with a grooved wooden handle. Thankfully, I didn't pass out. I walked over to Peter.

"Peter, I see you've tried to hurt yourself. Are you OK?"

"Yeah, I'm OK. It was stupid of me."

I had no medical training whatsoever, and offered what I could.

"Peter, do you mind if I pray for you?"

"No, not at all."

I prayed for Peter. Then Paul and I waited for the paramedics to arrive. I don't recall much after that—but I did run into Paul a few weeks later. In the lot. Two Cadillacs, two hoods up.

"Hey, man, how's Peter? Is he alright?"

"Yeah, man, thank God, he's going to be OK. He was depressed. Just got divorced. Lost a lot of money. He's been real sad."

I have been haunted by this story for years, and it's one I've shared with my students on numerous occasions. After that day, I've never quite looked at myself or the world the same. Here was a man, he lived right upstairs from me. I knew next to nothing about him. As far as I was concerned, he was a rich white guy cruising around playing golf and having the time of his life. I had no connection to him whatsoever. And all I knew of Paul was mostly superficial. Same for the cigarette girl on the porch. The Indian couple next door—I went over once for a Diwali celebration. Otherwise, I was clueless.

It occurred to me that in my self-absorbed quest to "do something with my life," I had taken for granted, what's the word? *People.* I had very little sense of connectivity to my neighbors, and here I was teaching politics and history to my students. I was so self-assured about all I knew about the country, its past, and its troubles—but I was utterly oblivious to the pains, heartaches, and lives of those who lived, ate, breathed, and slept around me. Somehow, I began to understand this not only as a personal failing but truly one with democratic implications. I think this book began, in its own way, in that bedroom in 1998, standing in front of a man, a knife, and a little circle of blood.

The great black scholar and activist W. E. B. Du Bois had something important to say about all of this, and I'm not sure we've taken him seriously. I'd like to do that in this book. Here is what Du Bois wrote in 1903 in his classic work, *The Souls of Black Folk*:

> In a world where it means so much to take a man by the hand and sit beside him, to look frankly into his eyes and feel his heart beating with red blood; in a world where a social cigar or a cup of tea together means more than legislative halls and magazine articles and speeches,—one can imagine the consequences of the almost utter absence of social amenities between estranged races, whose separation extends even to parks and streetcars.[1]

Was this merely a rhetorical flourish? Perhaps Du Bois was emphasizing just how separated blacks and whites were in Jim Crow America. And even if true one hundred and twenty years ago, surely cigars and teas can't mean more than "legislative halls" today. Danielle S. Allen put it this way in her powerful work on race and citizenship in America: "Is interracial distrust in fact a political problem, as opposed to, say, simply an embarrassment? The answer is clearly yes."[2]

The value of friendship as a fundamental quality of representative government can be traced as far back as the Greeks, up until the Enlightenment era, where revolutionary France placed "fraternité" on par with liberté and egalité. As Wilson Carey McWilliams wrote in his magisterial work, *The Idea of Fraternity in America*, "Greek philosophy saw fraternity as a necessity of life and politics. Life might be seen as a hierarchy of fraternities—the fraternity of blood yielding to that of association, which in turn yielded to that of the city."[3] The movement from Greek, to Christian *fraternitas* (the brotherhood and sisterhood of faith), to fraternité involved secularizing the idea of fraternity and "binding it to the calls for emancipation."[4]

The crucial distinction for the United States has been its size and diversity, twin obsessions of the founders. Where the Greek poleis and their more modern counterparts, the Italian city-states, shared in a republican vision for political rule, they were small, largely homogenous polities. Even the Roman republic, the principal guiding light for the early American experiment in self-government, dissolved into empire, and then anarchy. James Madison presumed that the expansiveness of America's territory would actually serve as an advantage for national unity, as opportunities for faction to work its mischief would be countermanded by the sheer multitude of differences, along with a compound federal form of government. All of this was made possible, though unmentioned in the Constitution, by the presumption of chattel slavery and the exclusion of Native Americans from political life. Whiteness, above all, was the bonding ingredient to the foundation of American citizenship.

Even one of the earliest and noblest examples of American democratic virtue, George Washington's Farewell Address, is tinged with the presumption of racial homogeneity as a prerequisite of national unity. "With slight shades of difference," he wrote, "you share the same religion, manners, habits, and political principles." While perhaps an exaggeration even then, that is certainly no longer the case. My little Central New Jersey apartment complex alone had such a dizzying array of differences that Washington would have been utterly stupefied. So, no, we don't share the same religion, manners, habits—and as recent events in American politics have shown—we barely share the same political principles. So, what way forward?

For McWilliams, the path to enlightened democratic citizenship was rooted in a local, communitarian vision of people who were bound neither by the burdens of a large centralized state, nor an impersonal slavishness to large corporations. His scholarly work and teaching were rooted in an "antifederalist" disposition, one directed toward deep participatory connectivity to one's neighbors and local institutions. Still, he harbored real doubts—doubts beyond those presented by race alone—that America was up to the task. "As always," he wrote, "the danger of the rebellions of the excluded and the fraternity of the embattled is that victory may be won—that men may create a place for themselves within the existing order without changing it, especially a nook of private gratification which helps conceal the knowledge of public indignity."[5] For McWilliams, the ironic conclusion was that fraternity had to be nationalized in a society whose very ethos of nationalized politics was anathema to his local sensibilities and sense of liberty located in community. "Under modern conditions," McWilliams concluded, "general political fraternity is impossible."[6]

While marginalized peoples have always needed space to be themselves and to create a world devoid of other-oriented measurements of self-worth, such acts, however revolutionary, don't exactly "begin the world over again," to use the language of Thomas Paine's *Common Sense*. Friendship in this sense is a refuge, but quite limited—particularly in a multiracial state premised upon white supremacy. If friendship and democracy are interwoven features of a good and just society, then democracy reserved for whites alone, with exclusive forms of friendship permitted among nonwhites (whether by choice or not), are reinforcing impediments to achieving this longed-for state. McWilliams's pessimism on this front echoes that of many Black Nationalists, who've deduced that the "modern conditions" McWilliams refers to are less modern than they are historic and endemic features of western civilization's obsession with whiteness.

Not all share in this pessimism. Danielle S. Allen's work, *Talking to Strangers: Anxieties of Citizenship since Brown v. Board of Education* (2004), provides a pathway out of democratic and fraternal forms of isolation. With the lessons of the civil rights movement as her historic guide, and Ralph Ellison's *Invisible Man* as an inspiration, Allen eloquently argues that barrier crossing among strangers is a fundamental prerequisite for rebuilding multiracial democracy.

Through interaction, even as strangers, citizens draw each other into networks of mutual responsibility. Engage a stranger in conversation

as a political friend and, if one gets a like return, one has gained a
pair of watchful eyes to increase the safety of the space one occupies.
Engage a stranger in conversation across a racial, ethnic, or class divide and one gets not only an extra pair of eyes but also an ability to
see and understand parts of the world that are to oneself invisible.
Real knowledge of what's outside one's garden cures fear, but only
by talking to strangers can we come by such knowledge. Wisdom
about the world we currently inhabit generally can't be gotten from
books, because they can't be written, or read, fast enough. Strangers
are the best source.[7]

Allen's vision is an indictment—but also an invitation—to citizens
like me, who have failed in the past to get to know their neighbors
well enough to identify their struggles across racial lines. For Allen, the
highest form of political rhetoric is produced in those very parking lots,
courtyards, and apartment complexes so many of us presume to be sites
foreign to democratic empowerment.

As someone who works in the field of American Political Development
(APD), I've written this book as an attempt to illustrate what this command to "talk to strangers" has looked like throughout American history. Indeed, the talismans of such experiences are steeped in these
forms of engagement, albeit between public figures. Benjamin Banneker
and Thomas Jefferson's exchange of letters; Frederick Douglass and
Abraham Lincoln's three White House meetings; even the story of Ella
Fitzgerald and Marilyn Monroe's socializing at the Mocambo Club—
these are all representative of attempts to disturb the prevailing notion of the time, namely that interracial friendship was, and ought to
be, discouraged, given the dictates of America's racialized democratic
order. As political scientists Desmond King and Rogers Smith have
invoked the highly salient model of "racial orders" to bring structure to
understanding American political history, so too, in *Stars and Shadows*,
do I express the history of racial fraternity as time marked by *closed*, *indeterminate*, and, ultimately, *open* periods where interracial friendship
may be expressed by political and cultural elites.[8] These fraternal racial
orders provide but another way of thinking about the role of political
and cultural leaders in shaping democratic discourse and possibilities

along racial lines, and they also are a window into why certain efforts have been more successful than others.

Allen is right: talking to strangers matters. While her work focuses on this dimension of American citizenship since 1954, my ten case studies span the entirety of American history. These are not of course, *the* definitive examples of the shortcomings and successes of multiracial democracy, but they are, I think, significant markers for gauging the transitions from one form of democratic society to something greater and, ultimately, more inclusive. How this has happened—the nuances of performing for the public what we might hope for along these lines—has been expressed from Jefferson's letter recognizing Banneker as one of his "brethren," to Ralph Ellison proudly noting that he and the writer Shirley Jackson were "now working in the same vein," to Barack Obama placing a Presidential Medal of Honor over a tearful Joe Biden.

My focus on cultural and political elites is not to negate the fact that throughout American history, ordinary citizens have always found ways to cross the bounds of racially proscribed forms of intimacy. Indeed, Harvard Law Professor Randall Kennedy has devoted an entire book to it, one focusing on sex, marriage, identity, and adoption.[9] What I am interested in conveying, however, is the manner in which public demonstrations of interracial friendship have been part and parcel of political efforts to convey to ordinary citizens just how far such relationships may go. The American state has long policed sexual intimacy between blacks and whites; but policing—or encouraging—interracial friendship, something not inhibited by law but deeply feared throughout our history, calls for more theatrical displays of instruction.

When Teddy Roosevelt failed in his effort to expand the horizon of interracial fraternity by sitting down to dinner with Booker T. Washington, it suggested the country was very much in an indeterminate period of interracial social relations and, by extension, the fulfillment of multiracial democracy; and when Eleanor Roosevelt placed a kiss upon the cheek of Mary McLeod Bethune, she sought to show the country—and herself—that such a period had to be brought to a close. All the world may be a stage, but in states formed though a commitment to white supremacy such as ours, it is a stage where the players

with the biggest roles occasionally attempt to go off script—to impro-
vise new possibilities for racial justice. Strangers must talk to one another—and we have come to learn that they often must be encouraged
to do so.

As is the case with my focus on public figures, my exclusive attention to interracial friendship among blacks and whites should not be
misconstrued. There are numerous expressions of interracial friendship's
significance for democratic possibilities between whites and other
groups, including Native Americas, Latinos, Asian Americans, and
others. I suspect such examples may well become increasingly significant in decades to come, as the demographic makeup of the country
continues to change. Yet these cases do not provide, at least at the present, the same kind of historical thread from the founding period to
today as those narratives presented by African Americans and whites.
Consider Desmond King and Rogers Smith's periodization of racial
orders. The founding period was defined by citizenship battles over
slavery; the post–Civil War period by contestations over the meaning
of the Fourteenth and Fifteenth Amendments and black rights; and finally, a civil rights period marked by transformative black (and white)
resistance to white supremacy.[10] Any attempt to grapple with racial justice and the status of democratic life in America must confront these
pivotal moments, ones I categorize again as closed, indeterminate, and
open, with respect to interracial friendship—a powerful proxy for the
health of America's multiracial democracy.

The political scientist Seyla Benhabib has argued that democratic
societies are "faced with the task of securing three public goods."
These include "legitimacy, economic welfare, and a viable sense of
collective identity."[11] The third pillar, collective identity, may well be
the most elusive—and, paradoxically, the one that sustains the other
two. If nothing else, this book places interracial friendship at the heart
of the democratic enterprise because it has been one of the greatest
impediments to—and, at times, most powerful models for—collective identity. Benhabib goes onto define democracy as "a model for
organizing the collective and public exercise of power in the major
institutions of a society on the basis of the principle that decisions affecting the well-being of a collectivity can be viewed as the outcome
of a procedure of free and reasoned deliberation among individuals

considered as moral and political equals."[12] It is as good a definition as any. It boils down to: *equals openly deciding together*.

Each of the case studies presented in this book centers around how this democratic project might have been made possible through the seemingly less political domain of social relations. Whether it be an invitation to W. E. B. Du Bois from William James to a private dinner at Harvard, for example, or marching together in Washington (once for "Jobs and Freedom") as did James Baldwin and Marlon Brando, or marching for Women's Liberation as did co-chairs Angela Davis and Gloria Steinem during the 2017 Women's March, or when Rev. Martin Luther King Jr. and Rabbi Joshua Heschel locked arms on the frontlines in Selma, displays of interracial friendship have frequently served as proverbial barometers as to whether *equals deciding together in public* was a viable enterprise. On occasion, such engagements have produced disagreement among the protagonists themselves, often around the meaning and significance of the respective endeavors. The business of friendship can be messy under ordinary circumstances. When imbued with the added pressure of consciousness-making politics, it can be nearly impossible.

In speaking of politics and friendship throughout the book, I hope to expand the ordinary meaning of both words. Friendship as a private social bond marked by amity and trust—perhaps the most important quality of all—is well enough. While I speak of friendship in *Stars and Shadows* in this sense, I also wish to implicate the larger sense of friendship as an essential characteristic of democracy and one of the more powerful responsibilities of citizenship. Friendship may be a more superfluous, albeit admired aspect of citizenship in ethnically or racially homogenous republics. This is not so for large, multiracial republics. Thus "politics," in the sense I employ it in the text, is also about the creation of meaning out of social realities and all efforts to reshape them. As Danielle S. Allen has argued in her reflections on Aristotle, "friendship is the bond of the city, and political friendship is not merely a serviceable aspiration, but a crucial one."[13]

One of the more impressive reflections on what this looks like in modern society emerges from the work of British historian Paul Gilroy, whose influential scholarship on the Black Atlantic has in more recent years been animated by what he describes as "convivial culture." In his 2005 book, *Postcolonial Melancholia*, Gilroy describes the dynamics of multicultural society in places like London, where racial animus and the aftershocks of empire are not so much extinguished but rather mitigated by genuine bonds of affection, love, and simple conviviality, across racial lines. Gilroy formally defines *conviviality*, a much better term than the ambiguous term *identity*, he argues, as "the processes of cohabitation and interaction that have made multiculture an ordinary feature of social life in Britain's urban areas and in postcolonial cities elsewhere."[14] Gilroy sees everyday expressions of conviviality in cross-racial sex, the permeability of Afro-Caribbean and Punjabi culture, and the popularity of Muslim entertainers as examples of the shifting tide against idealized remembrances of "empire" foisted upon the British public for so long. *Harry Potter* and its embrace of a traditional and highly classist British past may provide some succor in an age of melancholia over what has been lost, but it cannot do so for very long, he argues.[15]

In the United States, our racial lamentations over a bygone America, one in need of returning to ("Make America Great Again"), have led to denial, if not melancholy. Yet the same forces of social change underway in the United Kingdom and elsewhere imbue modern life in the United States with far greater possibilities for multiracial democracy than ever before. It is perhaps for this reason that democracy itself has been increasingly under threat, as demographic changes have been accompanied by increasing social intimacies among racial and ethnic groups.[16] Such a reality presents an affront to those vested in whiteness as a marker of national superiority and an indication of social and economic stability. When Donald Trump warned that "they" are coming to your suburbs during the 2020 presidential campaign, few were in doubt about who "they" were.[17]

New models for democratic politics, such as those presented by Allen and Gilroy, are powerful. They provide much-needed examples of what is possible to achieve, even in the darkest times. John Stauffer's *Black Hearts of Men: Radical Abolitionists and the Transformation of Race* is another example. Stauffer chronicles the friendship between two black and two white abolitionists—James McCune Smith, Frederick Douglass, Gerritt Smith, and John Brown—to show how their friendship "overcame existing social barriers" even as "they reimagined their country as a pluralist society."[18] Such histories have always been crucial in reframing the kinds of narratives Americans are exposed to, and those that hold sway. That such stories have taken different forms over time and in unique contexts begs greater attention to why, under any aegis—be it convivial culture, talking to strangers, or the guidance of stars and shadows—democratic citizenship is, at heart, a deeply personal and necessarily antiracist endeavor. The ten historical cases in this book offer a window into the recurring effort in America to dramatize the interconnection between multiracial democracy and friendship; between the personal and the political.

While researching for this book these past two years, I've sought out not only historical but also literary examples of what a robust, multiracial democracy looks like. Like countless others, I've been drawn to the story of Denver and Sethe in Toni Morrison's *Beloved*. Equally poignant is the bond between Ishmael and Queequeg in Herman Melville's *Moby Dick*. The best models all seem inherently premised upon friendship—a bond that, unlike romantic love, holds no physical allure over us; and unlike familial ties, obligations to our friends are essentially self-generated. Sex and blood titillate, but friendship is the stuff of democracy. It is sustaining because it is voluntary and visionary at the same time. It is also a delicate and difficult enterprise—particularly among people taught, trained, and conditioned to believe that, above all members of society, there is one group deemed intellectually, aesthetically, and politically superior to all. So, no, we cannot "friend" our way out of white supremacy—but friends can, and must, be part of its undoing.

The title of this book comes from what I believe to be a sacred and noble model—one not unclouded by its own time and points of reference, but a worthy one all the same. Mark Twain's *Huckleberry Finn* provides, at least to me, a glimpse of what the path to true and unequivocal friendship might mean for our country. "Stars and Shadows" comes from a passage in *Huckleberry Finn* where Jim and Huck are in flight at night, and about to board a raft to some still-unrecognizable freedom. Students of philosophy will appreciate that it is quite literally time for the two to decamp from the cave wherein they had been living. As in Plato's allegory of the cave, their vision is limited—they have only enough light to see with—but not enough to be discovered by.

"Stars and shadows ain't good to see by," Huck narrates, as the two continue their uncertain journey.[19] Like many, I was struck by how much Twain could get into such a simple sentence. As Jim and Huck were late nineteenth-century metaphors for what those with little standing in society could do in friendship, so it is with the idea that our efforts to remake our democracy today needn't be perfect, nor wondrously illuminated. The friendship between Jim and Huck *is* the path. *They* are the stars and shadows. The search for a direction out of white supremacy and all other manner of antidemocratic ills must first be an inward one. This is not to the exclusion of real and well-lit paths marked by law, public policy, and societal transformation. But the real light is nameless, it is internal, and it is the work of friends.

* * *

In September 2017, I received an email from such a friend. Daniel J. Tichenor was convening a gathering of scholars at the University of Oregon to workshop any recent work they had that was still in its developmental stages. He asked that I join, and I was eager to do so, given our friendship and Dan's influential support for me over the years. That December, I joined Dan and a terrific group of scholars that included Elizabeth Cohen, Cybelle Fox, Alison Gash, Karthick Ramakrishnan, and Debra Thompson. It was an intimate setting, where over a few days we read and lovingly critiqued each other's work. At the time, I was working on an article on the intellectual relationship and friendship between Du Bois and William James. I got great feedback on it—raw as it was—but I was enticed to do more with it. Much more. As we went around the room, a number of people suggested that there were many more potential cases to explore—so much so, that I ought to consider writing a book.

That friendly prodding led me to think about interracial friendship in the larger context of American political development. I considered the periods and cases in American history that illustrated the struggle for democratic expansion—and its moments of contraction—through the lens of this underappreciated ideal of fraternité. That consideration and research led me to consider cases that demonstrated movement from eras where such public displays of friendship among policymakers and elites were closed, then indeterminate, and ultimately open. By no means should these chapters reflect all there is to say on the subject. On the contrary, from the first day this idea was suggested in conversation back in Eugene, Oregon, I've been struck by how colleagues and friends have offered suggestions for chapter pairings. That includes my editor and friend, David McBride, who offered suggestions from his wife, Leah (Andy Warhol and Basquiat!). It seemed that as I shared more of my research, people were drawn to the subject—and to what these cases have meant politically. Including the many that I missed.

I think that is the hope and purpose of this book: to give readers an opportunity to reflect on the history of interracial friendship and the variety of examples that have meant so much to how democratic rule is demonstrated in the public arena. More importantly, I hope it inspires the kind of introspection required of citizens who all share in the responsibility of strengthening and sustaining democratic life. And so, I want to thank that talented and giving ensemble of colleagues and friends who met in Eugene, along with David, who has now supported my efforts in three books with Oxford University Press. Early readers of parts of the manuscript, or those who helped frame my thinking on the book, include Al Tillery, Jr., John Kaag, Harvey Cormier, Ermine Algaier, Anthony Clark Arend, John Baxter, Alexandra Filindra, Colleen Casey, Jane Junn, Michael Hanchard, and Tom Mayer, among others.

I'd especially like to thank those who allowed me to interview them, or simply get guidance on various chapters. These include Susannah Heschel, who was most generous with her time in sharing information about her father; Jonathan Greenberg, who offered a number of valuable suggestions for the chapter on Rabbi Abraham Joshua Heschel and Dr. King; Dr. Clarence B. Jones, who shared intimate and invaluable reflections on his time working with Dr. King; Rev. Richard Fernandez was also kind enough to share his insights into Dr. King, and his Riverside address in 1967. I'd also like to thank Avra Douglas, Executor, Trustee, and Archivist for Brando Enterprises, and Ryan Kernan, Vice President of Rights Representation and Merchandise Licensing at Greenlight Rights.

None of this would have been possible without the dedication of librarians and archivists who give so generously of their time. I wish to thank Anna Robinson-Sweet, Assistant Archivist at the New School for Social Research; Kirsten Carter, Supervisory Archivist at the Franklin D. Roosevelt Presidential Library; Kate Long, Research Services

Archivist, Smith College; Ellen M. Shea, Head of Research Services, Schlesinger Library, Radcliffe Institute; Edith Sandler, Manuscript Reference Librarian, and Valerie Haeder, Reference Librarian, Library of Congress; Natalia Schiarini, Librarian for Collection Services, Beiencke Library, Yale University; Bridgett Pride, Reference Librarian, Schomburg Center for Research in Black Culture; Anna Berkes, Reference Librarian, Jefferson Library, Jefferson Foundation; Meredith Anne Weber, Research Services Specialist, Eberly Family Special Collections Library, Penn State University; and Melanie Dance, Director of the Benjamin Banneker Historical Park and Museum.

My agent, Geri Thoma, as always, helped me think through this book over several years, providing the kind of faith and support all authors should have. Undoubtedly, I am leaving others out who, in some way, assisted me in this now three years' labor. I apologize for any oversights, and thank you nonetheless. As is plain to see, much of the archival assistance in research in the United States is done by women, in and out of the academy, many of whom go unnoticed—and yet their work is indispensable. They are, in their own ways, all-too-overlooked wellsprings of our democracy. Let's each do our part to change that. It goes without saying that any shortcomings in this work are mine alone.

On this final note of recognition, I'd also like to posthumously thank my dear friend, mentor, and confidante Ruth B. Mandel, whose passing this past year was a blow to the work of democratic politics and vision for an antiracist society. As Director of the Eagleton Institute of Politics at Rutgers University, Ruth was a tireless and powerful advocate for a society invigorated by the intellect, labor, and spirit of all Americans. And while much of her career was devoted toward ensuring that women were equal participants and leaders in the realm of politics and public policy, she was also a powerful advocate for racial justice. More than that, she was a principled, loving, and forgiving friend. This book is written in her memory. May it be a blessing.

Last but not least, I wish to thank my children, Gabrielle, Luke, and Daniel, who continue to show me what is most important in this short life—and from whom, through their own efforts to combat systemic racism, even at their tender age, I draw inspiration and instruction. I love you, and I admire you.

I

An Exchange of Letters
Benjamin Banneker and Thomas Jefferson

Introduction: Fraternity's Limits

The defensive missives would be there all of Thomas Jefferson's life. "Nobody wishes more than I do. . . ." Another, equally hopeful: "I shall be delighted to see. . . ." These are from letters written in 1791. One, written just after his presidency ended in 1809, is equally affirming: "Be assured that no person living wishes more sincerely than I do. . . ." And another such letter, eight months later: "Nothing was or is farther from my intentions. . . ." But the boldest of all of these came from a letter written in April 1820, some six years before Jefferson's death: "I can say," he wrote to John Holmes, "with conscious truth, that there is not a man on earth who would sacrifice more than I would to relieve us of this heavy reproach, in any practicable way." The pattern was one of assurance, hyperbole, and deflection.

To the untrained eye, these are incomplete thoughts, fragments unfairly excised from the writings of Thomas Jefferson. For many African Americans, however, these words resound today as the familiar rings of preemptive justification for racism. Indeed, when taken in their full view, as I outline in this chapter, these fits and starts by Jefferson concerning the intellectual capacity of blacks and the impossibility of ending slavery ("wolf by the ears," and all that) built the template for how liberal whites (or those hoping to be thought liberal on the question of race) would mask their role as willing conspirators in the great antidemocratic game of white supremacy.

Let's examine examples of more recent vintage. Take the following:

"I am the least racist person anyone is going to meet."
"I don't have a racist bone in my body."
"I am the least racist person you have ever interviewed."

These are the familiar and far more recognizable words of Donald Trump.

It is a difficult, and admittedly painful, thing to write about the political thought of Thomas Jefferson and Donald Trump at the same time, as if they were equals. But the sad truth is that the line between Jeffersonian denials of racism and those of Trump is, well, undeniable. However varying in degrees of formality and eloquence, when the discussion turns to race, Jefferson—and many subsequent white political leaders—have employed a reflexive defensiveness on the subject that says something about the history of race in America and the struggle for racial fraternity over time. If friendship as a first principle of standing in human relations cannot be achieved, how much more difficult will it be to achieve a functioning democratic society premised on natural law and equality? The answer to that question, if one can be had, has to begin with Thomas Jefferson. For it was Jefferson who practically invented the discourse on race in America—at least the one that claimed its irrelevance, while upholding its use as a political weapon. And, if any person of color had the potential to break into the fraternal orbit of Jefferson, it was Banneker.

The story begins on August 19, 1791. A free black man from Baltimore County, Maryland, named Benjamin Banneker has sat down and taken up his quill to write to then Secretary of State Thomas Jefferson, in Philadelphia. It was Jefferson who had hired Banneker to assist Andrew Ellicott of Baltimore, in surveying the territory along the Potomac River that was to become the nation's new capital. This was one month before the Frenchman Pierre Charles L'Enfant was hired by President George Washington to produce a survey. Banneker would go on to complete his role in the project in April, having arrived in Alexandria, Virginia, near Valentine's Day in 1791. Now, back at home, alone with his books and instruments, Banneker sought out a more daunting political project. He wanted to write to Jefferson, the author of the Declaration of Independence, to get America's great revolutionary thinker on the record about what he thought of black people, racial injustice, and the scourge of slavery. Banneker had decided to take the small scraps of negro empowerment he had available to him as a free black man—one who assisted in surveying the nation's capital and establishing lines for some of the major points in the city—and deign to ask Thomas Jefferson just what kind of white man he was.

Banneker was an unusual man by the standards of his time. He was sixty years old when he wrote to Jefferson, having spent the better part of his later years as a free man and tobacco planter, and taking up mathematics and astronomy. His grandmother was a white indentured Englishwoman named Molly Welsh, who settled in the Chesapeake area of Maryland. Upon completing her term of indentured servitude around 1690, Welsh purchased two slaves, one of whom was a man named Bannaka, thought to have descended from an African chieftain. Welsh soon granted both slaves their freedom and, at considerable risk to her livelihood and safety, married Bannaka—whose Anglicized name became "Banneky" thereafter. Welsh, now a Banneky, gave birth to four daughters, one of whom, Mary, married a free black man named Robert, who took on Welsh's new name. It was this union that produced Benjamin Banneker in 1731.

By his late twenties, Banneker had lost both parents, inheriting their tobacco farm in Ellicott, Maryland. While literate, Banneker's schooling ended fairly early as his responsibilities on the farm were unrelenting. In an otherwise uneventful life, Banneker gained a kind of regional fame for having manufactured by hand a wooden clock—what his biographer called a "miracle of untutored craftsmanship."[1] The clock, built by Banneker at the age of twenty-two from examining a watch he had procured, would prove to be accurate for the next fifty years.

Had Banneker's story ended here, he would remain but a footnote to African American history—a kind of anecdote to fill commercial spots during Black History Month. But today, Banneker's name is ubiquitous, if the man himself is otherwise less well known. Indeed, there are legions of prep schools, academies, public elementary, charter, and high schools named after Banneker. His name is also a fixture on many apartments, public housing projects, and senior living facilities—mostly in black neighborhoods. Harvard University even has a Banneker Institute created to train "undergraduate students of color for graduate programs in astronomy." Banneker is often linked with figures like Neil de Grasse Tyson—a kind of ready-made proto-celebrity of science from the distant past. He is a figure up for grabs, with African Americans, the scientific community, and more recently the LGBTQ community laying claim to Banneker's exploits (he was a lifelong bachelor, after all). In short, Banneker's legacy is useful for many purposes and political projects. But, at the end of the day, we have come to know Banneker because of his connection to Jefferson—one that was not only a boon to his popularity and enduring recognition but was the thing that made him a symbol of America's democratic possibilities.

To put it plainly, Benjamin Banneker was the first African American to formally dialogue with a founding member of the republic outside of the context of slavery or international diplomacy. Banneker's letter to Jefferson remains powerful now, as it was in its own time, because he had the audacity to presume that he was not only the moral equal of Jefferson but an intellectual one as well. And if he could make that presumption, it meant that he and Jefferson were social, as well as political, equals. And this in turn meant that in some abstract way, they could be more than fellow citizens. They could be friends. Taken together, this suggested that something fundamental about the nature of the country would have changed. This explains, at least in part, the significance of the many qualifiers Jefferson would employ over the years with respect to the intellectual capacities of blacks. And it would explain his reluctance to fully embrace the gifts of this most unusual free black man from Maryland, one to whom he wrote a letter signed with the customary valediction of the time: "Your most obedient humble servant."

"You Are Measurably Friendly and Well Disposed toward Us"

There is no telling precisely when Banneker decided to write to Jefferson. Perhaps he realized during his time surveying the new federal city that his assignment had larger implications. On March 12, 1791, the *Georgetown Weekly Ledger* noted that a member of the group in town assigned to survey what would become Washington, DC, was "Benjamin Banneker, an Ethiopian whose abilities, as a surveyor, and an astronomer, clearly prove Mr. Jefferson's concluding that race of men were void of mental endowments, was without foundation."[2] It is tempting to imagine Banneker in some Georgetown café or boarding house one morning, reading this account over coffee and deciding then and there to write to Jefferson—but there is no record that Banneker saw the article, or what he would have thought if he had. Clearly, Jefferson's views on race were widely known; his *Notes on Virginia*, written a decade earlier, offered a "scientific" account of black inferiority, ranging from the aesthetic to the intellectual. Even Phyllis Wheatley, the famed black poet of the revolutionary period, whom even Washington saw fit to praise, failed to escape Jefferson's disdain for black creativity and intelligence. "Religion indeed has produced a Phyllis Wheatley," Jefferson wrote, "but it could not produce a poet."[3]

Jefferson's dismissiveness of Wheatley is important because her status as a woman made friendship with her far less plausible; and, despite Jefferson's relatively more advanced views on the intellectual capabilities of women at the time, Wheatley was unlikely to ever be considered an intellectual figure capable of being on par with men, let alone whites. "The compositions published under her name," Jefferson concluded, "are below the dignity of criticism."[4] Jefferson seemed to offer some doubt that Wheatley was even capable of writing these poems—a charge he would later level against Banneker's work.

In any case, after *Notes*, Jefferson had gone from a kind of potential champion of black rights to an outright cynic. It is likely that Banneker was not only familiar with Jefferson as the author of the Declaration of Independence, but also as the author of the following passage from *Notes*:

> Comparing [blacks] by their faculties of memory, reason, and imagination, it appears to me that in memory they are equal to the whites; in reason much inferior, as I think one could scarcely be found capable of tracing and comprehending the investigations of Euclid; and that in imagination they are dull, tasteless, and anomalous.[5]

If Banneker was familiar with this Jefferson, and his letter suggests he very much was, then Banneker's status as a free black man and mathematician was a direct affront to Jefferson's conclusions, as the

Georgetown Weekly Ledger had argued. Indeed, as he noted in his letter, Banneker recognized that the white world had long looked upon his race as "rather brutish than human, and Scarcely capable of mental endowments." But what of Jefferson? Banneker opens his letter by letting him know that he is a free black man interested in having Jefferson commit to a stand on the equal intelligence of blacks:

> Sir I hope I may Safely admit, in consequence of that report which hath reached me, that you are a man far less inflexible in Sentiments of this nature, than many others, that you are measurably friendly and well disposed toward us, and that you are willing and ready to Lend your aid and assistance to our relief from those distresses and numerous calamities to which we are reduced.[6]

By granting Jefferson the position as a friend of the black race, one willing to work against racial oppression, he is ensnaring Jefferson in a bit of a trap. If Jefferson denies Banneker's flattering presumption of his interracial fraternity, then he is merely another racist, slaveholding Virginian; if he accepts Banneker's proposition, however, then he is bound, in a sense, to work—or, at the very least, to advocate—for the liberation of blacks in the United States. Of course, as we will see, Jefferson was a master illusionist and a veritable genius in extricating himself from such rhetorical commitments with respect to racial equality. But Banneker was trying his best.

His first appeal to Jefferson was religious. "[O]ne universal Father hath been given to us all," Banneker wrote, "and that he hath not only made us all one flesh, but that he . . . endued us all with the same faculties . . . however diversified in Situation or coulour, we are all of the Same Family, and Stand in relation to him." Despite authoring America's creed that "all men are created equal," Jefferson believed no such thing. At least not in the way Banneker hoped he did. For starters, Jefferson's attachment to the story of a biblical creation was untenable—his famous re-transcription of the New Testament eliminated any of Christ's miracles and was devoid of other unscientific postulates. As Jefferson wrote to John Adams in 1813, he favored the words of Jesus—while rejecting the miracles associated with him—viewing them as "easily distinguishable as diamonds in a dung-hill."[7] Far from being a biblical literalist, Jefferson was an Enlightenment-era deist—someone for whom religion had limited value, save only as a form of moral education.

Banneker's error was in assuming he and Jefferson shared a belief in the theory of a single creation for the birth of humanity. But as Jefferson makes clear in *Notes on Virginia*, he is uncertain how the physiological differences between blacks and whites arose. "I advance it as a suspicion only," Jefferson concluded in *Notes*, "that the blacks, whether originally a distinct race, or made distinct by time and circumstances, are inferior to whites in the endowments both of body and mind."[8] That blacks are a "distinct race" is the crucial point of Jefferson's. Why? Because it renders moot Banneker's claim of blacks and whites sharing the bonds of spiritual fraternity (owing to being common ancestors of a single creation). Jefferson thinks the idea irrelevant. In fact, in *Notes*, he refers to "*their* Creator" when considering the origins of blacks.[9] In Jefferson's world, there may well be a black God—but he sits in some alternate realm, outside of the bounds of whiteness.

Banneker's next tack was to appeal to Jefferson's sense of empathy, and at the very least, self-interest. "Sir, I have long been convinced, that if your love of Selves," Banneker wrote, "and for those inesteemable laws which preserve to you the rights of human nature, was founded on Sincerity, you could not but be Solicitous, that every Individual of whatsoever rank or distinction, might with you equally enjoy the blessings thereof." Here, Banneker invokes his own status as a free person to suggest an equal affinity for the type of liberty Jefferson was denied when "the British Crown" had "reduced you to a State of Servitude." With this lead-in, Banneker goes for the killer strike—employing the Revolutionary War and Declaration as witnesses for his defense of black liberation:

This Sir, was a time in which you clearly saw into the injustice of Slavery, and in which you had just apprehensions of the horrors of its condition, it was now Sir, that your abhorrence thereof was so excited, that you publickly held forth this true and invaluable doctrine, which is worthy to be recorded and remember'd in all

Succeeding ages. "We hold these truths to be Self evident, that all men are created equal, and that they are endowed by their creator with certain unalienable rights, that among these are life, liberty, and the pursuit of happiness."

If Banneker wrote to Jefferson for any reason, it was to deliver this passage.

Jefferson may have been called on the carpet by the French for his inability to convince his countrymen to abandon slavery; he may have been scorned by those Federalists and early white abolitionists who viewed him as hypocritical in his support for human equality while owning fellow human beings at the same time. But it was an entirely different thing to be effectively called to account for his moral temporizing on the question of slavery by an African American whose standing in society was fragile at best. But Banneker went further, using the kind of harsh language toward whites of Jefferson's standing that can only be described as unprecedented for the time.

> Sir how pitiable is it to reflect, that altho you were so fully convinced of the benevolence of the father of mankind, and of his equal and impartial distribution of those rights and privileges which he had conferred upon them, that you should at the Same time counteract his mercies, in detaining by fraud and violence so numerous a part of my brethren under groaning captivity and cruel oppression, that you should at the Same time be found guilty of that most criminal act, which you professedly detested in others, with respect to yourselves.

This is one of the more courageous passages in American political history, to be sure. When Frederick Douglass criticized the hypocrisy of white celebrations on the Fourth of July in 1852, he had become a popular and widely hailed figure of note, one with international recognition and support. And, while his acts were scarcely lacking in courage, Douglass had a movement behind him. Banneker was, in effect, a lone Negro in the wilderness—one whose freedom and life were most precarious. And here he was, calling the author of the Declaration of Independence and sitting secretary of state a criminal. Moreover, Banneker, like Douglass some sixty years later, used his platform for the liberation of others. Banneker had the choice to remain a local black curiosity—a free man of scientific merit and community standing. He was the kind of "articulate" black person who made his white neighbors proud. As a solitary and powerless figure in a slaveholding state, Banneker nevertheless chose to confront Jefferson on the most controversial subject of the day—and he did so without masking his disappointment and moral indignation for the Master of Monticello's hypocrisy.

After thoroughly admonishing Jefferson, Banneker softened his language—somewhat. He concluded by appealing to Jefferson's Christian sensibility, proposing that he, like Job, "Put your Souls in their Souls stead." Even this line carried a double meaning, however. The full scripture from Job 16:4 reads: "I also could speak as ye do: if your soul were in my soul's stead, I could heap up words against you, and shake mine head at you." With this, Banneker, as if reminding himself, turns to his original purpose of the letter, noting that his interjection of the black condition in America "was not originally my design."

Instead, Banneker has provided, along with his letter, an almanac "which I have calculated for the Succeeding year." Almanacs were ubiquitous in America throughout the colonial period and played an important role in providing farmers information about seasonal forecasts, along with astronomical calculations. Almanacs also included occasional political news, planting dates, tide tables arranged in a calendar, and a local directory. These were sometimes accompanied by moral teachings, humorous anecdotes, and stories.[10] They were, in a sense, the precursors of magazines or journals that covered important news while also seeking to entertain. The earliest almanac was produced in Cambridge, Massachusetts, in 1639 by William Pierce. By far, the most famous was Benjamin Franklin's "Poor Richard's Almanack," printed from 1733 to 1758.

That Banneker had produced an almanac was significant. It meant he had the ability to make the necessary mathematical calculations and record his astronomical observations with merit sufficient to be published. A kind of peer-review system for publication existed at the time, and Banneker's almanac had passed muster. Indeed, the almanac "gained the approval of the 'celebrated' scientist David Rittenhouse," whom Jefferson greatly admired.[11] For someone without formal education, and nearing the latter years of his life, it was a confirmation of Banneker's intellect—and a validation of the notoriety that brought him to Jefferson's attention in the first place. It was that acclaim that landed him the position on Ellicott's team of surveyors for the new capital. In presenting the almanac to Jefferson, Banneker did so as one scientist to another, without fanfare or any sense of separate social standing.

> This calculation, Sir, is the production of my arduous Study in this my advanced Stage of life; for having long had unbounded desires to become acquainted with the Secrets of nature, I have had to gratify my curiosity herein thro my own assiduous application to Astronomical Study, in which I need not to recount to you the many difficulties and disadvantages which I have had to encounter.

Banneker noted that he had almost failed to complete the almanac on time, reminding Jefferson that it was because of his work "at the Federal Territory." He also let Jefferson know that this was a pre-publication manuscript—the proofs, in contemporary editor's parlance. This was so Jefferson "might not only have an earlier inspection, but that you might also view it in my own writing." Undoubtedly Banneker anticipated Jefferson's disbelief in the ability of a black man, free or otherwise, to produce such a document. This was thus a kind of first instance of African Americans having to verify or authenticate their intellectual standing for whites. Banneker was saying, in so many words, "See my handwriting? I wrote this."

How could friendship of any depth develop from a social system where the basic intellectual capacity of one of the parties is perennially called into question? Of course, fraternity was not what was on Banneker's mind; the only friendship he sought from Jefferson—indeed, the only one truly available at the time—was "the friendly disposition" Banneker hoped Jefferson had toward African Americans. This too, was a hope at best. Not that Banneker lacked white friends. Banneker's white neighbor, George Ellicott, was a lifelong friend, so this was not an impossibility in American life at the time. Indeed, outside of his immediate family, Banneker's closest associates were white.

What made Banneker's connection to Jefferson so meaningful with respect to interracial fraternity was that it laid out the boundaries of what was possible in the realm of public friendships between whites and blacks occupying radically different positions of social standing. If Banneker and Jefferson could share some form of equal space—as men of science, perhaps—then it might be plausible to entertain something more, not only for them but for the nation as a whole. Jefferson's response was going to establish what those boundaries of opportunity were; but for now, Banneker was content to close. He had made his case for black freedom. He had shared his intellectual gifts with the greatest living American short of George Washington. And he showed no signs of obsequiousness or hesitancy in conveying his desire to share equally in the social and political gifts of citizenship that Jefferson could only take for granted. "And now Sir, I shall conclude and Subscribe my Self with the most profound respect your most Obedient humble Servant." And then he signed his full name.

"Our Black Brethren"

The first thing one notices about Jefferson's response to Banneker is its length. It is a pithy 190 words—less than one-seventh the length of Banneker's 1,394-word epistle. And, yet, as any Jefferson scholar will attest, there are great depths to probe in Jefferson's language; he was as politically astute, cautious in his rhetorical commitments, and penetrating in his use of words as any American before or since. So, in reading his letter, it is important to be careful not to over- or under-subscribe beliefs to Jefferson—particularly those with respect to race. This is why Banneker's letter's careful construction was so important. Trying to pin Jefferson down on the leading political question of his time was a tricky affair. One might say, on the question of race and slavery, it was Jefferson himself who was a wolf held by the ears.

Of course, it is worth noting that Jefferson was under no obligation to respond to Banneker at all, just as he was under no obligation to appoint him to serve as part of the team to survey the region that would become Washington. Jefferson's appointment of Banneker can be seen as part of the delicate, if not maddening, balance he seemed to consciously strike on matters of race. In the Declaration, blacks are "created equal." In *Notes*, they are intellectually inferior. At one point he inserts language in the Declaration opposing the slave trade; for the remainder of his public life, he is silent on the matter. He seems to think the problem to be one of innate inferiority. "But never yet could I find," Jefferson wrote, "that a black had uttered a thought above the level of plain narration."[12] Now, here he was responding to Banneker's eloquent letter, one challenging him on his public record on racial equality.

The historian Annette Gordon-Reed offered perhaps the best explanation as to why Jefferson appointed Banneker and in turn responded to his letter. It involves an anecdote told by Jefferson's grandson, T. J. Randolph. Randolph and Jefferson encountered a black man who removed his hat and bowed upon meeting the two men while walking. Jefferson returned the gesture, while Randolph did not. Jefferson later chided Randolph for permitting "a Negro to be more of a gentleman than myself."[13] In effect, responding to Banneker was the "gentlemanly" thing to do. Jefferson was willing to make the noble gesture with respect to matters of race, but he was unwilling to make the hard political sacrifices that would jeopardize his standing as a leading slaveholder, statesman, and spokesman for Southern interests. With respect to black liberation, for Jefferson, the tree of liberty would remain eternally parched.

Jefferson appears to have responded to Banneker immediately—his letter is dated August 30, 1791—some eleven days after Banneker's was written. After thanking Banneker for the almanac, Jefferson offers the first of two of his customary defensive responses he would employ in his letter. "No body wishes more than I do," he began, "to see such proofs as you exhibit, that nature has given to our black brethren, talents equal to those of the other colours of men, and that the appearance of a want of them is owing to the degraded condition of their existence both in Africa and America."[14] What appears to be at first glance a supportive line of reasoning is one that very much undercuts Jefferson's presumed belief in the inherent equality of human beings. Why does Jefferson need to "wish" that Banneker is not an anomaly— what black cultural writers have come to refer to as a "magical negro?" It is because he can't be certain that Banneker isn't the exception that proves the rule.

Banneker's "proofs"—his talent for mathematics, astronomy, the sophistication of his writing—may be the products of a freakish talent. Jefferson can't be sure they are representative of black talent more generally. He would like to believe, he tells Banneker, that the lack of exceptional black men (and Jefferson, like Banneker, is very much attached to the maleness of such talent) is owing to their oppression, not their nature. Jefferson doubles down on the idea, going back to his standard line, in the next sentence:

> I can add with truth that no body wishes more ardently to see a good system commenced for raising the condition both of their body and mind to what it ought to be, as fast as the imbecility of their present existence, and other circumstances which can not be neglected, will admit.

This sentence is a landmine of reasoning for anyone trying to understand where Jefferson stands on racial equality. But taken at its face value, Jefferson is telling Banneker that American democracy cannot serve the interest of black emancipation as the politics of the country are presently constituted. "The good system" for raising the condition of African Americans can only mean the elimination of slavery. This is a bizarre tautology—black life will be better when black existence is improved. But what can be the cause of this "imbecility" Jefferson refers to other than slavery? Jefferson hints at it when he writes that "other circumstances which can not be neglected," must be addressed. For Jefferson, it is his unspoken, but deeply held presumption, that blacks are not in a debased condition because they are enslaved; they are enslaved because their natural state is one of debasement. Blacks are inherently inferior, Jefferson suspects, however much he would like to believe otherwise. This is a point raised in a subsequent letter of Jefferson's, one written the same day as his response—but it is too unseemly for him to bring up to Banneker. By Jefferson's reckoning, Banneker is an outlier to this hypothesis.

Finally, Jefferson returns to Banneker's almanac. Just as Banneker suspected, it is a document of considerable political importance, as much as it is a work of scientific achievement. "I have taken the liberty of sending your almanac to Monsieur de Condorcet, Secretary of the Academy of sciences at Paris, and member of the Philanthropic society," Jefferson informs Banneker, "because I considered it a document to which your whole colour had a right to the justification against the doubts which have been entertained of them." Of course, Jefferson was one of the leading "doubters" of the age with respect to black intelligence. Nevertheless, his commitment to democratic progress accompanied these doubts, despite failing to remove them. As such, Jefferson's engagement with Banneker was like his overall engagement with the issue of race; he would come up to the line of championing black equality, before receding into the more politically comfortable (and economically beneficial) stance of supporting white supremacy.

Like Banneker, Jefferson signs off with the customary Enlightenment-era valediction recently popularized by Lin Manuel Miranda's musical "Hamilton": "I am with great esteem, Sir Your most obed. Humble servt., Th: Jefferson."[15] Like bowing to an unknown black man in Virginia, this close confers a level of respect and social equality customarily reserved for whites. And Jefferson did receive criticism for it. The social boundaries crossed by Jefferson in even responding to Banneker violated the code of white racial superiority—particularly in the South. A southern Federalist William Loughton Smith attacked Jefferson in 1796 for the suggestion of supporting racial equality. The criticism was designed to weaken Jefferson in the upcoming election. In his pamphlet, "The Pretensions of Thomas Jefferson to the Presidency Examined," Smith offered a scathing critique:

> Did [Jefferson] flatter himself that his letter to Banneker would escape publication and only be handed around among the free negroes who probably never read his *Notes*? . . . What shall we think of a Secretary of State thus fraternizing with negroes, writing them complimentary epistles, stiling (sp.) them *his black brethren*, congratulating them on evidence of their genius, and alluring them of his good wishes for their speedy emancipation?[16]

It's hard to know if Jefferson anticipated this kind of problem; in 1791 he was still five years away from seeking the presidency. That he did decide to suggest that blacks were his "brethren" was ample ammunition for his political enemies. Perhaps Jefferson wanted to be recorded as being on the right side of history. Then again, as Smith hinted at in his letter, perhaps Jefferson never imagined that his response would see the light of day.

His letter continued to dog him. Even after his reelection to the presidency in 1804, his Federalist opponents were using it to label Jefferson a traitor to his race. According to one source, "Thomas Green Fessenden, a Federalist satirist from New Hampshire, ridiculed Jefferson for allegedly abandoning his racial views from *Notes*, simply because of the 'wonderful phenomenon of a Negro Almanac (probably enough made by a white man).'"[17] Fessenden was writing in 1805—fourteen years after the exchange of letters. Attacks on Jefferson's presumed abandonment of white supremacy simply for writing a positive letter, amicably addressed to a black man, was sufficient grounds—in both the North and the South—to implicate Jefferson's honor and sense of racial loyalty. The early Federal period in America was one of closed interracial fraternity among leading white public officials. Jefferson's exchange of letters with Banneker hinted at the possibilities for a more open and genuine set of social relations between blacks and whites. But even these small gestures made by Jefferson crossed the line, proscribing such friendships as dangerous to a republic characterized by white political power.

As mentioned earlier, Jefferson did not end his thoughts on Banneker with his response of August 19. That very day he wrote to Condorcet about Banneker, sending him the almanac in a letter worthy of its own serious attention. Indeed, Jefferson followed up with several other letters to friends and associates about Banneker, and these offer a different kind of take on the political stakes for Jefferson—even after his political career was effectively over. That the gift of an almanac and a relatively friendly exchange between two men could set off a small firestorm explains an awful lot about the limits of racial fraternity in the late eighteenth and early nineteenth centuries in America. This was not about—at least not directly about—the far more pernicious fear of miscegenation, or sexual relationships between blacks and whites. On the contrary, this was a seemingly light encounter between two men of science. But the social dynamics of the time made it a veritable powder keg. Racial fraternity was, in a sense, its own form of revolutionary incitement in the Federal era. And Jefferson would do his best to walk back his more positive sentiments concerning the future between those whom he had once esteemed as his "brethren."

"A Mind of Very Common Stature Indeed"

Before he left thoughts of Banneker to return to other matters, Jefferson thought it opportune to write to the Marquis de Condorcet, Secretary of the Academy of Sciences in Paris. His intention was to inform Condorcet of Banneker's unique abilities, and to offer the almanac as a gift. Ten years earlier, in 1781, while Jefferson was delineating the countless ways in which blacks were inferior in *Notes on Virginia*, Condorcet had written an important pamphlet advocating for black liberation. In his *Reflections on Negro Slavery*, Condorcet could not have begun with a more different conclusion from that of Jefferson: "My Friends, Although I am not the same colour as you, I have always regarded you as my brothers. Nature formed you with the same spirit, the same reason, the same virtues as whites."[18]

By addressing blacks directly, and as friends, Condorcet was making public what Jefferson chose to only hint at—and that, in private— namely, that differences between blacks and whites were superficial, and where they existed at all they were the product of political and historical circumstances. Ever the Francophile, Jefferson's letter sought to link Banneker's letter and almanac to his broader support for democratic progress—and to, in effect, affirm his connections to the French Revolution's support for human rights broadly construed. And it is quite possible that Jefferson was, in fact, inspired by Banneker and his work and that, in the moment, he drafted a letter reflecting his progressive, albeit latent, position on racial equality.

After opening his letter by playfully chiding Condorcet for France's adoption of a confounding (at least to Americans) unit of measure, Jefferson got to the point of his correspondence:

> I am happy to inform you that we have now in the United States a negro, the son of a black man born in Africa, and of a black woman born in the United States, who is a very respectable Mathematician. I procured him to be employed under one of our chief directors in laying out the new federal city on the Patowmac, and in the intervals

of his leisure, while on the work, he made an Almanac for the next year, which he sent me in his own handwriting. Add to this he is a very worthy and respectable member of society. He is a free man. I shall be delighted to see these instances of moral eminence so multiplied as to prove that the want of talents observed in them is merely the effect of their degraded condition, and not proceeding from any difference in the structure of the parts on which intellect depends.[19]

Jefferson's framing of Banneker's accomplishments is critical to understanding the impediments to racial progress and fraternity in the United States at the time. First, Jefferson wants Condorcet to know that Banneker is, in effect, a "real" negro—both of his parents are black, and therefore his accomplishments are all the more remarkable. Indeed, Banneker offers a similar accounting of his undiluted blackness. "Sir I freely and Chearfully acknowledge, that I am of the African race, and in that colour which is natural to them of the deepest dye," he informed Jefferson.[20] Banneker thus excised ties to his white grandmother—it could only hurt the narrative he wished to establish. Jefferson's racial cosmology included the belief that blacks were "improved" by white blood. In an ironic twist, Banneker's dark complexion, and his black parents, were thus used as credentials to establish his humanity. If blacks could do what Banneker had done—without the aid of white blood or assistance—then it spoke to their potential for equality among whites.

While acknowledging Banneker's "elegant solutions of geometrical problems" and good standing in the community, Jefferson returned to his habitual optimistic denial of general black equality. "I shall be delighted to see," he wrote Condorcet, "these instances of moral eminence so multiplied as to prove that the want of talents observed in them is merely the effect of their degraded condition." Another way of phrasing this, and probably one closer to Jefferson's true sentiments, would be to say, "I have not seen other blacks like Banneker; and until I do, I can't be sure he isn't some anomalous negro." There is no record, at least that this author could find, of Jefferson offering any unqualified complimentary statement about African Americans or blacks anywhere. When confronted with Banneker's impressive talents—and Jefferson was undoubtedly impressed—he falls back into the comfort of his doubts.

Such doubts conferred political benefits; if blacks were of uncertain moral or intellectual ability, then assaults on white supremacy would be dangerous, or at the very least, premature. It was an argument of "liberal" racism—one used well into the twentieth century, as when the conservative writer William F. Buckley Jr. opined:

> The central question that emerges—and it is not a parliamentary question or a question that is answered by merely consulting a catalogue of the rights of American citizens, born Equal—is whether the White community in the South is entitled to take such measures as are necessary to prevail, politically and culturally, in areas in which it does not predominate numerically? The sobering answer is Yes—the White community is so entitled because, for the time being, it is the advanced race. It is not easy, and it is unpleasant, to adduce statistics evidencing the median cultural superiority of White over Negro: but it is a fact that obtrudes, one that cannot be hidden by ever-so-busy egalitarians and anthropologists. The question, as far as the White community is concerned, is whether the claims of civilization supersede those of universal suffrage. . . . NATIONAL REVIEW believes that the South's premises are correct.[21]

Using Jefferson's language ("born Equal"), Buckley saw the push to make equal citizens of African Americans an admirable, if not naïve political venture. As Jefferson cryptically alluded to in his letter to Banneker, there were "other circumstances which could not be neglected," ones preventing the political equality of the races. At least Jefferson had the decency not to enumerate them. Buckley, on the other hand, couldn't resist, resting his case for white supremacy on "the median cultural superiority of White over Negro." It was a fact that "cannot be hidden"—mirroring Jefferson's line about "circumstances which cannot be neglected."

Years later, as his presidency had come to a close, Jefferson again chose to reflect on the question of racial equality. In a February letter to the French abolitionist Henri Gregoire, Jefferson returned once more to his mechanical phraseology on the issue. "Be assured," he wrote, "that no person living wishes more sincerely than I do, to see a complete refutation of the doubts I have myself entertained and expressed on the grade of understanding allotted to them by nature, and to find that in this respect they are on par with ourselves."[22] It never occurred to Jefferson that, as a slaveholder, he was responsible for ensuring that the doubts he held concerning black intelligence would remain unimpeachable.

Jefferson did close this letter with perhaps his clearest advocacy for universal suffrage. "[W]hatever be their degree of talent," he wrote to Gregoire, "it is no measure of [black] rights. Because Sir Isaac Newton was superior to others in understanding he was not therefore lord of the person or property of others."[23] In this regard, Jefferson went further than Buckley, writing 148 years later. Jefferson would return to his exchange with Gregoire—this time in a letter to the American-born Joel Barlow, who would go on to live in France for seventeen years and become a French citizen.

In his October letter to Barlow, Jefferson chided Gregoire for his overly optimistic views on black equality. Noting how Gregoire "wrote to me also on the doubts I had expressed five or six & twenty years ago, in the Notes on Virginia as to the grade of understanding of the negroes, & he sent me his book on the literature of the negroes. [His] credulity has made him gather up every story he could find of men of colour (without distinguishing whether black, or of what degree of mixture) however slight the mention, or light the authority on which they are quoted."[24]

Jefferson's last words on Banneker would thus be familiar ones of doubt. Black accomplishments were spare, and when observable they were most likely owing to the presence of "white blood." As to the specific abilities of Banneker, Jefferson had now reversed himself. "We know [Banneker] had spherical trigonometry enough to make almanacs, but not without the suspicion of aid from Ellicott, who was his neighbor & friend, & never missed an opportunity of puffing him."[25] Jefferson was now apparently fully disenchanted with Banneker. "I have a long letter from Banneker," he wrote to Barlow, "which shews him to have had a mind of very common stature indeed."[26]

The best that can said of Jefferson in these exchanges is that his beliefs concerning black equality were dependent upon the audience he was addressing. When it was to his political advantage, or a function of his desire to ingratiate himself with a friend, Jefferson was more apt to emphasize either his doubts or convictions concerning black intelligence and abilities. That he had serious doubts about racial equality is undeniable. That he was a white supremacist in practice, and largely in belief, is also without question. The exchange of letters with Banneker is memorable, in part, because Jefferson expresses something approaching the universal ideals put forth in his Declaration but otherwise lacking in his personal and political life with respect to empowering African Americans. The other reason the exchange with Banneker is memorable is that that is what Banneker wanted. Notwithstanding Jefferson's position on race, Banneker was going to put forth his own narrative. And he would use the words of Jefferson, elusive and impenetrable as they often were, to advance, as best he could, the interests of his people and the possibilities for a more comprehensive democracy in America.

Conclusion: Benjamin Banneker and the Narrative of Racial Democracy

On a scorching hot July Friday afternoon, I drove into the parking lot of the Benjamin Banneker Historical Park and Museum. There was one other car in the empty lot beside my own, and when I went inside it was a cool but seemingly unpopulated refuge from the heat. But before long, Melanie Dance, the director, and a naturalist at the museum, emerged to assist me. "We're a bit understaffed right now," she told me. She was quick to direct my attention to some of the important holdings of the museum, an edifice tucked away in the suburbs of Baltimore. The Double "T" diner was the nearest landmark of note.

As I walked around a bit, my eyes were suddenly drawn to a small book encased behind glass. There it was—Banneker's almanac. At least one of them. This one was published for 1793—his second edition. It was worn, with the upper right corner somewhat of a peeled mess—but otherwise intact. The printing was fairly standard for the era, although there was an extravagant flourish of script for the word "almanac."

Benjamin Banneker's
PENNSYLVANIA, DELAWARE,
MARYLAND and VIRGINIA

Almanack

AND
EPHEMERIS,
FOR THE YEAR OF OUR LORD,

1793;

Banneker's Almanac. It had the ring of "Alfred Hitchcock's *Psycho*," or other authorially centered announcements. And, indeed, it was precisely that. Here was a work of scientific merit, and, as was customary for the time, these documents were presented with the fanfare designed to literally stamp the author with the credibility (if not celebrity) necessary for letting the reader know that the quality of the work was of a certain standard.

Banneker's publication of the almanac was a political enterprise. He followed it up with his letter to Jefferson, and upon receiving the hoped-for response from the Secretary of State, he immediately sought a publisher for the exchange of letters. They were, in fact, published as a pamphlet by the Philadelphia printer Daniel Lawrence and were widely distributed shortly thereafter. Banneker was also successful in having the popular periodical the *Universal Asylum and Columbian Magazine* publish the letters.[27] The publishers, William Goddard and James Angell, knew they had the potential for a phenomenon on their hands. In their introduction to Banneker's almanac, they were sure to let readers know just who the author was:

[A] COMPLETE and ACCURATE EPHEMERIS for the Year 1792, calculated by a sable Descendant of Africa, who, by this Specimen of Ingenuity, evinces, to Demonstration, that mental Powers and Endowments are not the exclusive Excellence of white People, but the Rays of Science may alike illumine the Minds of Men of every Clime (however they may differ in the Colour of their

Skin) particularly those whom Tyrant-Custom hath too long taught us to depreciate as a Race inferior in intellectual Capacity.[28]

The almanac was a huge success, and Banneker had to suddenly deal with fame that brought him unannounced visitors to his home.[29] The almanac's popularity led Banneker to include the exchange of letters between him and Jefferson in future editions, using Jefferson's response as a tool in the burgeoning abolitionist movement. As Banneker biographer Silvio A. Bedini noted, The Pennsylvania Society for the Promotion of the Abolition of Slavery used the almanac and letters for propaganda purposes.[30] Banneker's intention to exploit his correspondence with Jefferson for good had to meet, if not exceed, his greatest expectations. None other than William Wilberforce presented his almanacs in England in the House of Commons, for the purpose of supporting the cause of abolition.[31]

Banneker's almanacs continued to be published each year through 1797. They made him a cause célèbre. That his popularity had little impact on Jefferson's public views on race is less important than his influence on the antislavery movement and future civil rights leaders. By the 1880s, Frederick Douglass was advocating for a new biography of Banneker, arguing that "my newly emancipated people . . . are especially in need of examples of just such mental industry and success as I believe the life of Banneker furnish[es]."[32] Banneker was perhaps the first symbol of black excellence in America; he certainly was the most widely touted in his time, and like Crispus Attacks and Phyllis Wheatley before him, he became an iconic figure denoting black achievement in the United States.

But after 1791, Jefferson and Banneker would no longer correspond. Banneker died in 1806, some twenty years before Jefferson, and fifteen years after their exchange of letters. The politics of the period dictated a cordial but distant relationship between white public figures and African Americans—at best. And, even here, Jefferson was subject to paying a political penalty simply for responding to Banneker. The parameters of racial fraternity were entirely local, private, and depoliticized. The performance art of Banneker's letter to Jefferson was just that—an effort to suggest a collegial, if not personal connection—one that approximated friendship, if not its presumption. Even this went too far. The institution of slavery marred the potentiality of all relationships between blacks and whites in the United States. It was not only a question of differences in power, but also the assumed differences in intelligence, reasoning, and morals. That Banneker challenged this dynamic was rather extraordinary; that he was beaten back, less so. Nevertheless, his challenge to the closed system of racial fraternity in America advanced the cause of abolition and gave credence to the idea that blacks and whites could be part of the same social circles, given that blacks could exhibit the full range of human possibilities assumed by many to be the exclusive province of whites.

It was a deeply sick system.

Decades later, there would be another exchange between an American statesman and a free black man. This would take place in person, at the White House, rather than in letters. The two men would understand the unique circumstances of the moment—its politics and its social significance. And, yet, something more fundamental was at play in the relationship between Abraham Lincoln and Frederick Douglass. Something approaching an authentic dynamic that, at times, still remains elusive in American life, and none more so than in our relationships across racial lines.

In the end, Jefferson's unwillingness to push these bounds helped frame the social strictures of white supremacy. Months after the new American Constitutional Convention had taken place, Jefferson was explaining to a French abolitionist just why he could not join France's antislavery society. The familiar refrain continues to haunt his, and America's, racial legacy:

> I am very sensible of the honour you propose to me of becoming a member of the society for the abolition of the slave trade. You know that nobody wishes more ardently to see an abolition not only of the trade but of the condition of slavery: and certainly nobody will be more willing to encounter every sacrifice for that object. But the influence and information of the friends to this proposition in France will be far above the need of my association. I am here as a public servant; and those whom I serve having never yet been able to give their voice against this practice, it is decent for me to avoid too public a demonstration of my wishes to see it abolished.[33]

Where would America have been, if not for the vain wishes and decency of Thomas Jefferson, on matters of race?

Sometime after visiting the Banneker Museum, I drove out to see one of the original boundary stones thought to have been left by Banneker and his team, marking the parameters of what was to become Washington, DC. The stone, enclosed by an iron fence, sits in the quiet suburb of Falls Church, Virginia. The fence is marked by a National Landmark plaque from 1980. It reads: "Benjamin Banneker: SW-9 Intermediate Boundary Stone." Cyclists and pedestrians passed by as I peered in at this hefty but otherwise ordinary stone, surrounded by wrought iron. I'm not sure what it says about a nation that memorializes a stone placed by a black man over two centuries and a quarter ago.

But we do.

2

Three Meetings
Frederick Douglass and Abraham Lincoln

Introduction: "I Felt Big in There."

Frederick Douglass's only invitation to the White House was for a meeting with President Abraham Lincoln on August 19, 1864. What Lincoln shared with him that day shocked the great abolitionist and former slave. Lincoln asked Douglass if he would agree to help organize "a band of scouts, composed of colored men, whose business should be somewhat after the original plan of John Brown, to go into the rebel states, beyond the lines of our armies, and carry the news of emancipation, and urge the slaves to come within our boundaries."[1] With Lincoln's re-election in the balance, an air of desperation and doubt had set in among many pro-Union supporters in the North. The president himself was doubtful of his electoral prospects. In summoning Douglass, Lincoln was gambling that an infusion of newly liberated blacks into the North would invigorate the Union army, and further demoralize the South. Surprised and somewhat dumbfounded, Douglass nevertheless agreed to raise this band of black spies with the hope of contributing a death blow to the confederacy and the vile institution of slavery.

It was a crazy plan.

It was perhaps only slightly less desperate than John Brown's attempted raid at Harpers Ferry four years earlier. That the plan—despite being quickly jettisoned with news of General William Tecumseh Sherman's taking of Atlanta in September 1864—involved the nation's most well-known African American, says much about the distance the nation had traveled since Benjamin Banneker sat down to write to Thomas Jefferson, asking the then secretary of state to raise his voice against slavery.

Indeed, this second meeting between Douglass and Lincoln fell on the exact date of Banneker's letter to Jefferson – August 19, 1864. Nearly three-fourths of a century had passed, yet slavery still persisted. But the institution was on its deathbed, and the current occupant of the White House had put it there with an Emancipation Proclamation. And he was now enlisting the aid of a former slave, a free black man, to help him make that Proclamation stick. The meeting meant a great deal beyond politics to Douglass, who understood the connection between the personal and the political as well as any American who'd ever lived. "He treated me as a man," Douglass recalled later. "He did not let me feel for a moment that there was any difference in the color of our skins."[2]

The story of Douglass and Lincoln's political relationship cannot be separated from their personal feelings for each other. This is because, for different reasons, both men wanted it that way. Douglass would go on to memorialize his encounters with Lincoln over the remainder of his life. Lincoln, assassinated less than a year after his invitation to Douglass, nevertheless engaged in his own efforts to memorialize their relationship. It started early and somewhat innocuously. At that August 1864 meeting with Douglass, Lincoln twice rejected entreaties from his secretary to meet with Governor William Buckingham of Connecticut who was waiting outside the door for the president. "Tell the Governor to wait," said Lincoln, "for I want to have a long talk with my friend Frederick Douglass."[3]

A year earlier, Douglass's first word heard upon entering the White House was the word "nigger"—a far cry from "my friend." Douglass, like countless African Americans, had heard that former word nearly to the point of numbness. What struck Douglass during his encounters with Lincoln was the president's humanity. This would be the case for each of their meetings—the first and last, unannounced visits by Douglass. Indeed, the meetings between Lincoln and Douglass, like the exchange of letters between Banneker and Jefferson, reveal much about the state of racial affairs in America. They also shed light on how interracial friendship served as a proxy for what was politically possible. It is not too much to say that both Lincoln and Douglass were perhaps the two best political performers produced in the history of the United States. Each understood that the symbolism of their respective positions—Lincoln as president, Douglass as leader of his people—compelled them to shape public opinion through the art of politics. This meant using words, gestures, and memory as tools for conveying to their followers a vision for a better life—for illustrating what a truly democratic society would look like. They would each, in his own way, use the other to suggest a way forward. It was no easy task, as both men represented groups imbued with deep skepticism over the question of just how a multiracial democracy might emerge in a nation where the very possibility had been the source of its greatest calamity.

"I Felt Big in There!"

By the time Frederick Douglass met Abraham Lincoln for the first time in the White House on August 10, 1863, it was he, and not the president, who had spent the better part of his life in the public eye. Lincoln was elected to the presidency in 1860 as a relative unknown— his public debates with Senator Stephen Douglas in 1858 were to that point his most notable moment of national recognition. Douglass, on the other hand, was not only a prominent figure on his way to being the most photographed person in the nineteenth century, he was also internationally renowned, having delivered lectures in Ireland, Scotland, and England.[4] He was, as Douglass biographer David W. Blight has described him, "the most famous black person in the world."[5] Douglass's *Narrative of the Life of Frederick Douglass, an American Slave* turned him into a celebrated figure, if not an outright celebrity.

The book became an instant success, selling five thousand copies in the first four months. By the end of 1847, after Douglass' twenty-month tour of the British Isles, the bestseller had gone through nine editions and sold eleven thousand copies. And by 1860, it had sold thirty thousand and been translated into French and German.[6]

Meanwhile, Abraham Lincoln was a man with no political office, hoping to make a name for himself in the Republican Party and somehow seize the nomination for president in 1860. A vice-presidential nod seemed more in the offing—and even that looked bleak. When Lincoln visited Cooper Union in New York in February of 1860, there was reason to believe he'd be more likely to be laughed out of the city than to win over skeptical New Yorkers, who were somewhat bewildered by this odd-looking and high-pitched Westerner.[7] The *New York Times'* announcement of his visit was offered without fanfare, a short notice buried on page 8, sandwiched between the story of a man "seriously injured" after being thrown from a wagon, and another notice about 180 new brownstones being constructed uptown.

HON. ABRAHAM LINCOLN IN NEW YORK. —Hon.
ABRAHAM LINCOLN, of Illinois, will speak at the Cooper
Institute on Monday evening, on questions of National Politics. His arrival in the City on the 27th inst.
is anticipated. [8]

For a politician who had been thinking about his connection to the Framers of the Constitution since the earliest days of his political career, Lincoln had been only marginally successful in electoral politics. Yet, in the spring of 1860 the underrated and unschooled Kentucky-born lawyer had wrested the Republican Party nomination from men who'd been far more educated and entrenched party insiders.

When Lincoln met with Douglass three years later, Americans were living in a different country. The nation was not only divided politically, with eleven states having seceded; the country was also at war. It is likely that nearly 750,000 men died as a result of the conflict— a number considerably larger than previously thought.[9] And if anything could be more significant than that fact, for the first time in the nation's history the president of the United States had issued a proclamation declaring enslaved Africans "forever free." The Emancipation Proclamation was the terse, legalistic document its critics suggested it was at the time. Those slaves emancipated on January 1, 1863, were only those in bondage in states in rebellion to the Union. But the document was also profoundly liberating, as Douglass understood.

Speaking on the subject of the Proclamation at Cooper Union in February 1863, some three years after Lincoln's visit to the same hall, Douglass exuded tremendous joy and unbridled levity in his speech to the mostly white audience. As David Blight wrote in the *New York Times*, Douglass drew laughter as he ended his remarks, joking that he'd "felt whiter and combed his hair more easily," since January 1.[10] More substantively, Douglass addressed the arguments posed by some abolitionists, that the Proclamation didn't go far enough.

> It is again objected to this proclamation that it is only an ink and paper proclamation. I admit it. The objector might go a step further, and assert that there was a time when this Proclamation was only a thought, a sentiment, an idea—a hope of some radical Abolitionist—for such it truly was. But what of it? The world has never advanced a single inch in the right direction when the movement could not be traced to some such small beginning . . . [O]ur own Declaration of Independence was at one time but ink and paper.[11]

Nothing changed Douglass's attitude toward Lincoln as much as his September 22, 1862, notice of the forthcoming Proclamation. Douglass had been among Lincoln's harshest critics—denouncing the President for his timidity in attacking slavery. It is not that Douglass was entirely unhopeful about slavery's potential for demise under Lincoln as much as it was that Lincoln seemed more moved by politics to Douglass than by moral opposition to slavery. Taking the measure of Lincoln, after his inaugural address in 1861, Douglass declared the speech "a double-tongued document."

> Mr. Lincoln opens his address by announcing his loyalty to slavery in the slave States, and quotes from the Chicago platform, a resolution affirming the right of property in slaves, in the slave States. He is not content in declaring he has no lawful power to interfere with slavery in the Slave states, but he also denies having the least inclination to *"interfere"* with slavery in the States. This denial of all feeling against slavery, at such a time and under such circumstances, is wholly discreditable to Mr. Lincoln's head and heart.[12]

Douglass thought Lincoln's tone of reconciliation unfit for the occasion. American slavery's brutal legacy—etched on Douglass's back, as he often alluded to the scars of the lash he bore—could only be properly addressed by the moral will to declare slavery an evil and to attack it directly. "Some thought we had in Mr. Lincoln the nerve and decision of an Oliver Cromwell," Douglass wrote after the inauguration. "But the result shows that we merely have a continuation of the Pierces and Buchanans, and that the Republican President bends the knee to slavery as readily as any of his infamous predecessors."[13]

Events would dictate a different outcome, however. Eighteen months after the inaugural address, Lincoln would issue the Emancipation Proclamation. And less than a year after that, Douglass would be in Lincoln's office for the first time. Despite this first meeting's contentiousness over the issue of equal pay for black soldiers, it would leave Douglass feeling very differently about Lincoln, as the two men forged a political alliance, and later a friendship, that would reorder American race relations, giving greater meaning to Lincoln's closing words at his first inaugural address: "We are not enemies, but friends."

Lincoln had prevaricated on the question of slavery over the years. Like Jefferson, he had been only in favor of emancipation that led to colonization. The thought of racial equality among blacks and whites in the United States eluded his imagination. If there was any credit to be had, he was at least honest about it, where Jefferson was evasive. Roughly one year before Douglass's first visit to the White House, Lincoln invited five black leaders to sit with him and discuss the future of the two races. It was an astounding conversation, with Lincoln proposing a colonization and resettlement plan in Africa as the solution to the nation's racial woes. "Why should [blacks] leave the country?" he asked, rhetorically. "You and we are different races. We have between us a broader difference than exists between almost any other two races. Whether it is right or wrong I need not discuss." Lincoln went on to explain how both groups were presently suffering under the weight of each party's presence. "It is better for us both to be separated," he concluded.[14]

Was this August 14, 1862, meeting a last-ditch effort on Lincoln's part to offer an acceptable "out" to blacks before issuing the Emancipation Proclamation? Some forty days later the Proclamation would be announced, and everything would be very different. But Lincoln's shocking proposal would shape Douglass's views of the president leading up to their first meeting. "Mr. Lincoln assumes the language and arguments of an itinerant Colonization lecturer," Douglass wrote.[15] If Lincoln valued anything, it was the preservation of the Union. He had, to this point, expressed a personal opposition to slavery, albeit one that did not rise to the level of attacking it where it already existed. This containment policy infuriated Douglass. In the days leading up to his unscripted meeting with the president, it was but a piece of all his doubts that the man occupying the White House was just a more homespun version of the white supremacists who'd governed the country from its inception.

By August 1863, Douglass had two sons, Charles and Lewis, fighting in the Union Army. It was now an army of liberation, with victory being tantamount to realizing the goal of forever eradicating the institution of slavery from American soil. Lincoln had said as much at Gettysburg. This "new birth of freedom," however, remained a distant object. Black privates were still being paid only $10 per month, while white soldiers were paid $13. To add insult to injury, $3 would be further deducted from the pay of black privates to cover the expense of clothing them.[16] For Douglass, it was another maddening result of Lincoln's reluctance to take a strong stand against racial inequality.

Douglass paid a "flying visit" to Washington, as he described it in his letter to his friend George L. Stearns, to try to turn the tide of discrimination against black soldiers in the Union.[17] His chief objective was to get to Lincoln. As a black man without an official portfolio, Douglass's route was necessarily circuitous. On the morning of August 10, 1863, Douglass first met with Kansas Senator Samuel C. Pomeroy, who agreed to escort Douglass over from his office to the White House. But their first stop was the War Department. Douglass was granted a thirty-minute meeting with Secretary of War Edwin M. Stanton, whom Douglass found "cold and businesslike." Yet, Stanton listened as Douglass prefaced his request by imploring Stanton to disregard caricatures of blacks as either "angels or demons" or "cowardly or brave." What did this have to do with the question of the black presence in the Union army, Stanton inquired. "I answered, Douglass recorded, 'In the unequal pay accorded to colored soldiers and in the fact that no incentive was given to the ambition of colored soldiers and that the regulations confined them to the dead level of privates or non-commissioned officers.'"

If equality meant anything to Douglass, it meant accepting individuals for who they are, not who we imagine them to be. Black soldiers shouldn't have to perform more heroically than whites to command the same pay. Nor should they escape reprimand when they fall short. Stanton agreed, reminding Douglass that he had proposed a bill for the equal pay of black soldiers that passed in the House but did not have enough votes in the Senate to become law. The conversation ended with a surprising request. Stanton asked Douglass to join General Lorenzo Thomas in "raising colored troops on the Mississippi." In thirty minutes Douglass had gone from an aggrieved outsider to someone authorized by the secretary of war to raise black troops. The power of Douglass's presence, his personal history, and his standing among blacks as well as white abolitionists gave him unprecedented status for an African American. Stanton told Douglass he was going to prepare and "send [Douglass] the sufficient papers immediately."

Douglass was pleased with this meeting with Stanton, although "there was nothing from him to me, nor from me to him," Douglass wrote two days after their encounter. Douglass was keen to not only report on the official results of his interactions with whites in power—but also their attitude and demeanor toward him. Stanton was an emotional cipher, but a sympathetic one. Douglass left the War Department with Pomeroy, stopping only to pick up Douglass's pass to go through army lines. John Usher, secretary of the Interior Department, presented the pass to Douglass, which read:

> Frederick Douglass is known to us as a loyal, free man, and is hence, entitled to travel unmolested. We trust he will be recognized every-where as a free man and a gentleman.[18]

It was now on to the White House. When they arrived, Douglass and Pomeroy quickly joined the line of patronage seekers waiting to see Lincoln. Not long after handing his card to an attendant, Douglass was invited in, recalling hearing someone call out "nigger" as he made his way inside.[19] This familiar indignity soon dissipated in significance, as the meeting with the president proved to be extraordinary. Indeed, the contrast in personal warmth exhibited by Stanton and Lincoln would prove most striking to Douglass. For centuries in America, blacks have had to become expert readers in the countenance, body language, and emotional state of whites. This was especially true during slavery, and such assessments had to be drawn immediately. It was no different for Douglass, who took his measure of Lincoln within seconds.

> [I was] received cordially and saw at a glance the justice of the pop-
> ular estimate of his qualities expressed in the prefix "Honest" to the
> name of Abraham Lincoln. I have never seen a more transparent
> countenance. There was not the slightest shadow of embarrassment
> after the first moment.[20]

Douglass observed no discomfort in Lincoln—no betrayal of "embar-rassment." How many whites had Douglass been around—including the most high-minded of abolitionists—who could not help but evince some displeasure or unease in the presence of blacks? Lincoln's face was indeed "honest"—but why should it matter? For Douglass, it indicated that regardless of what was to come out of the president's mouth at this initial meeting, it would be truthful. More significant still, it would come from a man who bore no vestige of perhaps the most pervasive feature of white supremacy in American life: the subtle shade of disgust at having to be in the presence and personal space of black people.

Douglass then recounted the practical points of the meeting. After thanking Lincoln for issuing a retaliatory order binding Union commanders to punish Confederate prisoners for acts of bru-tality administered to captured black Union troops, Douglass noted how Lincoln jumped into a defense of his slavery policy, "instantly upon my ceasing to speak." Lincoln told Douglass that he issued the Emancipation Proclamation only after Union victory at Antietam be-cause he did not wish to erode Northern support for the war or the measure itself. "It would be said," Douglass wrote, recounting Lincoln's explanation, "'Ah! We thought it would come to this. White men were to be killed for negroes.' His general view was that the battles in which negroes had distinguished themselves for bravery and general good conduct was the necessary preparation of the public mind for his proclamation."[21]

But what made the greatest impression on Douglass was Lincoln's rejection of criticisms of him as a vacillator. "No man can say that having once taken the position I have contradicted it or retreated from it," Lincoln told Douglass. "This remark of the President I took as our assurance that whoever else might abandon his anti slavery policy President Lincoln would stand firm to his."[22] Lincoln had challenged Douglass on his record. He defended himself as any politician might, under similar circumstances. But Lincoln did so with Douglass as an equal. Whereas Jefferson offered platitudes to Banneker decades ago, refusing to honestly engage him on his stance concerning slavery, Lincoln talked politics with Douglass—as a means of not only explaining his policy but achieving the larger goal of emancipation.

Months later, on December 4, 1863, Douglass would offer the first public memorialization of his meeting with Lincoln. In front of a large crowd of African Americans gathered at the American Anti-Slavery Society in Philadelphia, Douglass drew out the details of the meeting, explaining how Lincoln was seated, legs stretched out with papers strewn all about him. And then he "began to rise, and continued to rise until he stood over me," Douglass said to laughter.[23] And the beginning of Douglass's message was really the end unto itself. "[P]erhaps you may like to know how the President of the United States received a black man in the White House," Douglass said teasingly to the crowd. "I will tell you how he received me—just as you have seen one gentleman receive another," Douglass said. "With a hand and a voice well-balanced between a kind cordiality and a respectful reserve." And then a line that would come down though the many decades, because it said so much—and says so much about the gaping hole in race relations in the United States. "I tell you I felt big in there!" Douglass said.[24] Although it was the start of his talk, truly nothing more needed to be said.

"My Friend Douglass"

"[E]very man who wishes well to the slave and to the country should at once rally with all warmth and earnestness of his nature to support

Abraham Lincoln."[25] Those were the words of Frederick Douglass, written a little over a month after his second meeting with Lincoln. The letter, sent to the great abolitionist William Lloyd Garrison, reflected the startling about-face Douglass had undergone with respect to Lincoln. The President had impressed Douglass in their first meeting; their second encounter—this time at the invitation of Lincoln—created perhaps the first great bond between an American president and the leader of a social movement.[26]

Whereas Douglass's first visit to the White House had come in the aftermath of Union victory at Gettysburg and the admission of black troops into the Union army, his second visit came amid the uncertainty of the summer of 1864. The Wilderness Campaign saw unprecedented bloodshed as General Ulysses S. Grant relentlessly pursued his Confederate counterpart, Robert E. Lee, in Virginia. The loss of life and seemingly endless nature of the war placed Lincoln's reelection in grave jeopardy—with former Union general and Democratic candidate George B. McClellan running under the banner of compromise with the South and the perpetuation of slavery. Douglass later recalled this second meeting as a profound reflection of Lincoln's newly radical posture toward slavery.

Lincoln began by sharing with Douglass the dire situation: white opposition to the war in the North was growing—namely because it was being increasingly seen as a war over slavery. Lincoln feared being put into the position of having to accept a compromise with the South, with slavery still in place for those blacks unable to get to Union lines. Douglass recalled Lincoln telling him in a "regretful tone," " 'The slaves are not coming so rapidly and so numerously to us as I had hoped.' "[27] Douglass replied that slave masters were skillful at keeping information from their slaves. Many slaves had no knowledge of the policy granting freedom to those able to get to Union lines. "Well, I want you to set about devising some means of making them acquainted with it, and for bringing them into our lines." Douglass was moved by Lincoln's concern—and for his plan to enlist Douglass in a secret mission to inform enslaved blacks in the South of the policy—to, in short, bring as many to freedom as possible. "What he said on this day," Douglass later wrote, "showed a greater moral conviction against slavery than I had ever seen before in anything spoken or written by him."

Douglass agreed to the plan, leaving the White House as a newly minted covert agent tasked by an American president with helping to strike a death blow to slavery. Moreover, Lincoln had met with Douglass for about an hour, twice delaying his meeting with a Republican governor for "his friend Douglass." It was not the last time Lincoln called Douglass his friend within earshot of others. Nor was it their last meeting. But Douglass had one regret related to this meeting. A day or more after, Lincoln invited Douglass for "tea out at the Soldiers' Home, the presidential summer retreat within the District of Columbia."[28] A White House messenger delivered the note personally to Douglass, a carriage outside, ready to take him. This was apparently a social call— "a simple gesture of friendship."[29] Douglass couldn't make it, declining so he could attend a speaking engagement he'd agreed to. It was a decision that would haunt him.

Douglass did follow up with his only letter to Lincoln. Written on August 29, 1864, ten days after their meeting, Douglass informed Lincoln that he had come up with a plan to inform blacks enslaved in the South that the Union was granting safety and freedom once they reached Union lines. Douglass wanted Lincoln to hire an agent in charge of recruiting some twenty-five sub-agents who would be authorized to scout out escaped slaves behind "rebel lines." These men would be authorized to hire others to help effectuate the plan. These "squads," as Douglass called them, were but part of what he acknowledged to be "an imperfect outline of the plan." He signed the letter, "Your Obedient Servant, Fdk. Douglass." It was the only official correspondence between the two men.[30]

Whatever hopes Lincoln had after meeting with Douglass this time were superseded by deep concern about his and the country's future prospects. "This morning, as for some days past," Lincoln wrote to himself in a private memo, "it seems exceedingly probable that this administration will not be re-elected. Then it will be my duty to so cooperate with the President-elect as to save the Union between the election and the inauguration."[31] That next inauguration would be attended by Douglass—and it would be Lincoln's inauguration, not McClellan's. Events turned in favor of the Union as the war of attrition in Virginia pushed the Confederate army to the brink of collapse in the fall of 1864. Notably, in this moment of great despair, Lincoln had invited Douglass into his circle of influence. And he wanted—seemed intent on getting—Douglass and others to know that Douglass's value to him was not, strictly speaking, political. Douglass was becoming an intimate—in Lincoln's words, a friend. That friendship was clearly not of the kind that either man had cultivated with others over their many combined years. But it had the unique character of being tied to the great project of expanding representative democracy to those historically locked out. And both men seemed to appreciate that it was not likely that the country could have a political democracy without erecting a social one as well.

Years later, reflecting on this second visit to the White House, how he had insisted Lincoln see Governor Buckingham of Connecticut, even as Lincoln insisted otherwise, Douglass offered high praise for this most unusual man. "I have often said elsewhere what I wish to repeat here—that Mr. Lincoln was not only a great President, but a GREAT MAN—too great to be small in anything. In his company I was never reminded of my humble origins or of my unpopular color."[32] Somehow, it had always been the province of whites, no matter how sympathetic, to remind Douglass of his place. It was not an uncommon experience for African Americans during slavery and Jim Crow—and not altogether a relic of American history even today. But Douglass marked it out as an essential quality of Lincoln's leadership—of his humanity—that he could see Douglass's race, while also seeing him as his equal.

"A Sacred Effort"

As Lincoln biographer Ronald C. White Jr. notes, days after Lincoln's assassination, Douglass spoke at a memorial for the slain president in Douglass's hometown of Rochester, New York. There, on Saturday, April 15, 1865, he quoted verbatim and from memory, an extraordinary passage from Lincoln's second inaugural address. It was the master stroke of what many consider to be Lincoln's greatest speech—and it moved Douglass unlike anything Lincoln had ever said. What could Douglass, the former slave from the same Maryland region of Benjamin Banneker, have thought when he heard the sunken-eyed Lincoln speak these words?

Fondly do we hope—fervently do we pray—that this mighty scourge of war may speedily pass away. Yet if God wills that it continue, until all the wealth piled by the bond-man's two hundred and fifty years of unrequited toil shall be sunk, and until every drop of blood drawn with the lash, shall be paid by another drawn with the sword, as was said three thousand years ago, so still it must be said "the judgments of the Lord are righteous altogether."[33]

What American president had ever equated slavery with a moral evil so grave as to warrant divine retribution? Thomas Jefferson did attempt something similar in 1781, when he expressed that "I tremble for my country when I reflect that God is just: that his justice cannot sleep for ever: that considering numbers, nature and natural means only, a revolution of the wheel of fortune, an exchange of situation, is among possible events: that it may become probable by supernatural interference!"[34] Of course, Jefferson's "exchange of situation" where whites suffered under conditions similar to those of enslaved blacks, was entirely prospective. And Jefferson's fear, expressed decades before his presidency, was confined to his *Notes on Virginia*; it was not offered for the type of national discussion ensured by placement in an inaugural address. But Lincoln went further: the suffering of whites during the Civil War, was *earned*. It was indeed a requirement of justice, as Jefferson had suggested many decades before. While Jefferson's vision was one where blacks had turned the table on whites, Lincoln's interpretation of divine retribution was premised on the reality of a conflict where upward of 750,000 whites had lost their lives at the hands of men who looked like them.

Jefferson's "divine retribution" for American slavery was the least likely of his two possible turns of fate. The other he alluded to was demographic change—what he called "numbers, nature and natural means only." Blacks at some future point, may well outnumber whites. That future never materialized; it was, in the end, the political failure to address slavery's incompatibility with representative government that was the true impetus for "God's will" to present itself. No matter, what Lincoln said was powerful—and nearly an unimaginable utterance for an American president today. The passage cemented in Douglass's mind something ineffable about Lincoln's leadership and his sincerity about racial equality. Douglass had long been deeply skeptical of American Christianity and its complicity with slavery. As he wrote in his *Narrative*:

> The slave auctioneer's bell and the church-going bell chime in with each other, and the bitter cries of the heart-broken slave are drowned in the religious shouts of his pious master. Revivals of religion and revivals in the slave trade go hand in hand together. The slave prison and the church stand near each other. The clanking of fetters and the rattling of chains in the prison, and the pious psalm and solemn prayer in the church, may be heard at the same time.[35]

Lincoln's speech shattered this odious relationship, at least in that moment. Reflecting on the second inaugural address years later, Douglass said, "The address sounded more like a sermon than a state paper."[36] It was the kind of sermon sorely missing from the churches most Americans attended.

As Douglass recounted in his *Autobiography*, Lincoln saw Douglass at the inauguration in the front of the crowd before Chief Justice Samuel Chase administered the oath of office. At once, Lincoln tapped Vice President Andrew Johnson, pointing Douglass out to him in the front of the crowd. Immediately, Douglass discerned in Johnson "the true index of his heart . . . one of bitter contempt and aversion." Johnson quickly tried to cover it up with a "bland and sickly smile," Douglass recalled, but it was the type of facial distortion Douglass was deeply familiar with.[37] Once again, Douglass was merging a personal observation with the political. The social dynamics of white supremacy went hand in hand with its political practices. This is what made Lincoln great, and Douglass so hopeful; it is also what jarred him about Lincoln's assassination. The torch was not only being passed from the Great Emancipator—it was being delivered into the hands of a bitterly racist man. "Whatever Andrew Johnson may be," Douglass told the woman next to him at the inauguration, "he is no friend of our race."[38]

When Lincoln completed his remarks, Douglass decided he must attend the inaugural reception at the White House to offer his congratulations. He had a hard time getting any of his black friends to join him, however, as they didn't want to face what they knew would be the enumerable indignities associated with trying to attend an all-white reception. They proved to be right. As Douglass approached the door of the executive mansion, "two policemen stationed there took me rudely by the arm and ordered me to stand back for their directions were to admit no persons of my colour."[39]

Douglass was nevertheless insistent.

"I told the officers I was quite sure there was some mistake," Douglass recalled, "for no such order could have emanated from President Lincoln; and if he knew I was at the door he would desire my admission."[40] It was an uncanny conviction—perhaps the first for an African American regarding an American president. Douglass was nevertheless detained, and then misdirected, as the officers brought him in, only to redirect him down the hall, and then, in the direction of a large window where planks had been placed to allow for egress outside. At this point, Douglass had had it.

"You have deceived me," Douglass told them. "I shall not go out of this building till I have seen President Lincoln." At this moment, Douglass recalled seeing someone passing by who recognized him, and called out to them to inform the president that "Frederick Douglass is detained by officers at the door." Somehow, Douglass soon found himself headed to the East Room of the White House "amid a scene of elegance such as in this country I had never seen before." There, the statesman and the prophet met for the last time.

Like a mountain pine high above all others Mr. Lincoln stood, in his grand simplicity and home-like beauty. Recognizing me, even before I reached him, he exclaimed so all around could hear him, "Here comes my friend, Douglass!" Taking me by the hand he said, "I am glad to see you. I saw you in the crowd to-day listening to my inaugural address. How did you like it?"

Douglass tried to demure, but Lincoln was having none of it. "No, no. You must stop a little, Douglass," Lincoln chided him. "There is no man in the country whose opinion I value more than yours. I want to know what you think of it?"

"Mr. Lincoln," Douglass replied, "that was a sacred effort."

The two had played their parts exceptionally well. Lincoln calling out Douglass by name, "There's my friend Douglass!" It wasn't for Douglass's benefit as much as it was meant for the white policeman who had detained him, the white guests who perhaps felt superior to him, and the soul of a nation that rejected the personhood of Douglass and his people. "My friend" cut the air of formality and placed not only Douglass, but every black person, in the East Room of the White House in that moment. This was the reconstruction of the soul that Lincoln knew must be undertaken by whites—who had four years been instructed by the "sword," as he had made plain in his inaugural speech.

And then there was Douglass, in his role—the Joseph-like figure stolen away into Egypt and now in its corridors of power and "elegance," as he described it. But this was a good pharaoh—a man of the people—and Douglass respectfully declined to give his opinion at first, out of respect for the office as much as for the man. For now this was an office that his people would have to begin to respect; to deal with. There was power in the corridors of the building Douglass was nearly thrown out of. And he had to model respect—but a respect without fear or awe. And so when pressed, he gave Lincoln the answer, really the only answer commensurate with the address and the moment. The "sacred effort" was the speech; but it was also the journey of Douglass and blacks to arrive at this threshold of freedom; and it was the work of these two men, who understood that the new democracy they were both constructing in the moment required something beyond bandages and soldiers' pensions. It required a deeper bond. As Douglass said in his own words upon reflecting on this final visit with Lincoln, "My colored friends were well pleased with what to them had seemed a doubtful experiment, and I believe encouraged by my example to follow its example. I have found in my experience the way to break down an unreasonable custom is to contradict it in practice."

Lincoln and Douglass together had contradicted hundreds of years of social custom in their three meetings. But their last was an opportunity—one that arose out of the indignities of the social custom of segregation—that provided the stage for them to act out what a better custom looked like. It was an extraordinary moment—one that would not be replicated for many decades, for its sincerity or for the commitment of its protagonists to defy convention and absorb the risks that come with it.

Conclusion: "Taking Him for All in All"

A few months after Lincoln's assassination, Douglass received a package at his Rochester home. It contained a note from Mary Todd Lincoln, the widowed wife of the late president. The letter accompanied an unusual token: Abraham Lincoln's favorite walking stick. The cane is held today at the Frederick Douglass National Historic Site in Washington, DC. It is the home where Douglass lived from 1877 until his death in 1895. Overwhelmed by this gesture, Douglass wrote to Mary Todd Lincoln to thank her. He did so drawing the same connection between the personal and the political he had been making ever since he met Lincoln for the first time two years before.

> I assure you, that this inestimable memento of his Excellency will be retained in my possession while I live—an object of sacred interest—a token not merely of the kind consideration in which I have reason to know that the President was pleased to hold me personally, but as an indication of his humane interest in the welfare of my whole race.[41]

The warmth Douglass felt in Lincoln's presence was significant. When coupled with his transformation on the question of slavery and his political commitment to black equality, Lincoln became a most unique figure for Douglass. Friendship without political equality was insufficient; with it, the nation had untold possibilities going forward. Both men understood this. It would take arguably another hundred years before an American president and black advocate for racial justice shared a common vision for multiracial democracy in the United States. The lost opportunities were generational: Booker T. Washington and Teddy Roosevelt; W. E. B. Du Bois and Woodrow Wilson; FDR and A. Philip Randolph. These all were reflections of the dominant story in American interracial fraternity—political obfuscation, insincerity, and compromise with white supremacy. For a brief moment, Lincoln and Douglass pointed the way. "I know that damned Douglass," President Andrew Johnson would declare after meeting with Douglass and a delegation of blacks in February of 1866. "[H]e's just like any nigger, and he would sooner cut a white man's throat than not."[42] Tragically, the door that Lincoln and Douglass had begun to open was soon closed, as the Jim Crow era's rules of interracial engagement soon crept into the protocols of presidential behavior. Their three meetings nevertheless remained a hopeful symbol of interracial friendship and multiracial democracy in an otherwise closed society.

Douglass never let his affection and admiration for Lincoln get in the way of frank assessment of his legacy. He saw Lincoln's flaws as well as his strengths, placing them beside each other so as to draw out the significance of what Lincoln had achieved. His most earnest re-flection came in 1876, in a centennial oration in Washington, DC, for the erection of what was the first true "Lincoln Memorial," otherwise known in its time as the Emancipation Memorial. The unveiling of the statue was on April 14, some twenty-one years to the day of Lincoln's assassination. With President Grant in the audience, Douglass spoke, as he so often did, with cutting honesty and searing insight. He first reminded his audience that only twenty years prior, such a gathering of whites and blacks in the nation's capital would have been unthinkable, resulting in all likelihood in "an excuse for opening upon us all the flood-gates of wrath and violence."[43]

Perhaps invoking Lincoln's closing words of the second inaugural address ("with malice towards none"), Douglass said he did not mean to "refer to the past . . . in malice, for this is no day for malice; but simply to place more distinctly in front the gratifying and glorious change which has come both to our white fellow-citizens and our-selves, and to congratulate all upon the contrast between now and then." But then Douglass went to the heart of the matter—as he had done in 1852 during his oration to celebrate Independence Day. "What to the Slave is the Fourth of July?" went on to become one of the greatest speeches ever delivered by an American, its greatness insepa-rable from its brutal honesty. And Douglass was no less honest in front of this audience.

It must be admitted, truth compels me to admit, even here in the presence of the monument we have erected to his memory, Abraham

Lincoln was not, in the fullest sense of the word, either our man or our model. In his interests, in his associations, in his habits of thought, and in his prejudices, he was a white man.

He was pre-eminent the white man's President, entirely devoted to the welfare of white men. He was ready and willing at any time during the first years of his administration to deny, postpone, and sacrifice the rights of humanity in the colored people to promote the welfare of the white people of this country.

Like a dinner guest dredging up bad news from the past, Douglass went to the heart of Lincoln's failings as a statesman. And who could doubt his veracity? Weeks before issuing the Emancipation Proclamation, Lincoln was hosting black leaders in the White House with the hope of convincing them that a back-to-Africa movement would better serve both races than any effort at racial equality in America. Emphasizing his point, Douglass said, "The race to which we belong were not the special objects of his consideration. . . . First, midst, and last, you and yours were the objects of his deepest affection and his most earnest solicitude. You are the children of Abraham Lincoln. We are at best only his step-children."

If one of Lincoln's forms of genius was his ability to compel introspection in his countrymen—as he did most forthrightly in the second inaugural address—then it was a genius shared by Douglass. Both men eschewed the cheap fraternity of platitudes and apolitical niceties. Friends not only sup together—they have the unique ability to be frank with one another, unafraid that their love and bond will suffer. Recognizing that Lincoln upheld the Fugitive Slave Law for as long as he needed to keep support from the border states, Douglass nevertheless acknowledged that "under his rule" blacks found their emancipation. The refrain "under his rule" gave African Americans a greater role in the history of slavery's abolition than the statue standing before Douglass and his audience that day suggested. The memorial included a cowered slave underneath Lincoln, who benevolently seemed to call for his rise. Douglass thought the memorial statue more of a relic of subservience than a dignified portrayal of a newly liberated race. But these observations did not shortchange Lincoln's ultimate contribution.

His great mission was to accomplish two things: first, to save his country from dismemberment and ruin; and second, to free his country from the great crime of slavery. To do one or the other, or both, he must have the earnest sympathy and the powerful co-operation of his loyal fellow countrymen. Without this primary and essential condition to success his efforts must have been vain and utterly fruitless. Had he put the abolition of slavery before the salvation of the Union, he would have inevitably driven from him a powerful class of the American people and rendered resistance to rebellion impossible. Viewed from the genuine abolition ground, Mr. Lincoln seemed tardy, cold, dull, and indifferent; but measuring him by the sentiment of his country, a sentiment he was bound as a statesman to consult, he was swift, zealous, radical, and determined.

Douglass evaluated Lincoln politically in terms keeping with the reality that he had led a nation historically committed to white supremacy. He evaluated him personally, as a man based on his internal qualities and private conduct. "[T]aking him for all in all," Douglass concluded, "measuring the tremendous magnitude of the work before him, considering the necessary means to ends, and surveying the end from the beginning, infinite wisdom has seldom sent any man into the world better fitted for his mission than Abraham Lincoln."

As Douglass biographer David W. Blight notes, years later Douglass would reflect on Lincoln's assassination and the moment he spoke in Rochester before a largely white audience to eulogize Lincoln. Thinking about his audience that day, Douglass articulated a sentiment that illuminates what Lincoln meant to him as a man, and to the country at large. "I had resided long in Rochester and had many speeches there which had more or less touched the hearts of my hearers, but never to this day was I brought into such close accord with them," Douglass recalled. "We shared in common a terrible calamity, and this touch of nature made us more than countrymen, it made us Kin."[44]

During the Second World War, a national competition was held to create a mural for the Recorder of Deeds building in Washington, DC. The contestants had to have a scene from African American history as its subject. Seven finalists were selected—including one whose subject was Benjamin Banneker. The winner was William Eduard Scott, whose 1943 mural was "Frederick Douglass Appealing to Lincoln and His Cabinet." In it, Douglass's arms are outstretched, palms upward, with a troubled countenance on his face. Lincoln is seated opposite Douglass, and equally grave. Two unnamed cabinet members look on. It is a portrayal of Douglass's 1863 meeting with Lincoln, where he sought equal pay for black soldiers—though the mural suggests it was a meeting to enlist black soldiers into the Union army. No matter; in the end, the contest sought to cull from the limited national reservoir of historic unity, something grand to aid the nation in its greatest crisis since the American Civil War. And what better image of democracy's possibilities than that of Douglass and Lincoln in the White House? Their short-lived friendship was, in its time and for decades to come, a symbol burdened by the nation's inability to achieve in politics what its subjects were able to achieve in life. Their effort was indeed sacred, and for many years thereafter, tragically unmatched.

3

Color Lines

W. E. B. Du Bois and William James

Introduction: Consciousness Among Friends

Three years into his graduate studies at Harvard University, W. E. B. Du Bois received an invitation from William James, his brilliant philosophy professor. The occasion was a dinner to be held on Valentine's Day, 1891.

> Dear Mr. Du Bois,
> Won't you come to
> a philosophical
> supper on Saturday,
> Feb. 14th, at half past
> seven o'clock?
> Yours Truly,
> William James

Despite his outstanding undergraduate record at Fisk University, the historically black college in Nashville, Tennessee, Du Bois remained a curiosity at Harvard. While not the first or only black student at Harvard, Du Bois became the first African American to receive a PhD from the institution. He lived a decidedly segregated existence in Cambridge, as evident from an absence of white friends to the denial of his acceptance into the university's glee club. The latter was an inexplicably insulting blow. "Following the attitudes which I had adopted in the South, I sought no friendships among my white fellow students, nor even aquaintanceships," Du Bois wrote. "Of course I wanted friends, but I could not seek them. My class was large, with some 300 students. I doubt if I knew a dozen of them. I did not seek them, and naturally they did not seek me. . . . Only one organization did I try to enter, and I ought to have known better than to make this attempt. But I did have a good singing voice and loved music, so I entered the competition for the Glee Club. I ought to have known that Harvard could not have a Negro on its Glee Club traveling about the country. Quite naturally I was rejected."[1]

Du Bois was, by his own estimation, "in Harvard, but not of it."[2] Nevertheless, James's invitation had to have elevated his spirits as much as it elevated his standing as a budding scholar.[3] Many years later, in his autobiography, Du Bois would write, "James and one or two other teachers had me at their homes at meal and reception," but only James would be named.[4] With James's invitation delivered just shy of Du Bois's twenty-third birthday, Du Bois became a member of Harvard's Philosophical Club—an affirmation of his outstanding intellect—and, by implication, recognition that social equality among the races was a real possibility.

It was Du Bois who famously wrote, "The problem of the twentieth century is the problem of the color line."[5] Yet, halfway through Barack Obama's second term as America's first (and only, thus far) African American president, the *Washington Post* reported that three-fourths of all whites had no black friends, while slightly less than two-thirds of blacks surveyed had no white friends.[6] The report came almost fifty-one years to the day after Du Bois's death was announced at the March on Washington. In his seminal work, *The Souls of Black Folk*, published in 1903, Du Bois had written, "In a world where it means so much to take a man by the hand, to sit beside him, and look frankly into his eyes and feel his heart beating with red blood; in a world where a social cigar or cup of tea together means more than legislative halls and magazine articles and speeches—one can imagine the almost utter absence of such social amenities between estranged races, whose separation extends even to parks and streetcars."[7]

While James's views on race reflected some of the deeply held and problematic presumptions of black equality during his lifetime, he likewise extolled the movement toward progressive politics that would counter the more retrograde beliefs of the period, one defined by *Plessy v. Ferguson's* (1896) dictate of "separate but equal." Indeed, James took pride in his younger brother Wilky's participation in the 54th Massachusetts Infantry Regiment's assault on Fort Wagner during the Civil War. Among the regiment's one thousand black soldiers were Charles and Lewis Douglass, the sons of Frederick Douglass. Garth Wilkinson James, or "Wilky," was seriously wounded during the battle. Many years later, James would memorialize the assault and the black soldiers who died making it, in a famous oration at the Robert Gould Shaw memorial in Boston, named for the white colonel who died leading the charge on the fort.

James was one of the most extraordinary intellectuals produced in American history. Before his career as a philosopher he entertained one as an artist—his sketch of Wilky's recovery after Fort Sumter is a small but poignant reminder of his talent; he also abandoned a path toward medicine, graduating Harvard Medical School in 1869, the year after Du Bois's birth. He would never practice medicine. Instead, after recovering from a period of serious depression, James pursued psychology, helping to establish the discipline in America. His *Principles in Psychology* (1890) remains a classic in the field. If that weren't enough, James moved quickly on to philosophy, becoming a founding theorist in what would become known as pragmatism. Finally, James would write what arguably became the most influential scholarly study in religion by an American in the twentieth century. His work *The Varieties of Religious Experience* (1902) remains required reading for many undergraduates today.

When Du Bois met James in his philosophy class in 1888, he was a much heralded and financially strapped young man with high aspirations. Du Bois never quite lost an elite bearing in his life—fastidiously dressed, formal, studious—a manner cultivated at Harvard and during his later study-abroad experience in Berlin. But he was still a Negro, bourgeois though he may have been. He was a figure lurking behind "the veil," a metaphor Du Bois would often employ to describe the experience of black life in America. James's invitation was an opportunity for both men to lift the veil, to have that "social cigar" Du Bois would write about in *The Souls of Black Folk*. Their short time together at Harvard could have been no more than that, but Du Bois internalized his time with James as much more—and he would go on to immortalize it as an object lesson in what intellectual and social equality among the races might look like in a just society. Du Bois was no ordinary student, and through a kind of alchemy, he memorialized one of the most important interracial friendships in American history. Some of it was even true. All of it was part of the creative project of building American democracy.

"An Extraordinary Aggregation of Great Men"

Writing nearly fifty years after receiving his doctorate from Harvard, Du Bois reflected on his time there and what it meant to him. "The Harvard of 1888 was an extraordinary aggregation of great men. Not often since that day have so many distinguished teachers been together in one place and time in America," Du Bois wrote in his biography of race in America, *Dusk of Dawn* (1940). Undoubtedly, Du Bois saw himself as part of that collection of "great men"—though he held the highest regard for James among the illuminated field of intellectuals he encountered, one that included the highly influential philosophers George Santayana and Josiah Royce, and the incomparable historian Albert Bushnell Hart. "By good fortune, I was thrown into direct contact with many of these men," Du Bois wrote. "I was repeatedly a guest in the house of William James; he was my friend and guide to clear thinking."[8]

It was Du Bois's interest in philosophy that "landed me squarely in the arms of William James of Harvard, for which, God be praised."[9] Du Bois would not describe any of his other professors with such affection—and James is the only one he called a "friend." But first, James was his instructor. In his notes from James's second half of his 1888–1890 Philosophy course, Du Bois records, "James believes in conscience as a separate faculty as a fact but claims that upon its dicta as to conduct are not alone to be depended on: we must appeal to consequences."[10] What we *feel* we must do is insufficient grounds for action; right actions can only be determined by considering how our behavior might affect the real world. In a sense, this brief insight explains James's practical advice to Du Bois before graduating—if he wanted the best prospects for a job, one that would affect the most change in society, he should move from the pursuit of philosophy toward history and social science.

"If you must study philosophy you will," Du Bois recalled James telling him, "but if you can turn aside into something else, do so."[11] Du Bois nevertheless gained immeasurably from his experience with philosophy with James as his professor, a point I will come to in the next section. Du Bois took his professor's advice. The young scholar proved to be a person of action as much as he was one of ideas, helping to found the National Association for the Advancement of Colored People (NAACP) in 1909, while editing its influential paper, *The Crisis*. In addition to his prolific career as a writer, Du Bois would go on to lead anti-lynching campaigns, organize numerous conferences of black intellectuals and leaders, all while serving as a tireless ambassador in the global struggle for racial justice. But Du Bois was, first and foremost, a scholar and a thinker.

Who knows how often Du Bois attended those Philosophical Club dinners at James's home? By Du Bois's account he went fairly regularly. Beyond these august gatherings, we have Du Bois's account of a trip he and James took to Roxbury, Massachusetts, to visit none other than Helen Keller in 1892. Du Bois recalled the trip vividly decades later:

> When I was studying philosophy at Harvard under William James, we made an excursion one day out to Roxbury. We stopped at the Blind Asylum and saw a young girl who was blind and deaf and dumb, and yet who, by infinite pains and loving sympathy, had been made to speak without words and to understand without sound. She was Helen Keller. Perhaps just because she was blind to color differences in this world, I was intensely interested in her, and all throughout my life I have followed her career.[12]

One can't help but wonder what the conversation was like between Du Bois and James before and after this meeting. Du Bois's account leaves us with the impression of two friends sharing a powerful moment of great cultural and sociological significance. Yet James biographer Robert D. Richardson offers a less intimate and more complete account. The May 1892 visit to Keller was a "field trip" organized by James. And Du

Bois was but one of sixteen students who joined the Harvard professor to interview the twelve-year-old Keller. James brought Keller an ostrich feather, telling her, "I thought you would like the feather, it is soft, light, caressing." For whatever reason, Du Bois provided little detail of this trip, nor did he make mention of others in attendance. In his account, Du Bois and James had the wondrous Keller to themselves.[13]

A good deal of Du Bois's recollections of his time with James appear not so much as untruthful, but rather, carefully tailored to depict a close, personal relationship. Why Du Bois might have chosen to do so is another matter—but for now, suffice it to say that Du Bois wanted the historical record to reflect his deep fondness for his professor, one defined by the bonds of education and friendship. Of course, friendships between faculty and students at Harvard were hardly natural occurrences, particularly in an era guided by Victorian notions of propriety and rank. Even the great George Santayana, Du Bois's senior by only five years, who, after receiving his doctorate from Harvard in 1889 and joining the faculty thereafter, found the great philosopher more than difficult to approach. "I for instance, was sure of his goodwill and kindness, of which I had many proofs; but I was also sure he never understood me," Santayana would recall, noting that James's bearing made "spontaneous friendship impossible."[14]

As Kim Townshend's *Manhood at Harvard* (1996) notes, "the Civil War brought about a narrowing of the common definition of manhood," with the word *masculinity* appearing for the first time in the 1890 Century Dictionary.[15] The Harvard of James and Du Bois began to epitomize the staid, strong, virile conception of masculinity—and Santayana, a closeted gay man, found the institution uncommonly difficult to navigate at times. It was a period marked by masculinity's presumed opposition to "womanish" behavior—and this made certain friendships likely more difficult to come by. Yet James had little trouble establishing a close relationship with Josiah Royce, for example, despite disagreements on important philosophical matters.[16] Because the Philosophical Club was one of those American "rooms where it happens," we are not privy to how Du Bois was received by James or others in that space. What's important is that Du Bois believed his inclusion significant—all the more so because of its signifier of a special bond with James.

In 1890 Du Bois received his second bachelor's degree, from Harvard College, after two years of study—a quirk of Harvard's sometime requirement to compel completion of coursework with its faculty when transferring from another institution. The occasion gave Du Bois the chance to deliver the commencement address, when he was selected to speak. He chose Jefferson Davis as his subject, presenting the president of the Confederate States of America as an exemplar of "Teutonic" civilization. The subject was sufficiently "manly" and the address was widely hailed. *The Nation* magazine recorded that Du Bois—"the slender, intellectual looking mulatto"—had "handled his difficult and hazardous subject with absolute good taste, great moderation and almost contemptuous fairness."[17] Du Bois may have been "at Harvard, but not of it"—but he was clearly sensitized to its peculiar tastes. More importantly, Du Bois's time at Harvard, and with James in particular, had helped him develop the language and conceptual framework for explaining the duality of racial identity like no other person in American history. Before graduating, Du Bois would receive a fellowship to study in Berlin. His experiences there would complement his burgeoning sociological understandings of race, as well as interracial intimacy and friendship. Over the course of the next decade, Du Bois would incorporate these experiences and studies into a masterwork that remains unrivaled in its influence.

Double Consciousness

From the works of Ralph Ellison to those of Jordan Peele, whose films have explored the psychic duality found in African Americans, the metaphor of double-consciousness remains W. E. B. Du Bois's most enduring popular expression of black life in America.[18] Indeed, much of the significance of Du Bois and James's friendship revolves around this intersection of the two men's work. It has often been speculated that the closeness of Du Bois and James contributed to the felicity with which Du Bois is said to have appropriated the idea from his professor, whose work in psychology touched upon something James called the "split-off," or "hidden self."[19] For Du Bois, double consciousness—"the sense of always looking at one's self through the eyes of others"—was a novel development in human history, insofar as America's poisonous racial practices brought about a hollowed-out sense of self for African

Americans. The feeling of "two-ness," of being both an American and a Negro, as described by Du Bois, was really a search for a true self, now lost in the refraction of the white gaze.[20] In effect, black people could never quite come to know themselves, except through the prism of what they believed whites thought of them.

Because there is no similar far-reaching concept of Du Bois's associated with any of his other Harvard professors, his relationship with James takes on added importance. But did Du Bois get this "Jekyll–Hyde" metaphor from James? Martin Raitiere is one of a number of historians who chronicle the origins of the term *double consciousness* in America. Raitiere notes that the term goes back at least as far as 1838 when Herbert Mayo used it to describe the "depression of the cerebral forces."[21] Others trace the earliest usage of the term to 1817.[22] The most proximate, relevant usage as far as Du Bois is concerned belongs to that of the French psychologist Alfred Binet, whose book *On Double Consciousness*, William James was familiar with. In 1890, the year Du Bois received his undergraduate degree from Harvard, James published an article in *Scribner's* on "The Hidden Self." The article was an assessment of Binet's unusual methods for tapping into the dream-state of his patients—all women—who were experiencing various states of multiple levels of consciousness. "It must be admitted therefore that, in certain persons at least," James wrote, "the total possible consciousness may be split into parts which coexist, but mutually ignore each other and share the objects of knowledge between them, and—more remarkably still—are complementary."[23] James saw this phenomenon as limited in application but universal in scope. "How far this splitting up of the mind into separate consciousness may obtain in each one of us is a problem."[24] For Du Bois, double consciousness was the *inner* problem that reflected the external problem of race in America.

Neither James's nor Du Bois's interest in consciousness was unique in the history of American political thought. Dickson D. Bruce Jr. notes that Ralph Waldo Emerson used the term *double consciousness* in his 1843 essay, "The Transcendentalist." In it, Emerson wrote, "The worst fear of this double consciousness is, that the two lives, of the understanding and of the soul, which [one] leads, really show very little relation to each other: one prevails now, all abuzz and din; the other prevails then, all infinitude and paradise."[25] Why should James, as opposed to Emerson, be seen as the source for Du Bois's expression of double consciousness? As Alexander Livingston has argued, "critics are correct to warn against any direct parallelism of James and Du Bois's account of double consciousness. But this alone does not repudiate the possibility of reading Du Bois as appropriating and reworking Jamesian concepts in an innovative manner."[26] The bottom line is that James was involved in research related to double consciousness while Du Bois was his student. It's reasonable, if not definitive, to believe that Du Bois learned, or augmented his understanding of, double consciousness from James.

What is undisputed is that Du Bois's use of the expression was truly innovative—connecting the dimension of racialized experience in America to dissociative thinking.

Where Emerson and James used the idea to explore spiritual and psychological struggles, Du Bois married the concept to social forces very much at work in his own life, and the lives of his oppressed brethren. Double consciousness was transformed into something quite new in racial discourse—and perhaps within the field of psychology itself.

In considering the Du Bois–James relationship, it is worth viewing the two outside of the professor–student context and, more broadly, as intellectual interlocutors and, indeed, effectual collaborators, even if unintended. For obvious reasons, Du Bois's own personal experiences with race shaped his intellectual map in ways that escaped James. Du Bois's confrontation with race within the color line invited the formulation of constructs not only useful for navigating the social sciences, but primarily useful for navigating the murky waters of black life in America. It is not so much that James was ignorant of race's role in American life; but what he, and so many of the white progressive thinkers of the period, missed was its central role in national political development. In this light, James's silence on the connections between race and consciousness is staggering—primarily because of his exposure to Du Bois. I'll get to more on James and race shortly.

Most students of Du Bois recognize *double consciousness* as a term used in *The Souls of Black Folk*, published in 1903. But Du Bois's first use of the term in his writings was in 1897, in *The Atlantic* magazine. In his "Strivings of the Negro People," Du Bois begins his essay by writing:

Between me and the other world there is ever an unasked question: unasked by some through feelings of delicacy; by others through the difficulty of rightly framing it. All, nevertheless, flutter round it. They approach me in a half-hesitant sort of way, eye me curiously or compassionately, and then, instead of saying directly, How does it feel to be a problem? they say, I know an excellent colored man in my town; or I fought at Mechanicsville; or, Do not these Southern outrages make your blood boil? At these I smile, or am interested, or reduce the boiling to a simmer, as the occasion may require. To the real question, How does it feel to be a problem? I answer seldom a word.[27]

In recent years, the phrase "between the other world and me" has become familiar, popularized by Ta-Nehisi Coates in his best-selling book of that title—one inspired by Du Bois's question and James Baldwin's *The Fire Next Time*. In "Strivings," Du Bois captured the chasm between the black and white worlds in language that has not been improved upon to this day. "It is a peculiar sensation, this double-consciousness, this sense of always looking at one's self through the eyes of others, of measuring one's soul by the tape of a world that looks on in amused contempt and pity," he wrote. "One feels his two-ness,— an American, a Negro; two souls, two thoughts, two unreconciled strivings; two warring ideals in one dark body, whose dogged strength alone keeps it from being torn asunder."[28]

Du Bois continued his study of race after Harvard, albeit interrupted with a stint in Germany, where his intellectual and personal experiences with race added depth to his perspective on the most searing issue of his time. As the philosopher Kwame Anthony Appiah has suggested, Du Bois's growing use of the terms *soul* and *striving* may have arisen from his exposure to their German equivalents (*geist* and *streben*) while a student in Berlin. In Germany the words carried heavy meaning, with broad, communal application. Again, Du Bois transformed their meaning into an American context where blackness suffused them with new power.[29] Du Bois would experience different forms of "two-ness" in Berlin. On the one hand he was treated better in Germany than he was in America, adopting the dress and manner of an upper-crust gentleman—cane, gloves, top hat, and all; on the other hand, despite his ability to "escape" race at times, he would otherwise be painfully reminded on occasion that such departures from reality were short-lived. As a professor of German History, Kenneth Barkin, has pointed out, Du Bois believed there were only two periods in his life during which he did not suffer overt racism: his childhood in Great Barrington, Massachusetts, and in Europe, by which he meant Germany."[30]

It was in Germany, Du Bois wrote, "that I began to realize white people were human."[31] Du Bois rounded out this statement by later adding, "I had a strong affection for Germany because in the days of my *Strum und Drang*, this was the land where white people treated me as a human being."[32] Indeed, in Germany, Du Bois had several interracial romantic relationships with white women. One was apparently with a woman named Amalie Lebenfeldt, with whom Du Bois lived for a time. Their relationship ended for unknown reasons, though Du Bois would write cryptically in his *Autobiography* that he felt remorse for having caused her "(perhaps) life-ruin." One could only speculate about what this means.[33] The other, more serious relationship was with Dora Marbach, the "raven haired" daughter of a family Du Bois stayed with in Berlin. She took Du Bois dancing about town, as it were, and Du Bois confessed years later to his wife that he had fallen in love with her. When Marbach proposed to Du Bois, he declined, as the prospects of returning to America with a German bride and all the attendant difficulties that would present were too much to bear. He would tell himself, if not Dora, "*Es war so schon gewessen/Es hat nicht sollen sein.*" It would have been so lovely/It could not be.[34] Double consciousness was also an arbiter of love.

William James and Race

William James lived, learned, and taught at the dawn of American imperialism. In the late nineteenth century, the world's most successful democracy was poised to engage with the rest of the world, and this engagement was to follow along the lines of European colonialism—a competition for the world's resources, territory, and, ultimately, power over its peoples. This was made possible by America's growth in industrial might and rapid advancement in scientific discovery. It was philosophically augmented by belief in racial superiority, particularly those derived from scientific theories purported to support northern European biological advancement over other races. After the Civil War, the push to advance American power enlisted the support of both blacks and whites. As the historian John Pettegrew pointed out, popular journalistic accounts of the Spanish–American War were used to unify black and white sentiments concerning American imperialism. "Although the tributes to black soldiering did not last very long past the end of the war against Spain," Pettegrew wrote, "the ideological formulation that heroic masculine character rather than race determined true American identity would be used effectively throughout the twentieth century to mobilize an increasingly heterogeneous U.S. citizenry to foreign war."[35] Of course, many black soldiers would return to the United States to learn something quite different—and Du Bois would be further disillusioned after America's victory in the First World War to learn that where biology vanished as an obstacle to win black support *for* the war, it returned with a vengeance to limit the rewards once the shooting stopped. For Du Bois, the Great War had been "the jealous and avaricious struggle for the largest share in exploiting the darker races."[36] Black folk had been duped once again.

While James was an opponent of American imperialism, it can be said of him, as Eddie Glaude Jr. has written of John Dewey, that James "failed in some significant way to address the evils of white supremacy in his work."[37] Despite the possible reconsideration of his racial stereotypes during his visit to Brazil and the Amazon at the age of twenty-three with Louis Agassiz, America's leading biologist-naturalist-racialist, there are few meaningful accounts of James pondering race with any degree of depth.[38] In an 1865 letter to his parents from the expedition along the Amazon, James wrote of the Indians he encountered. "We slept on the beaches every night and fraternized with the Indians who are socially very agreeable, but mentally a most barren people."[39] Such pithy and presumptive insights raise the question: what kind of friendship was James capable of having with Du Bois—or any other nonwhite person in his life? Was James largely unchanged (or uninterested) in matters of race after meeting Du Bois in 1888 and being in contact with him up until 1907?

James did have occasion to address the issue of race in his Memorial Day oration of 1897 at the unveiling of the Shaw monument commemorating the assault on Fort Wagner, as discussed earlier. At the unveiling, James referred to the "social plague of slavery" and honored the black soldiers who gave their lives to preserve the Union. James's oration, which addressed the black soldiers' contributions somewhat tangentially, nevertheless went further than a great many similar literary and oratorical remembrances. The poet Robert Lowell recalled James's words:

Two months after marching through Boston,
half the regiment was dead;
at the dedication,
William James could almost hear the bronze Negroes breathe.[40]

James's humanizing of the black soldiers was rare for the time. Was this evidence that James did not believe in race as a valid scientific concept, as James scholar Harvey Cormier has suggested?[41]

It's difficult to say. Maria DeGuzmán may have put James's encounters with race best in her essay on "Anglo-American Identity." Noting James's membership in the Anti-Imperialist League, DeGuzmán writes that James did not engage in racial stereotyping with respect to Spaniards or Spanish-speaking people as did his peer and self-proclaimed 'anti-imperialist' Charles Francis Adams." This is an important observation and some indication of James's aversion to socio-racial classifications. "Nevertheless," DeGuzmán continues, "James did not entirely abandon the enterprise of racial stereotyping promoted in his day as a respectable form of 'knowledge' by scholars such as the Harvard based naturalist Louis Agassiz to whom James had served as an assistant. Although James's writings do not amount to a critique of racial typing, they do reveal a concern with the end that discourse was serving: justified imperialism."[42] Agassiz's influence was quite significant, as the Swiss-born naturalist—a member of Boston's earlier intellectual club, the Metaphysical Club—found his teachings on race and black inferiority welcome sources for debate and rumination among the intellectuals of his era.[43]

In fairness, Du Bois himself regretfully recognized his own standing as a fledgling imperialist in these early years. "I am less sure now of this war attitude," Du Bois wrote in *Dusk of Dawn* (1940), in a moment of self-criticism, as he recalled his support for "Our Country" during the Spanish–American War at the outbreak of the Second World War.[44] But Du Bois's concern with race, and to be sure American imperialism (certainly by the publication of *Souls*), appear to have had little impact on James's systematic thinking or predilections concerning race; certainly not nearly as much as Agassiz's.

Some historians have tried to add greater complexity to James's relationship to Du Bois, given James's mixed record on race. Trygve Throntveit has pointed out James's "casual racism" as reflected in his private allusions to the great black industrialist and educator, Booker T. Washington, as "the darkey."[45] Other scholars have excused this epithet. One James biographer goes to some length to depict the descriptor as actually a form of *respect* for Washington by James, rather than one of opprobrium.

> I interpret James's use of *darkey* differently. . . . Using *darkey* was James's way of trying not to be stilted, artificial, or sentimental, but to indicate that he was himself relating with respect and admiration to a person whom many described, whether endearingly or otherwise, as a "darkey." I think it was not condescension but rather James's show of confidence that in *his* use, a word like *darkey*, could take on positive connotations. Because of this confidence, he could afford to show, to his brother [Henry, to whom he was writing] anyway, a lack of fear toward a borderline epithet.[46]

It's one thing to try to view James's language within the context of the times; but it is quite a feat to turn "darkey" into a term of endearment. While James's slur of Washington should be weighed against James's profound life's work with respect to democratic theory and egalitarianism (along with his philosophic pragmatism), we also needn't be compelled to overlook every thorn for every rose of James's, either. The allure of interracial fraternity shouldn't be so blinding.

Making Memories

In his June 6, 1903, letter to his brother Henry, James made a passing reference to Du Bois. "I am sending you a decidedly moving book by a mulatto ex-student of mine," James wrote, "Dubois, professor [of] history at Atlanta (Georgia) negro College. Read Chapters VII to XI for local color, etc."[47] Despite the poor rendering of Du Bois's name, the letter is an expression of the genuine impression Du Bois made on his professor. It recalls Jefferson's shipping of Benjamin Banneker's almanac to France as proof-positive of Negro excellence, if not equality. While James's letter to Henry was not particularly effusive, James was unlikely to have heaped much praise on a recent graduate. That said, it's hard to identify close, or even passing friendship in it. It certainly doesn't compare to Du Bois's written expressions of fondness for James over the years. James's view of his relationship with Du Bois seemed to be more in line with collegiality; Du Bois's with admiration and affection. The historiography that makes Du Bois and James friends may be on par with the same kind of effort that makes Benjamin Banneker "the architect of Washington, DC." It's an understandable wish—but a stretch.

Incidentally, Henry James, one of America's greatest writers, liked *Souls* very much, although his praise for it was made in the context of his view of a dearth of culture in the American South. "How can everything so have gone that the only 'Southern' book of any distinction published for many a year is 'The Souls of Black Folk,' by that most accomplished member of the Negro race, Mr. W. E. B. Du Bois?"[48] Maybe Du Bois was pleased with this review. He didn't say. But it was the kind of assessment at once complimentary but also critical. A backhanded compliment—*white folk's praise*.

In William's letter, Du Bois is a "mulatto ex-student"—a designation worth considering, given that the prevailing belief since Jefferson's time had been that blacks were "improved" by white "blood," while whites were genetically damaged by it. It was James's mentor Louis Agassiz, after all, who wrote, "[I]t is not difficult physiologically to understand why mulattoes with their peculiar constitution should be attractive physically, even though that intercourse should be abhorrent to a refined moral sensibility."[49] It is no small wonder Banneker wanted to be clear in his letter to Jefferson that he was a dark-skinned black man. He didn't want his accomplishments to be "diluted" in the eyes of the white world.

For whatever reason, Du Bois almost always played up his closeness to William James over the years. He is said to have told the literary critic and biographer Arnold Rampersad that "the two most important people in my life were my mother and William James."[50] Granting his memory the benefit of the doubt, the author of this unpublished work, Eugene Taylor, is effusive in ways that go beyond what Du Bois has written. The "indication [is] that James and Du Bois were something more than just casual acquaintances," Taylor wrote. "In fact, James appears to have been one of Du Bois's spiritual mentors."[51] That's quite a lot. Even Francis Broderick's mid-century interview with Du Bois where the aging scholar-activist recalls James as his "favorite teacher and my closest friend," doesn't quite capture the intimacy conveyed in Taylor's description.[52] Did Du Bois "unconsciously" adopt even James's writing style? Taylor seems to think so. Indeed, for Taylor, friendship was James's chief influence upon Du Bois. "Could James's real impact on Du Bois's thinking have been in just such an atmosphere of intimacy and friendship, with all the notebooks and published references providing us with empirical but only peripheral clues?"[53]

Few scholars have gone so far as Taylor, but we can glean an aspirational tone in some of the language around friendship surrounding James and Du Bois—language that goes well beyond what either of them said or wrote of the other. Du Bois's "my friend and guide to clear thinking" rendering of James is found in almost any discussion of note where their relationship is touched upon. But the line is rarely, if ever, interrogated, and friendship hangs as a presumed state. It can be found in Louis Menand's *The Metaphysical Club*, for instance, where James's influence is emphasized (pushing Du Bois away from the impractical field of philosophy into the social sciences).[54]

Would James have ever referred to Du Bois as his "friend"? It does not appear he ever did. This may be altogether immaterial in evaluating the depth of the relationship, particularly in an inherently unequal one between professor and student. Nevertheless, Du Bois does invoke the term. While James seems not to have used it, his sentiments toward Du Bois, in more staid terms to be sure, suggest something cooler, but not without meaningfulness: something more like fondness. James's 1891 letter inviting his then graduate student Du Bois to a "philosophical dinner" at his home on February 14 is as austere as can be. But it is clear that it meant a great deal to Du Bois—and it was but one of numerous occasions where Du Bois and James conversed together outside the bounds of the academy. James wrote to others besides Henry about Du Bois, including a letter to Sarah Wyman Whitman. James wrote pridefully to the pioneering artist and writer about "my old pupil Du Bois, whose 'Souls of Black Folk' is a very remarkable literary production—as mournful as it is remarkable."[55] That letter, coming two days after James's letter to Henry, adds a bit more depth to understanding the relationship—but scholars are prone to draw more meaning from it and similar missives than is perhaps warranted. Herbert Aptheker posits a different tone in his edited volume on Du Bois's correspondence, describing "the relationship between Du Bois and William James [as] always cordial."[56]

In the end, we should also consider whether Du Bois's language of friendship toward James may have been an effort to fold himself within the great intellectual canon of American letters. By associating himself so closely with James, perhaps Du Bois was choosing to do what other liberal white scholars and thinkers would not do—namely, graft Du Bois into the American philosophical tradition as a first-rate thinker on par with James and the rest. As Lincoln's public exclamation of "My friend Douglass!" served a political purpose, Du Bois's "my friend William James" served an intellectual one. Friendship matters.

Conclusion: The Purposes of Friendship

William Edward Burghardt Du Bois was the first black man in America to be taken into the inner councils of America's intellectual society as something approaching an equal. There had been widely hailed intellects and talents such as Phyllis Wheatley and Frederick Douglass; Booker T. Washington was a grand industrialist and educator. Marcus Garvey was a mass mobilizer and organizer. But it was Du Bois who first carried all the credentials and trappings of elite white education, all while embracing his blackness and contention for a kind of leadership of his people. His friendship with William James was the imprimatur establishing those credentials. That he could, and did, socialize with James and other leading white minds of his time meant that the door was potentially open for other blacks to enter. Political equality was a possibility, however remote, not because Du Bois was so brilliant, though brilliant he was; it was possible because he could sit down at supper and discuss philosophy with whites. And he would never let anyone forget it.

James left teaching at Harvard in 1907 and died a few years later in 1910. The *New York Times* obituary headline described him as "Long Harvard Professor. Virtual Founder of Modern American Psychology and Exponent of Pragmatism and Dabbled in Spooks." [57] I confess to having laughed at the final descriptor—a somewhat ironic reference to James's interest in séances and the metaphysical world. *Dabbled in Spooks.* I wonder if Du Bois would have chuckled at that as well. But friendship was serious business in a world where having to prove one's humanity hinged on what others made of you. Du Bois's relationship with James was, in that sense, most practical—dare I say, pragmatic. The *Times* obituary may have put it best about Du Bois's embrace of James over the years. Describing Jamesian philosophy, the *Times* wrote that James "became the chief American advocate of 'pragmatism,' a trend in philosophical thought that holds that 'that is true which works.'" In this sense, James and Du Bois were the closest of friends.

Du Bois outlived James by fifty-three years and one day (James died on August 26th, Du Bois on the 27th). Together they established, largely through the work of Du Bois after James's death, that race is no impediment to intellectual greatness, nor should it be a barrier to friendship. In *Souls*, Du Bois would write about how one of his classmates, a white girl, "a tall newcomer," spurned his greeting card in his little New England schoolhouse.[58] It left a lasting impression upon Du Bois, a mark of his "otherness." That card's symbolism was supplemented, if not replaced, by the one Valentine's Day invitation to a philosophical supper William James would deliver to him many years later.

4

First Ladies

Mary McLeod Bethune and Eleanor Roosevelt

Introduction

The friendship and political alliance between Mary McLeod Bethune and Eleanor Roosevelt came to public prominence in the 1930s, a purgatory period for African Americans, between Reconstruction and the onset of the civil rights movement of the 1950s. A generation after slavery, the Supreme Court established the constitutionality of racial segregation in the *Plessy* decision (1896); a generation after that, the federal government of the United States remained a segregated domain, with black activists forced to desperately seek an audience with policymakers and presidents, as Frederick Douglass had so many decades earlier. They were, once again, supplicants in a newly arranged white power structure, and by some lights Douglass was permitted more influence in his short time at the elbow of Abraham Lincoln than any other African American would enjoy over the next fifty years.

What complicated matters was that the Democratic Party—the chief institutional force for progressive change at the time—was held together by a coalition of Southern white supremacists and Northern white ethnics and labor. Franklin D. Roosevelt's New Deal support was thus premised upon locally administered and racially discriminatory programs in the South in exchange for continued support for FDR's progressive policies. This left the president's black supporters where they had been in the previous Democratic administration of Woodrow Wilson: deeply compromised.

There were two important distinctions between Woodrow Wilson and Franklin D. Roosevelt on race, however. First, Roosevelt initiated greater outreach to African American voters and sought a more direct, albeit quiet, advisory role for blacks in his administration; second, Roosevelt's New Deal policies, while largely discriminatory, did provide some degree of economic relief to African Americans.[1] Thus, blacks were told that appeals for racial justice, such as presidential support for an anti-lynching bill, would jeopardize liberal economic programs, which were of some practical and much needed benefit. As a result, advocacy for more visible and unapologetically racially based justice was channeled through the first lady, Eleanor Roosevelt, who was more personally moved by racial injustice, and less politically compromised, than her husband. By some accounts, Eleanor Roosevelt's role as an intermediary between the White House and black activists earned her the title of "the most hated woman in the South since Harriet Beecher Stowe."[2] As much as anyone, Eleanor Roosevelt modeled the shift away from a closed period of interracial friendship among leading public figures toward a more open one. The source of hatred for her among some whites reflected the political implications of the crossing of such closely guarded racial lines.

The most important relationship Eleanor Roosevelt cultivated toward this end was the one she forged with Mary McLeod Bethune. For over a decade, Bethune and the first lady engaged in a political dance that sought to advance mutual, and at times discordant, goals. On the one hand, Bethune fought to increase the numbers and influence of African Americans in government; she likewise sought to empower black institutions, while advancing their economic standing. These objectives often clashed with the president's agenda, including the need to maintain Southern white support for the New Deal, diminish the symbolic and practical power of black protest, and later, win the support of African Americans in the war effort.

These interconnected, and at times contradictory, objectives made the friendship between Roosevelt and Bethune the most significant interracial relationship in the United States since Booker

T. Washington's truncated friendship with Theodore Roosevelt. It was also the most successful partnership of this kind since Lincoln and Douglass. Between 1935 and 1945, Bethune became the highest paid African American in government, the only female member of FDR's "black cabinet" of unofficial advisors, and the president's special advisor on minority affairs. The appointment came after Bethune's first meeting with FDR, where she attended a gathering at Hyde Park. At that meeting, she told Roosevelt, "I speak Mr. President, not as Mrs. Bethune, but as the voice of 14,000,000 Americans who seek full citizenship." A tearful FDR is said to have reached across the table, declaring that he was "glad I am able to help contribute something to help make a better life for your people."[3] FDR would formalize Bethune's role within his administration as the director of the Division of Negro Affairs of the National Youth Administration (NYA). In these capacities, Bethune was an advocate, patronage seeker, and, at times, moderator of black political expectations. Likewise, the first lady sought to advocate for, and at times temper, the requests of Bethune within the administration.

It was unlike any other political relationship to that point in American history—two women, black and white, shaping the contours of possibilities for African Americans, and, by extension, American democracy, during the nation's most dire moments since the Civil War. And throughout, there were seemingly small interventions that reflected the vulnerability of black life in America, while also demonstrating the practical importance of Roosevelt and Bethune's relationship.

An example occurred during a tuberculosis outbreak in Florida in 1942. Bethune, then president of Bethune-Cookman College, wrote to the first lady, seeking to get beds built in the State Sanatorium for Negroes. The Public Works Administration and the Public Health Service seemed to be passing the buck over who had responsibility for building the space for two hundred beds. "These poor people are in such dire need of facilities for the salvation of their lives," she pleaded in her letter to Eleanor. "Do make one more effort to get this project through," she wrote. "We know you will do all you can—we can always depend upon you."[4] It was the type of plea—premised upon friendship and a shared sense of justice—that would be made over and over again, for many years.

Advisory Roles

Mary McLeod Bethune was born the fifteenth of seventeen children to Patsy and Samuel McLeod in July of 1875, in Mayesville, South Carolina. The first of the McLeods to be born into freedom, she would meet Eleanor Roosevelt over fifty years later at a conference of women club leaders, in 1927.[5] As the historian Patricia Bell-Scott notes, once her husband was elected president of the United States, Roosevelt would greet Bethune at the White House, "'always running down the driveway to meet her, and they would walk arm in arm into the mansion' to talk for hours about the needs of African Americans." White House usher J. B. West observed, "Few heads of State received such a welcome."[6]

It was one of the most unlikely paths to political influence in American history. Bethune's work as an educator in her adopted state of Florida began to earn her early recognition as a powerful voice for African Americans, as she began an industrial school for the training of black girls. Bethune displayed an early talent for winning the support of powerful benefactors, including Booker T. Washington, and John D. Rockefeller, who contributed to what would ultimately become Bethune-Cookman College, in 1931.[7] Bethune parlayed her skill as an institution builder and tireless advocate for racial justice into no small degree of political influence at a time when African Americans were virtually shut out of power in Washington. By the time she became the minority director of FDR's National Youth Administration's Division of Negro Affairs in 1936, she had already been appointed by President Calvin Coolidge to the White House Conference on Child Welfare, and by President Herbert Hoover to the American Child Health Association.[8]

Bethune's move from Republican to Democratic administrations mirrored the larger transition undertaken by black voters nationally, as the New Deal became the first federal program to inspire the kind of sustained progressive change African Americans had sought since Reconstruction. Bethune cut her teeth at the NYA, where she presciently identified the work of a young Lyndon Baines Johnson, Roosevelt's tireless director of the program. "I have found what I have been hoping to find for colored girls," Bethune remarked after visiting

Texas, where Johnson directed the training of youth for jobs. "I believe I know the Negro condition in the southern states, and no one would be more delighted to see them have the kind of training that Mr. Johnson is setting up in Texas." Bethune was struck by Johnson, a "very outstanding young man," in her estimation, one who was "going to go places."[9]

Bethune was not being Pollyannaish about the struggle for blacks to achieve parity in the equitable distribution of New Deal programs. On the contrary, recent research has supported the idea that Johnson's time as NYA director was formative of his ultimate advocacy for civil rights as president. Bethune was keen to observe that Texas was comparatively more progressive than other southern states with respect to the racial integration of NYA programs.[10] I'll return shortly to Bethune's time at the NYA and its relevance for Eleanor Roosevelt and Bethune's developing relationship.

For her part, Roosevelt's path to advocacy for racial justice and her friendship with Bethune were more complicated. Even after many years of friendship and collaborative work, Roosevelt remained a creature of the American system of white supremacy, one she vociferously opposed and yet in some small ways remained infected by. As Jill Watts writes, it was Roosevelt's "habit to give her women friends a friendly peck on the cheek when she greeted them. Yet she didn't kiss Mary, and she knew it was because she didn't feel comfortable kissing a black person." When Eleanor decided to break this seemingly minor, yet significant, personal taboo with Bethune, Eleanor's daughter Anna would report years later, it was a milestone for her.[11]

"From my earliest childhood I had literary contacts with Negroes, but no personal contacts among them," Eleanor wrote in *Ebony* magazine's November 1960 issue. Reflecting upon her life and early privileged upbringing, she noted that her initial knowledge of African Americans came from the Br'er Rabbit stories of plantation life read to her by her Georgia-born aunt. Roosevelt confessed in the nation's leading black publication that "I was more than 15 and in Europe [before] I actually met a Negro."[12] As Doris Kearns Goodwin notes:

When Eleanor first moved to the segregated city of Washington, D.C., with her young husband, her primary contact was with black household staff members, whom she persisted then in calling darkies and pickaninnies. Her sympathetic comprehension of the Negro situation in America had been a gradual awakening, a product of her exhaustive travels around the country and her developing friendships with Negro leaders, which one black historian has written, "began to resemble a crash course on the struggle of blacks against oppression."[13]

However well born Eleanor was, she was nevertheless the victim of trying life circumstances. By age ten she had lost both of her parents, and was raised by her maternal grandmother before attending boarding school in England. Her memories of her mother were marred by the kind of verbal cruelty that can only be heightened when coming from a loved one. Her appearance was mocked; she was called "Granny" and described as so plain, by her mother, that "she had best develop manners."[14] It wasn't until her time at the Allenswood Academy in England that she began to feel a semblance of self-confidence; this was largely owing to the influence of the school's headmistress, Marie Souvestre, who encouraged Eleanor's evident talents. Nevertheless, she remained daunted by a poor self-image, as when visiting Florence, Italy, at sixteen with Souvestre, who encouraged Roosevelt to walk the city's streets alone and take it in. "Perhaps [Souvestre] realized that I had not the beauty which appeals to foreign men and that I would be safe from their advances," Roosevelt wrote many years later in her autobiography.[15]

Personal strength and intelligence were thus offset with a nagging sense of physical inferiority; the mixture was at the heart of Roosevelt's early adulthood—and it was a linkage of sorts to Bethune's own self-understanding, where as a very dark-skinned black woman, she had to endure an unending chain of personal slights and antagonisms both in her youth and as an adult. According to Bethune biographer Joyce A. Hanson, Bethune "often described herself as the 'homely one' of the McLeod Children because unlike her siblings—who had her mother's soft, fine features, she had coarse, dark skin, and a very low hairline."[16] Thus, despite the enormous social and economic chasm separating Roosevelt from Bethune, there was a shared bond of cultivated pride in the face of gendered physical antipathy. The two women were reared and educated in a Victorian age replete with time-honored racist, sexist, and misogynistic values. It was an ironic connection to build a friend-ship upon—but first there was a shared political partnership at stake.

From the NYA to the "Black Cabinet"

Over the years, Bethune's time at the NYA has received its fair share of criticism, not the least of which from African American scholars, and indeed, those in her time, who felt she was too much of an accommo-dationist in the tradition of Booker T. Washington. She has been vary-ingly portrayed as a "Janus-faced figure who presented a public position to bi-racial and white groups which often differed appreciably from her privately expressed attitudes," and someone who was, in the words of the famed black congressman Adam Clayton Powell, "sentimental and naïve."[17] These are harsh assessments, to be sure. And yet, Bethune's tendency toward "accommodation"—call it acceptance—was the only tenable position for any African American seeking to wield influence within the American government in the pre-war era (and, arguably, for years after).

Take, for example, her July 10, 1941, letter to Eleanor Roosevelt, where she writes:

> My dear Mrs. Roosevelt:
> I am sending this note to let you know how happy I am over the many things that are taking place in such a quiet way yet so far reaching. I was most happy that we were able to ward off the march on Washington. We can never express our appreciation to you for your interest in the whole affair and the signing of the Executive Order by our President on June 25. Not since Abraham Lincoln spoke on that memorable day of the emancipation of the slaves has such a far-reaching Executive Order come forth for the benefit of my people.[18]

On its face, Bethune expressed the sentiments of a White House in-sider, rather than someone fighting as an advocate for black equality, exulting over how "we were able to ward off the march on Washington." Yet the two roles weren't mutually exclusive—certainly not for this period. Indeed, as Ira Katznelson has written, FDR's fears over such a large gathering of blacks on the nation's capital, led by A. Philip

Randolph, the president of the Sleeping Car Porters union, led him to issue Executive Order 8802 on June 25, 1941, "banning discriminatory employment practices because of race, color, creed, or national origin in government service, defense industries, and by trade unions."[19] As Gary Younge noted, despite "some in the movement [condemning] him for demobilizing so many, [Randolph's] standing grew as a result of the victory."[20]

Warding off the march was as much about preserving the civil order of the polity for the sake of FDR and the New Deal's political standing as it was about winning the concession of anti-discriminatory policies from the White House. The fact of the matter was that the imbalance of power between Eleanor Roosevelt and Bethune meant that their friendship's political dimension could only be one where Bethune played a somewhat servile role. Her entreaties to have Eleanor speak on the behalf of Bethune-Cookman College for fundraising purposes are but one example of this dynamic. There were friends, and then there were *friends*, when it came to black inequality. "I would like to have a big meeting here for Negro people and as many of the white friends as we can get at one of the large churches," Bethune wrote to Eleanor in February 1943, seeking another fundraiser for the college.[21] White friendship was a pathway to white philanthropy.

Bethune biographer Joyce A. Hanson described Bethune's approach well. "Bethune purposefully pursued a dual strategy to ameliorate racial discrimination that became a double-edged sword. She encouraged and assisted African Americans in building strong black political power bases while she unrelentingly sought to reshape white political agendas and influence white liberals."[22] As Hanson notes, Bethune would occasionally win concessions, sometimes against the opposition of FDR's aides, including a personal visit to an NYA conference of black leaders organized by Bethune. "Do you think he has to see them?" asked Marvin McIntyre in a memo to the president's adviser and executive director of the NYA in 1938. "Frankly, I do *not*," McIntyre concluded.[23]

FDR concluded that he *did* have to see them. As the historian and Roosevelt biographer William E. Leuchtenburg has written:

> The NYA through the noted Negro leader Mary McLeod Bethune, funneled funds to thousands of young Negroes. Negro intellectuals might fret at the inequities of the New Deal, but the masses of

Negroes began to break party lines in gratitude for government bounties and nondiscriminatory treatment.[24]

"Negro intellectuals" were not incorrect about the disparate treatment African Americans received with respect to the doling out of New Deal largesse, which often excluded them. But there was reason for the crossing of party lines as well. By 1943, the NYA was claiming in its final report that 300,000 young African Americans were given employment and training by the organization since its inception.[25]

As the first black woman to serve in an advisory role to the president, Bethune used the position and her relationship with Eleanor Roosevelt to give her unvarnished opinions to the president. As part of her role as a member of FDR's "black cabinet" she advocated for racial justice, while mindful that Roosevelt was as likely to be moved by the political considerations of the issue as by its moral significance. In 1939 Bethune wrote to FDR to advocate for anti-lynching legislation, while warning the president about the insecure status of the black vote as late as 1939:

> I have found deep affection for you and Mrs. Roosevelt among colored Americans in all walks of life. . . . But over and above this personal regard for yourselves is a widespread and growing feeling of despair, distrust, and even bitterness because of the apparently increasing control of party policy, so far as Negroes are concerned, by southern congressman, senators and others who are bitterly anti-Negro. . . . It is my conviction that it would be a serious mistake to believe that the Negro vote is irrevocably fixed in the Democratic ranks.[26]

Bethune would go on to prioritize federal anti-lynching legislation, along with increased numbers of federal appointments and jobs for African Americans, as critical to continuing to win black political support for Democrats, in her letter. While there would be some small steps toward racial justice over her time as a member of FDR's unofficial cabinet, anti-lynching legislation would not be among them. Nevertheless, Bethune used her status and standing as an expert witness for black suffering and political sentiment as best she could. While the triangular nature of her friendship with Eleanor Roosevelt tried both parties at times, there is little evidence that it ever truly jeopardized their relationship. The stakes were too high, and the value of the friendship for all parties—including its significance to FDR—was immeasurable.

The Black Cabinet

Historians of the period have long understood that the term "black cabinet" doesn't quite capture the complexities of black administrative and political service during Roosevelt's time in office. As B. Joyce Ross wrote forty-five years ago in the *Journal of Negro History*, few of the dozen or so "members" of the black cabinet served contemporaneously; "indeed it might well be argued that there were several Black Cabinets during Roosevelt's extensive tenure."[27] In 2020, a full-length study of the black cabinet was published, owing to the group's and period's continuing significance for understanding what some have labeled the "early civil rights movement."[28] What is common in nearly all studies is the centrality and enduring quality of the role played by Bethune in shaping White House policy.

"Contact is the thing." This is what Bethune is said to have later told the civil rights activist and statesman Ralph Bunche about the importance of personal, and in person, influence in the White House. Bunche was part of what became, in 1936, the Federal Council of Negro Affairs. Bethune cultivated contact with Eleanor Roosevelt into a political art, winning the first lady's support for racial justice when opposition to engaging questions of civil rights among FDR's inner circle was seen as potentially far more harmful to the administration than helpful. Reflecting on the black cabinet's influence—a group that included his college friends Robert Weaver and William Hastie, along with Eugene K. Jones of the Urban League and William Pickens of the NAACP—Bunche declared the moment "a radical break with the past."[29]

Eleanor's path to racial justice and friendship with Mary was hardly one anyone would have predicted. As the bond between them grew, political opposition to crossing the social line between the races intensified as well. As Jill Watts, author of *The Black Cabinet*, recounts:

The Georgia Woman's World reprinted photos of Bethune and Roosevelt together, alleging that African Americans were "taking

over the White House." The President's press secretary, Stephen
Early, was alarmed by the affection shared by the black educator and
the First Lady. White House southern relations rested in his hands,
and in 1936 he ordered Eleanor Roosevelt to "*NOT* visit the colored
school with which a Mrs. Bethune is associated."[30]

In an often recounted episode that illustrates her precarious position,
Eleanor sought, both figuratively and literally, a happy medium between supporting Bethune and the cause of racial justice, and not
antagonizing her husband and his white supporters. In November 1938,
Roosevelt attended the Southern Conference for Human Welfare in
Birmingham, Alabama. The Conference was "an interracial gathering
of liberals who met to discuss health, economics, housing, labor, race
relations, voting rights, opportunities for young people, and agricul-
tural issues affecting the region."[31] The integrated gathering violated
local law, and Eugene "Bull" Connor, in fact, enforced the ordinance
by separating black and white attendees several days into the gathering.[32] In doing so, he placed the first lady in a precarious position.
Yet, "[w]hen the police ordered ER to move, she had her chair placed
between the white and black delegations. And it was there that she
sat, symbolically outside of racial strictures, for the remainder of the
conference."[33]

Such gestures of solidarity were not always possible and, more often
than not, Bethune's specific entreaties to FDR—almost always made
through Eleanor—would be rebuffed. A tragic example is the case of
Odell Waller, an African American in Virginia who was put on death
row for shooting his landlord and employer, Oscar Davis, a forty-six-
year-old white tenant farmer, under dubious circumstances, on July
15, 1940.[34] The young and influential black activist Pauli Murray, who
would cultivate her own powerful friendship with Eleanor Roosevelt,
pleaded with A. Phillip Randolph to bring the case to the attention of
Bethune, who, hope against hope, might be able to influence Roosevelt
to put the case before the president of the United States. The expecta-
tion was that FDR might make an appeal to Virginia Governor Colgate
Darden, on the grounds that "Waller had not been tried by a jury of his
peers and that Negro morale would be adversely affected unless there
was an impartial examination of the issues."[35]

Randolph telephoned and wrote to Bethune on June 22, 1942. The Waller case was nearing its second full year; by the time of his death, Waller would serve some 630 days on death row—the longest period in Virginia's history at the time. Randolph asked Bethune to try to arrange a conference with himself, Bethune, and representatives from the *Richmond Times-Dispatch*, Freedom House, the Workers Defense League, and Walter White of the NAACP. The meeting was to be held as soon possible as Waller was granted a stay by the governor lasting until July 2. Randolph wanted to impress upon Eleanor "the implications of this case and to secure her promise to speak with the President about the case, in order that he will speak with Governor Darden before June 29th."[36]

Eleanor had been aware of the case since its earliest days; Pauli Murray wrote her own appeal to the first lady Thanksgiving weekend of 1940.[37] Eleanor did not meet with Waller's mother, Annie, as Murray had encouraged; she was keen on not upsetting the delicate balance of power holding FDR's coalition together. She chose instead to share Murray's letter with Virginia's governor, hoping that he would "look into the case and see that the young man has a fair trial."[38] FDR did write to the Virginia governor, obliquely suggesting he commute the sentence to life in prison. A rally would be held for Waller at Madison Square Garden. Many letters and gatherings were held on his behalf, and the issue drew national media attention. Nevertheless, despite significant protest and pleading from black organizations and back-channel efforts from Bethune and others, Waller's sentence was upheld, and he was put to death on July 2, 1942.

Eleanor Roosevelt's phone call to the small group of black cabinet members was a haunting reminder of the limits of the group's relationship to Eleanor and the president. "Mr. Randolph, I have done everything I can possibly do," the first lady explained. "I have interrupted the President twice. He is in an important conference with Mr. Hopkins and will be displeased with me if I interrupt him again. He had said that this is a matter of law and not of the heart. It is in Governor Darden's jurisdiction and the President has no legal power to intervene. I am sorry, Mr. Randolph, I can't do any more."[39]

As FDR biographer Robert Dallek noted, the episode further strained an already difficult relationship between Eleanor and the president. She is said to have become "angry with Harry Hopkins, who was acting as a buffer for the president, when he refused to plead her case with Franklin for a last-minute intercession with the governor."[40] But the entire black freedom struggle to that point in American history involved nearly impenetrable chains of command between the masses of black people and those with some standing among whites in power, such as Bethune. Customarily, Bethune and others had to make their way through additional links in the chain. In the case of Eleanor Roosevelt, as first lady and a widely admired national figure among liberals and minorities, her standing was considerable, but hardly determinative. Hopkins was but the latest in a long line of white officials—including the president himself—who presented formidable obstacles to racial progress—often in the name of other, more expedient political objectives. Given that the Second World War had become the new existential crisis facing the nation, Bethune and others in the black political community began turning their attention to the war effort, hoping that somehow, this new crisis might best serve the strategic exploits of friendship.

The War Effort

As the United States approached the summer before its entrance into the Second World War, it became increasingly apparent to all that the nation's entrance into the broiling conflict in Europe was all but inevitable. As was the case during World War I, black activists shifted their strategy toward joining support for the war effort with equal citizenship for African Americans. Bethune wrote to President Roosevelt in June 1940, with this objective in mind, and with the specific goal of empowering the standing of black women in the nation. Bethune began her letter by linking "the basic principles of democracy" and black "faith in your leadership" as integral to representing the best image of America, now threatened by fascism and Nazism. "Now we come as a group of loyal, self-sacrificing women who feel they have a right and a solemn duty to serve their nation."[41]

Later, when the war was well under way, Bethune would write to Secretary of War Henry Stimson, taking the War Department to task for failing to invite black women's organizations to participate in addressing the welfare of the nation's GIs. Bethune's letter was a window into her anger and frustration, something she rarely expressed with either Eleanor Roosevelt or the president.

> We are anxious for you to know that we want to be and insist upon being considered a part of our American democracy, not something apart from it. We know from experience that our interests are too often neglected, ignored, or scuttled unless we have effective representation in the formative stages of these projects and proposals. We are not blind to what is happening. We are not humiliated. We are incensed![42]

If African Americans could not be part of the war effort, many black leaders rightly surmised, it was unlikely they'd be able to claim any increased standing in the post-war world they'd inhabit. Of course, the logic was deeply flawed, as it presumed that a system of white supremacy would be responsive to demonstrations of loyalty and courage during war than it otherwise would during peacetime. But African Americans had long worked with these dilemmas of collective action in a racist state. With the exception of a small number of black radicals, most activists thought there was little choice than to be insistent in making demands upon the government, despite its historic unresponsiveness.

It was an at times confusing enterprise, trying to assess the limits and possibilities for black empowerment—perhaps more so in a liberal administration. One case in point involved Bethune's outreach to Eleanor in in the early days of the war. Bethune had begun work in late 1941, in enlisting black craftsmen and technicians to serve in a production plant in Scotland, Louisiana. The proposal's focus was getting qualified African Americans involved in the manufacturing of war material; the facility would be a small boat and shipping plant operating under black management. The detailed plan, put forth in a four-page memo to Mrs. Roosevelt, was led by the heading: "A plan to utilize in defense industry the now unused available Negro manpower, thereby increasing the production of war material and at the same time furnishing Negro craftsmen and technicians employment."

It was swiftly rebuffed by Roosevelt. "Dear Mrs. Bethune," she began, "I am afraid the plan which you left me would meet with objection in certain quarters from Negroes, because this is segregation, and what they want is the opportunity to work in the newly established plants with other people."[43] Bethune accepted Eleanor's decision, if not her reasoning. Bethune's objective was to create jobs and, by extension, the favorable disposition of the federal government toward black labor and its loyalty during wartime. Integration, for Bethune, who had long fused the desire for civil rights as espoused by W. E. B. Du Bois, with the economic nationalism of Booker T. Washington, was not an end in and of itself.[44] Whether Eleanor Roosevelt felt compromised by competing objectives among black organizations or simply could not, or chose not to, agree to the proposal can only be guessed.

Indeed, later in the year, Bethune cautioned Eleanor against making any public statements concerning efforts to raise a "mixed brigade of white and colored peoples," from the Interracial Association of the University of Michigan's Ethel Levine. Bethune's reasoning was simple: interracial brigades would draw far greater opposition from whites than all-black ones. It would be better to have unchallenged, yet segregated, black units than no black participation at all. "I would advise her sincerely make no statement regarding the Mixed Brigade," Bethune wrote to Eleanor's personal secretary, Malvina Thompson. "Opinions on this are varied and I do not think she needs to make any statement concerning it, whatever her opinions may be."[45] Bethune felt strongly enough to encourage the first lady to decline a future invitation from the organization in her letter to Thompson.[46]

Roosevelt found other projects related to racial justice to support during the war. In her role as assistant director of the Office of Civilian Defense, she supported the funding of what would become the Tuskegee Airmen. Bethune had lobbied FDR for years to end the military's " 'flagrant discrimination against Negroes,' and allow them to fly as pilots."[47] It was an idea Roosevelt supported wholeheartedly, and she visited the training school, taking the added step of flying with Charles Anderson on March 31, 1941. She was photographed in the seat behind Anderson, and wrote in her nationally syndicated column, "My Day," "These boys are good pilots."[48]

The Second World War increased opportunities for African Americans while simultaneously revealing the perpetuation of their second-class status. Bethune's efforts to use her relationship with Eleanor Roosevelt toward the advancement of "her people"—a term she often employed—had their limits. A year before the war's end, Bethune received a request from a black attorney in New York, asking her to seek the first lady's support in getting FDR to reverse an order to deport his Japanese American secretary, Yoneko Nakazawa. "I would submit this to Mrs. Roosevelt personally," White wrote, "but the very delicacy of the situation demands that someone of prestige, and in whom our President has the utmost confidence, entercede [*sic*] in this young lady's behalf."[49] I could find no response from Bethune to White. In January 1948, Congress canceled all deportation hearings for Nakazawa, granting her the right to remain in the country.[50] The fight against white supremacy in America remained a complex, tiring, and often multidimensional game, one where even victories carried the stench of deep injustice.

The Post-War World

"Have you found anything for Mrs. Mary McLeod Bethune?"[51] That short sentence made up the entirety of Eleanor's July 21, 1943, memorandum to the president. The National Youth Administration was newly abolished, and Bethune was in need of a job. Bethune described her feelings to Eleanor as those of "a mother at the burial of her murdered child."[52] Over the years, Bethune had "subtly reoriented the program so that black local and state administrators reported directly to her, thereby giving a federal agency at least limited control over state distribution of funds."[53] No other African American had wielded as much power in government to that point in American history. With the abolition of the NYA, that power was now gone.

Bethune wrote to Eleanor Roosevelt, hoping to arrange a meeting where her future could be discussed. She was no longer president of Bethune-Cookman College, and the NYA had been the center of her political power in Washington. She was, however, to continue her work as founder and president of the National Council of Negro Women, using the platform and her national recognition as a way to continue the work of racial justice. Getting Eleanor on her calendar proved difficult, however. Eleanor was confronted with Franklin's desires for her to take a low profile as an election year (1944) approached. Eleanor turned down one request—an invitation to speak at Knoxville College, a historically black institution, because of these concerns. Her secretary wrote to Bethune: "Mrs. Roosevelt, after careful consideration, decided she would not do much traveling now because of so much criticism, especially in Congress. As you know, she does not mind personal criticism, but feels it might hurt other more important things, if she gave the opposition any more ammunition."[54]

It wasn't until late December of 1943 that Eleanor wrote that she would not be able to find a position to match Bethune's interests or talents. It was a direct message, one that effectively ended any chance of Bethune's work within the administration. After writing that she would not be able to speak with the president about offering Bethune a position—even one she could refuse for the sake of demonstrating a degree of dignity, Eleanor cut to the chase. "I do not feel that would be honest," she wrote. "I think the President should either offer you something he wants you to take or an honorary position which would give you prestige." There was no such position FDR had in mind. And with respect to her trouble raising funds for Bethune-Cookman College, Roosevelt told Bethune that there'd be little likelihood of federal funds coming its way. "I hate to say this to you," Mrs. Roosevelt wrote, "because I know it is your life's work in one sense, but your life's work is the young people you have trained and sent to different parts of the country, so you must not feel, even if the institution is used in a different way, that your life's work has, in any way, been impaired."[55]

The news did not end the friendship—or, more importantly, the relationship. Bethune would continue to write to, and work with, Roosevelt. She managed to have Eleanor attend a YWCA Conference in Washington on "Building Better Race Relations." She likewise continued to submit names of qualified African Americans to serve in government. As such, Bethune remained a kind of good-will ambassador between the administration and African Americans, whom the president very much needed to keep inside the New Deal coalition. Such entreaties included advocacy for black physicians to serve in the Department of Public Health, and an invitation to Lena Horne to the White House ("the most outstanding star of our race. . . . She is considered tops," Bethune wrote).[56]

In May 1945, Bethune joined NAACP members W. E. B. Du Bois and Walter White as "associate consultants" to the founding charter of the United Nations.[57] The consultant role had to be fought for, however, as no African Americans were appointed to the official U.S. delegation in April. Bethune used the occasion to support an international bill of rights opposing colonialism and racism, while also "emphasizing the importance of having black women take a significant role in rebuilding the postwar world." Bethune's appointment, however late and limited, was nevertheless historic; as the only black woman in the American delegation in San Francisco for the charter's conference, she brought a unique perspective to the proceedings.[58] Writing shortly after the conference, Bethune reflected on her work, noting that "I never failed to voice the hopes and aspirations of the Negro people. I interviewed and conferred with many important persons, delegates, experts, and consultants, winning them to sympathy and support for a liberal position with regard to the abolition of colonialism, the international bill of rights, and the inclusion of an adequate educational and cultural program into the Charter of the United Nations."[59]

The black freedom struggle grew in intensity and in opposition in the post-war period. The Cold War presented opportunities to argue for racial justice in the presence of an anti-democratic enemy, while at the same time fears of radicalism drew new antagonisms to black organizations and individuals deemed insufficiently patriotic. Bethune suffered such attacks, and was accused of communist sympathies. The accusations began as early as 1943, when congressman Martin Dies of the House Un-American Activities Committee hurled the charge. Bethune defended herself, dismissing the charges as merely an attack against her "incessant efforts in seeking for all Americans the constitutionally guaranteed rights of full citizenship regardless of race."[60]

Nevertheless, Bethune periodically faced the brunt of such accusations over the years, leading Eleanor Roosevelt to take up her defense in her syndicated "My Day" column in 1952, after a school organization in Englewood, New Jersey, rescinded an invitation for Bethune to speak. Roosevelt described the attacks as "a pernicious thing that we are allowing to bedevil us—guilt by association." It was the type of defense from a powerful person many similarly branded Americans could not muster—certainly few African Americans. Ironically, the tenor of the times was making the cause of racial justice one of allegiance to the flag—one under which blacks fought and died and received little reward for. "I know the danger of Communists in this country," Eleanor

Roosevelt concluded, "and I know the subversives can do us harm. But it does us much more harm to tear down the fabric of justice and fairness and trust in our fellow human beings who have a life record to disprove an idle accusation."[61] It was a strong defense, one from a still highly admired former first lady and stateswoman—above all, a friend.

Conclusion: Passing the Cane

Mary McLeod Bethune was first mentioned in the *New York Times* on January 23, 1915. She was visiting New York seeking financial support for her technical college for girls in Florida from a wealthy white benefactor, one Mrs. Orme Wilson, born Caroline Schermerhorn Astor, a great-granddaughter of John Jacob Astor.[62] Bethune would spend the next forty years of her life in and out of white homes, philanthropic societies, and government halls. Her friendship with Eleanor Roosevelt brought her to the White House, giving her a standing few African Americans had received to that point. Of course, any interracial friendship of that period—certainly any public one—necessitated the acceptance and presentation of acceptable roles. These were inherently unequal relationships. Bethune understood this and was compelled to maximize not only her own talents but the presumptions of whites about what "helping Negroes" looked like. The next time Bethune appeared in the *Times*, the headline screamed the established virtue of white support for black causes: "Mrs. Bethune's Daytona School a 'Civilizer.'"[63]

"Mrs. Bethune, a negro woman, is the founder of the Industrial Training School for Girls at Daytona," the *Times* wrote, introducing the nation to Bethune. "She understands the failings of her people and is working hard to eliminate their undesirable habits." For her part, Bethune assumed the assigned role—what other choice did she have? "I consider the Daytona school a civilizer. I do not know a better name to give it," she said.[64] There'd be other similarly benevolently racist (and indeed, sexist) features on Bethune over the years (she was described as the "Booker-Washington of her sex" in one story). Like nearly every black woman of her time, she was forced to endure untold indignities and repress them. Yet, in her obituary, the *Times* recounted the many achievements of "Dr. Bethune," including her presidency of

Bethune-Cookman College, her time as director of the Division of Negro Affairs for the National Youth Administration, her founding of the National Council of Negro Women, and her appointment as associate consultant to the delegation of the United Nations in San Francisco. And, of course, the pivotal relationship in her public life could not go without mention: "She was a close friend of Mrs. Franklin D. Roosevelt."[65]

As the civil rights movement developed in earnest, Bethune's style of leadership grew in disfavor. The great black sociologist E. Franklin Frazier lamented her "ego problem," while disagreements abounded "among some of the black literati about whether her occasionally supplicating demeanor was an artful manipulation to accomplish her goals in a racially segregated, male-dominated society. Or just too much bowing and scraping."[66] The "dual strategy" of seeking black empowerment while also embracing integration meant that Bethune had to present different faces to those she sought help from, as well as those who were closest to her. As was the case with Eleanor Roosevelt, they were, on rare occasion, the same person.

Eleanor did not describe Mary as her "friend" in her "My Day" article about Bethune's passing in 1955. "I would like to be at her funeral but I doubt if that will be possible," Roosevelt wrote. "I have many commitments that would mean disappointment to various causes, which I think Dr. Bethune would be the first to feel should come before one's personal desires. Nevertheless, I will cherish the spirit she lived by and try to promote the causes that she believed in, in loving memory of a very wonderful life."[67] Part of the black experience was the uncertainty about whether the acts of whites were *sui generis*, or somehow the result of racial bias or racially based considerations. Maybe Roosevelt *was* too busy to attend.

Many accounts of Bethune over the years feature her possession of a cane that once belonged to FDR. It was a symbol of her power—her connection to friends in high places. It recalls to mind the cane Mary Todd Lincoln had delivered to Frederick Douglass months after Lincoln's death. Such personal connections to white power were highly prized. They conferred a status on the bearer beyond their rank and station in life. You pass on a cane, or an article of clothing—maybe a piece of jewelry—to someone close, a friend, a loved one. The value of interracial friendship in America, at least in its political context, depended upon how the relationship could symbolize what might be possible on a national level; how friends and citizens could live together in a democracy. By the middle of the twentieth century, however, there was increasing hope—indeed, a growing demand among African Americans—that one day soon, they would have canes of their own to hand down.

Post-war America thus began to reflect the advances made since the height of the Jim Crow era, as black activists and leaders of the "early" civil rights movement made increasing demands on the nation's political leaders as new avenues of access to power had been won. Bethune's role as a bridge between the White House and advocates for racial justice on the outside typified the intermediate, and "shadow," quality of the progress that had been made since the days when Douglass and Lincoln met during the Civil War.

5

Veins

Ralph Ellison, Shirley Jackson, and Stanley Hyman

Introduction: An Intellectual Democracy

When Ralph Ellison was the editor of the *Negro Quarterly* in 1942, he reached out to an up-and-coming literary critic who'd caught his eye, to write for the new and fledgling journal. The man was Stanley Edgar Hyman, an impressive and brilliantly cutting writer who also happened to be the husband of Shirley Jackson, who would later be recognized, albeit all too slowly, as one of the great American writers of the twentieth century. But in 1942, she was still very much "Mrs. Stanley Hyman," and Ellison was still a little-known and unheralded writer in his own right. Nevertheless, Ellison wanted the *Quarterly* to be a powerful journal on race and the American experience. As he wrote to Hyman in his letter, "As we visualize the Quarterly it is elastic enough to allow for the only real democracy now possible in America, an intellectual democracy."[1] Hyman accepted the offer.

Thus began one of the great literary friendships in American history—a triangle of intellectual power with plenty of charisma to boot. It helped shape one of the greatest American novels ever written—Ellison's *Invisible Man*—but it also gave depth to Jackson's writings on race. And it gave Hyman a black intellectual interlocutor he was otherwise lacking. If only there was more room for Jackson in this "intellectual democracy." The chasm of race was hard enough to close; the one between men and women would prove even harder. But there was enough closeness between Jackson and Ellison to make up for it. And that closeness, however limited by time and custom, made a difference in growing the kind of democracy Ellison hoped for.

Ellison had previously met Hyman in December 1941, when he and his first wife, Rose, attended the wedding of a mutual friend.[2] Despite their differences—Ellison was a black man from Oklahoma City, and Hyman was a Jew from New York—the two men shared a common political ideology. Both were figures on the far left, with Ellison a member of the Communist Party and Hyman a Marxist of sorts, and former member of the Young Communist League.[3] The two men grew fond of each other from the start and before long were sharing Christmases, borrowing and lending money to each other, serving as godparents, taking up summers together, and traveling in the same high-brow social circles New Yorkers loved writing and hearing about in the 1950s.

In a word, they were friends. And their friendship naturally brought their wives into their circle of closeness, in effect enlarging the dynamic to four, with Shirley and Ralph's second wife, Fanny, rounding out this unusual quartet in the deeply segregated political and literary world of America at midcentury. The relationship was especially significant because Ellison's novel, *Invisible Man*, is one of the greatest ever written by an American and Jackson's "The Lottery" may well be the greatest American short story ever written. These two towering works were made possible by a deep understanding of the dark underside of American life by both authors. Moreover, these works have become part of the canon of American literature, shaping the way Americans view difference, race, terror, tradition, and identity for the better part of sixty years now.

Could either have been written to the same effect without this friendship? Perhaps. What's most important is that the politics of racial fraternity in America had been undergoing a transition; with the end of the Second World War and the defeat of Nazism and Fascism, the ironies of racial oppression, along with the repression and alienation of American women, made for uneasy assessments of democratic life. The violent and turbulent passions that would later be channeled into the civil rights movement and women's rights movement of the 1960s and 1970s were already present, however latent, in the late 1940s and early

1950s. Few writers gave greater voice to this mood and condition than Ellison and Jackson. And they each admired it in the other, even if they chose not to express it directly to one another in writing. Despite being men who abhorred stale custom elsewhere, Hyman and Ellison wrote to each other, and each other only, with Ellison's letters frequently shouting out to Jackson. "Tell Shirley" became a kind of mantra over the years. You didn't write to another man's wife.

That Ellison and Jackson didn't correspond directly over the years is one of the great shames left by enduring patriarchal society in America. But at least Ellison got something of profound importance off his chest, after reading Jackson's *Lottery*. After making his own critique of the story to Hyman—a closer review of which I'll take up later in this chapter—Ellison concluded that he and Jackson had far more in common than perhaps even he realized. "Let me know if she's done anything else of the kind," Ellison asked his friend; "we're beginning to work the same vein."[4]

Ralph and Stanley

Is it possible that had Stanley Edgar Hyman and Ralph Ellison not become friends, the quintessential novel about race and American identity might not have been written? It seems a distinct possibility. *Invisible Man* certainly would have been a different novel. And as Jackson biographer Ruth Franklin surmised, "the influence flowed both ways," with Ellison offering his own commentary on Hyman and Jackson's works.[5] At some point in the middle of the last century in North Bennington, Vermont, townsfolk were raising more than a furtive brow at the comings and goings of a lone Negro, Ralph Ellison, into the home of a radical New York Jew, and his crazy writer-witch-wife, Shirley. As one of the Hyman children put it, adopting the townsfolk's perspective: "It was, 'That Shirley Jackson's a witch, married that Jew from New York. That nigger comes to visit them once in a while, he teaches at the Commie place up the hill, where the girls are.'"[6] It was a remarkable triangle to say the least.

It began with Hyman. He was born in an era when Jews were still fighting for entrée into the leading socio-political and cultural institutions of America. Post-war America was still very much a country of ruling white Protestants. The list of townspeople in Jackson's 1948 short story "The Lottery" is a good indication of the monochromatic society whose darkness Jackson was trying to draw attention to. Hyman's early career as a literary critic was, in part, owed to his Jewish identity and his ability to speak to the kind of ethnic distinctiveness that "urbane" readers wanted but were otherwise unfamiliar with. Hyman's early work found a home in *Commentary* magazine, a once left-leaning but presently conservative publication devoted to featuring work on Jewish identity and affairs. Requests for Hyman to participate in symposiums on "The Jew's relation as writer and reader to a literary tradition from Chaucer to T. S. Eliot" and his writing on "the problem of Jewish identity" are representative of this sort of appeal.[7] It was not always a good fit. Just as Hyman did not bring his Marxist leanings into the lecture hall, he likewise did not wish to be confined to writing about Jewish identity. Ellison's journal offered something different. When he reached out to Ellison to write a review for the *Negro Quarterly*, it pleased Ellison greatly, as he had been struggling to find white critics for the journal.[8]

It soon became apparent that both men, while hardly rejecting their ethnic or racial identities, saw them as vehicles for expression, not as ends in themselves. Ellison wrote to Hyman very early on that he hoped the *Quarterly* would help "break down the double ghetto in which both Negro writing and American writing (generally) fall because one is not sufficiently aware of the other."[9] In a sense, Hyman was equally engaged in escaping the "double ghetto" of identity-based writing. He was lightly chided for a piece for the Oxford Dictionary, in which he described himself as "an infidel in the Jewish faith, too."[10] He was asked to strike it out. And Shirley Jackson's reflections on her own "ghettoized" world of female domesticity became defined by its power to eviscerate the sense of tranquility and security that had long accompanied the genre. These three were iconoclasts—nearly in the literal sense of the word—as each shattered, in their own way, the mythology of their seemingly most obvious self-identification.

One of the most important factors shaping the relationship between Ellison and Hyman, and, indirectly, Ellison and Jackson, was the mutual friendship with the philosopher and literary critic Kenneth

Burke. Ellison was struck by Burke's speech at the New School for Social Research at the Second American Writer's Congress in June 1939, on Hitler's rise to power. "The Rhetoric of Hitler's Battle" would go on to become a highly influential essay, but the speech was reviled by many in the crowd that day for its principal subject—yet it struck a nerve with Ellison for its "Marxist and Freudian analysis."[11] It was also the type of critical analysis that moved Hyman. Once they discovered their mutual admiration for Burke, Hyman and Ellison were having weekly lunches together, where they, in Hyman's words, were busy "expounding the revealed word of Burke."[12] As Ellison biographer Arnold Rampersad observes, "To converse with Burke and young disciples of Burke gave a fresh, human dimension to [Ellison's] reading. Now he was ready to embrace ideas that would supplant the influence of pure Communism, weakening the persisting distractions of black nationalism in his thinking, and give order to the impulses toward liberal humanism that he had suppressed in his radical writing."[13]

Of course, Ellison could hardly forget his blackness, even if he wanted to—perhaps no more than Hyman could, or wanted to, jettison his Jewish heritage, or Jackson her womanhood. As Ellison explained in a letter to Burke in 1945, "I certainly agree with you that universalism is desirable, but I find that I am forced to arrive at that universe through the racial grain of sand, even though the term 'race' is loaded with all the lies that men . . . warm their values by."[14] Ellison was quite literally captivated by race, and it shaped his strong desire to pursue his own individuality in life and literature. His character, Emerson, in *Invisible Man* is at least partly symbolic of whites' ability to embrace the uniqueness of personhood in ways nearly impossible for African Americans. Both Burke and Hyman were stalwarts in embracing the self against every agitation to conform, to be part of "the group."

For these reasons, Ellison was drawn to Hyman's work on folklore and ritual; it was the underlying historical—indeed, anthropological—explanation for the formation of "races" and the cruel acts that flowed from these primal divisions. It was the shared interest in ritual and folklore that tied Hyman, Jackson, and Ellison to each other intellectually. Along these lines, Ellison wrote to Hyman a few months after Jackson's "The Lottery" appeared in *The New Yorker*. Ellison wanted to "say something about [Hyman's] folklore piece," a reference to a recent article Hyman had published on the subject. "It is my belief," Ellison wrote, "that it is not accidental that this field has been neglected, but in keeping with the character of our scholarship generally, for any delving into folklore brings the investigator into immediate contact with the painful and tragic elements which Americans have not been too anxious to touch."[15]

The shocking quality of Jackson's "The Lottery," a subject I will turn to later, was not only related to the story's gruesome ending; it had much to do with the fact that Jackson suggested white-shirted and blue-jeaned Americans were tribal, and thus as prone to the vagaries of violent ritual as anyone else. Blood wasn't supposed to matter in America—and it was the confrontation with this obfuscation that gave Ellison's *Invisible Man*, Jackson's "The Lottery," and Hyman's work in literary criticism their radical texture. As Arnold Rampersad has written, Ellison's shift in focus to ritual and myth gave him entrée into a "forbidden world and the literary styles, including surrealism, that it inspired. He was coming close to acquiring a literary language appropriate to his vision of chaos.".[16]

For all of the intellectual heft involved in the exchange of ideas between Ellison and Hyman, the two were friends, in the most ordinary sense of the word. They looked out for one another. Ralph was tasked with driving Shirley to the hospital during one of her pregnancies.[17] In lean times, Stanley would borrow money from Ralph.[18] And before Ralph's career skyrocketed, Stanley would reciprocate ("Thanks a hell of a lot for sending that money order," Ralph would write when pressed, in 1945).[19] The Ellisons and Hymans (as they were known) ate, drank, and partied together. They spent a good deal of leisure time in each other's company over the years. At least this author couldn't find a harsh word between Ellison and Hyman—not at least until a long late letter in 1970 from Ellison, which I will discuss later. On the whole, from the early days when Hyman began writing reviews for *Negro Quarterly* and Ellison began lecturing at Bennington College, at Hyman's invitation, there was great chemistry and affection shared by all. What remains most lamentable is the scant written record between Jackson and Ellison. For it was truly this pair that made the lasting imprint on what being an American—from the outside, looking in—felt like.

Ralph and Shirley

"Sometimes we have such good luck in acquiring our friends that it's impossible not to suspect that fate had a hand in their appearance," Ralph Ellison reflected later in life.[20] In all probability this thought was tied to the passing of Stanley Hyman in 1970, but it well could have applied to Ellison's friendship with Shirley Jackson. Despite having to live in the shadow of her husband as "Mrs. Stanley Hyman," Jackson was the spouse with the early literary success. At twenty-six, she had her first two stories published in *The New Yorker*. "After You, My Dear Alphonse," a sly and marvelously perceptive story of liberal white racism, stood out—and it was an indication that Jackson was most attuned to the type of pedestrian racism common to her social circle. Nevertheless, it was Jackson's attention to the black child's perspective that struck Ellison. "[U]nlike most New Yorker stories in which Negroes appear, Alphonse succeeds in being 'about' the Negro child almost as much as it is about the cheap liberalism of the white kid's mother," Ellison wrote to Hyman.[21]

This was but the first of many letters to Hyman that included the "Tell Shirley" mantra. Despite the indirect communication, it is clear that Ellison felt close to Jackson—both as a writer and as a friend. Yet the social etiquette of the time frowned upon personal communication between married friends. Instead, spouses transferred their perspectives through intermediaries. Kenneth Burke's wife, Libbie, for example, corresponded with Jackson about Ellison's well-received essay on Richard Wright. "Ralph Ellison's pamphlet on Wright is positively the best, the most profound, the wisest thing I have ever seen on the black-white issue," Libbie wrote Shirley. "He is really seeing things from a higher level, and thereby seeing a deeper level of the underlying set-up."[22]

Whether "Alphonse" reflected Jackson's attention to the Ellisons' place as occasional interlopers into the lily-white setting of Vermont, or the cocktail scene of New York's publishing world, her observations were uncanny. As Ellison biographer Arnold Rampersad has written:

> Even if [the Ellisons] had the money to entertain stylishly, Ralph and Fanny understood the delicate rules of racial etiquette for liberal

whites. Almost always, Negroes formed only a token presence at social gatherings hosted by whites. Adding even one other black couple
might compromise the tone of the gathering. Whites rarely played a
token role in social gathering dominated by blacks. To place white
friends in such a situation was to risk their friendship.[23]

Hyman and Jackson paid no matter to what their white friends or
neighbors thought. They had become unapologetic friends with the
Ellisons—and, just as important, readers of each other's work.

In June of 1947, Ellison was beginning to put the finishing touches
on *Invisible Man*, even as his old publisher had the rights to the prospective novel. Ellison was pitching it to Random House, hoping for a
better deal at a bigger house. In a joking reference to Shirley's "witch-
craft," Ellison wrote to Hyman asking him to "tell Shirley to hex 'em
up so they won't like it"—"they" being the publisher Ellison wanted
out from under.[24] Jokes aside, Ellison had just offered feedback to
Jackson on her short story, "Pillar of Salt." In the same letter to Hyman,
he asked his friend to "tell Shirley congrats on selling *Pillar of Salt*, and
I'm very glad that some of my comments made sense to her conception
of her novel."[25] The kindness would be repaid with Jackson's help—
crucial at the time—in helping Ellison complete *Invisible Man*.

The rise of Jackson and Ellison as acclaimed authors would come in
short order. It began with Jackson and the appearance of "The Lottery"
in *The New Yorker* in June 1948. Jackson's meditations on myth over
the years was a strong influence on her telling of the story of a small,
plausibly New England town set in the present, bound together by the
ritualistic stoning of one of its members sometime near the summer
solstice. As Jackson biographer Ruth Franklin notes, Jackson's "interest in myth and ritual date[d] to her collegiate reading of *The Golden
Bough*, anthropologist Sir James Frazer's compendium of ancient rites
and customs."[26] The book saw a resurgence of interest when Director
Francis Ford Coppola's camera panned over it slowly near the end of
Apocalypse Now.[27] Jackson was one of many writers over the decades
drawn to its insights.

It was the modern setting of the ritual in "The Lottery" that conveyed,
in Jackson's words, the kind of "not very rational order struggling in-
adequately to keep in check forces of great destruction, which may be

the devil and may be intellectual enlightenment."[28] Before I explore the great democratic products of the Hyman-Jackson-Ellison friendship—namely, the masterworks "The Lottery" and *Invisible Man*—it is worth reviewing Ellison's immediate reaction to the story. In a letter to Hyman written two months after the story's publication, Ellison was both critical and praiseful:

> Incidentally (again) I read Shirley's The Lottery with a great deal of interest, though I did not think it as successful as most of her stories. I understand also that she upset the middlebrow readers who discovered there was something they knew little about. Good! . . . My own objections, subject to revision when I re-read the story, is that it has presented the rite in too specific a form for the contemporary reader, unfamiliar with such rites and the mystery they entail, [to] make the full identification between himself and the "dedicated and set aside" scapegoat. My other objection is over the understatement, for while I believe the <u>ritual</u> may be understated (providing that the reader understands and makes the willing suspension of skepticism that marks belief) the <u>tragic action</u> can never be. . . . What do you think? It is a rich story, perhaps it is the placing of it in the form of a past situation rather than in terms of its contemporary equivalent that caused my trouble. Let me know if she's done anything else of the kind, we're beginning to work the same vein.[29]

Today, Ellison's letter has a touch of the feeling of someone *mansplaining* the shortcomings of perhaps the greatest American short story ever written. There is no record of Jackson's response to Ellison or what she thought of this criticism—or even if this came up in conversation, aside from the congratulatory benedictions between friends. Nevertheless, the last line of Ellison's letter to Hyman is a testament to his understanding of Jackson's work's relevance to his own. For it is a powerful concluding motif in Ellison's *Invisible Man* that the connections between the oppressed—and indeed all humanity—run very deep. Those connections, what his nameless character refers to as "frequencies," is a reminder that aside from the progressive nature of this interracial friendship at the dawn of the American civil rights movement is the fact that Ellison, and undoubtedly Jackson, understood that their works meant something far greater than storytelling for telling's sake. Their work also involved a kind of political mission. Indeed, after learning that the government of South Africa had banned the story, Hyman recounted that Jackson "felt that *they* at least understood the story."

Masterworks

In the famous battle royal scene in *Invisible Man*, Ellison depicts a white woman being assaulted by the same white men who, for sheer sport, torture the nameless black narrator and his companions in the ring. After "sinking their beefy fingers into her soft flesh" the men toss her into the air, when suddenly, the narrator observes "the terror and disgust in her eyes, almost like my own terror."[30] It is impossible to know all the derivative influences that went into this passage, but I've always associated it with Ellison's understanding of gender's closely felt relationship with racial hatred. Even more, I've wanted to associate the passage with Ellison's friendship with Jackson—someone who lived with her own quiet torments, many of them based on the simple fact that she was a woman.

I'm probably wrong. Almost all guesses into authorial intent are fool's gold. But, still—Jackson's gothic perspective was prolific, and Ellison clearly grasped her intuitive sense of how daily life is brimming with small gestures and practices tied to a darker past. That Ellison understood what more contemporary academics have described as the intersectionality between race and gender is unsurprising; what is novel is that he and Jackson lived it as friends and proverbial outsiders, despite their great success.

"The Lottery" works on many levels, and for many reasons—not the least of which is the familiarity of its world not only to readers over seventy years ago but also to those reading it for the first time today. Its town square's post office and bank reflect the public and private sectors in American life, its black box the symbol of democracy—for what can be more "fair" than the random selection of names? The men wear "clean white shirts and blue jeans"—a presaging of the American uniform created by Ralph Lauren many decades ago. There are oaths of office, a census of sorts for heads of households. It does looks awfully like America, with great mainline Protestant names like Adams, Warner, and Hutchinson abounding. The rich guy who runs the coal business runs the town. You get the idea. Yet, it's the subtlety of it all that allows the story to sneak up on you and overwhelm your sense of security. Of course, this is precisely what terror feels like—the grave interruption of daily life. Had "The Lottery" simply been a macabre story, it would have been chilling enough.

Jackson had other things in mind. The story itself famously emerged out of an ordinary moment in her domestic life. Jackson is said to have conceived "The Lottery" while out with her two-year old daughter, Joanne, for an early summer morning stroll. With the story on top of mind, she went home and wrote what would become nearly the final version of "The Lottery" in a few hours.[31] For many American high school students the story has been a rite of passage.[32] Moreover, people remember it. Its plot is simple: on a summer day local towns-people assemble in the town square for the annual lottery. Men, as heads of households, draw sheets of paper from a shabby old black box, administered by the de facto town leader, Mr. Summers. Onlyone of the folded papers inside contains a black dot, colored in with pencil. The prize? Whoever draws the paper with the black dot is to be stoned to death by the other villagers. We discover this gruesome detail at the very end. There is no explanation about why.

Tessie Hutchinson, a woman bearing the name of the real historical figure, the ostracized Quaker woman Anne Hutchinson, is the one who ultimately "wins" the lottery. Chillingly, she protests the unfair-ness of the system, even as the first stones begin to strike her. It is, by any measure, a grotesque and infinitely satisfying story. It satisfies be-cause Jackson so realistically depicts the unbelievable premise. Indeed, many readers of *The New Yorker* were aghast that such practices "still existed." The story's small touches edify the gruesome; they provide signposts as to the structure of the society, and how such terror is administered.

At base level, this is men's work. They run the lottery, the civic events, and the social activities. Women are relatively sequestered—the "faded house dresses" are the giveaway here. The "girls stand apart" as the boys gather stones; the work of women is about "dishes in the sink" and caring for children. While Ellison likely picked up on the "tuneless chants" and "ritual salute" described in the story—undoubtedly owing to his study of myth—we don't see much of any discussion on his part (or Stanley's, for that matter) about the role of gender in this society. And yet, that early scene in *Invisible Man* provides some solace, that Ellison was indeed attuned to the violent and repressive role of patriarchal culture in American life. As Jackson biographer Ruth Franklin observes, "If 'The Lottery' can be read as a general comment on man's inhumanity to man, on another level it works as a parable of the ways in which women are forced to sacrifice themselves: if not their lives, then their energy and ambitions. The story is at once generic and utterly personal."[33]

In an ironic twist of fate, "The Lottery" catapulted Jackson to fame about the same time that Hyman's great work in literary criticism, *The Armed Vision*, was published. In a world in which she was still "Mrs. Stanley Hyman," Jackson's success was awkward for her, and for her husband, even if it was welcome. When she gave birth to their third child, her profession was listed at the hospital registration desk as "Housewife." She had requested "Writer."[34] Nevertheless, while Hyman's work struggled to gain readers and critical acclaim, Jackson and "The Lottery" grew in notoriety. Still, aside from plumbing the dark side of American life, Jackson shared with Ellison a bit of unwelcome recognition for being associated with "only" one great work. This was less fair to Jackson than it was to Ellison, who despite having published a number of valuable essays, never came close to repeating the greatness of *Invisible Man*. Ellison came to appreciate Jackson's gifts as a writer over the years. "Tell Shirley that I hope she's back at her typewriter, and although I've never said it," he wrote to Hyman in 1961, "she should know her productivity has been a source of strength to me as I creep along at my snail's pace."[35] It was self-deprecating, true, and kind. The kind of thing one friend would tell another.

Ellison was working on the finishing touches of *Invisible Man* when "The Lottery" was published, and he was not having an easy time of it. In a 1949 letter to Hyman, Ellison shared his frustrations with his friend:

I'm now fighting out the political and final section of my book, all full of doubts and stubbornness, like a man juggling boulders into a pile which he hopes will be a house. I haven't lost sight of my form, but I must admit that I am somewhat swamped by the proportions of the thing—and by the many possibilities of which I cannot possibly take advantage. I'd like very much for you to see whats [sic] here. I want to get the dam [sic]thing ready for Fall publication.[36]

Hyman had helped Ellison plow through an effective outline of the novel in its early days. Now, with most of the work done, Ellison was looking for an effective close. One of the most vexing challenges was the novel's transitions. Ellison credited Jackson with helping him solve this puzzle, writing to his friend, the literary jazz critic Albert Murray, "I had been worrying my ass off over transitions; really giving them more importance than was necessary, working out complicated schemes for giving them extension and so on. The I read her page proofs [for her novel *Hangsaman*] and saw how simply she was managing her transitions ad how they really didn't bother me despite "and-so-and-then-and-therefore"—and then man, I was on."[37]

In a sign of the personal and professional closeness of the Ellisons and Hymans, Ralph and Fanny were asked to be godparents to Stanley and Shirley's newborn son, Barry Edgar Hyman, the day the galleys for *Invisible Man* arrived.[38] Ellison had finished the novel at the Hymans' place in Westport, Connecticut. The result was one of the most important and influential works in American literature. The genius of *Invisible Man* lay in Ellison's ability to somehow, through a single narrative voice, encapsulate the African American experience from the end of slavery to the rise of the civil rights movement, while at the same time conveying a universal struggle for human recognition.

All the characters and set-pieces are there: black conservatism, Communism, nationalism, Negro preachers, pimps, buffoons, "handkerchief-heads," the Great Black Migration, wizened veterans, and. in the end, personhood-seeking individuals. Ellison told this history—indeed "history" is at once a liberating theme but also a trap in the novel—while making the singularity of this "invisible" character compelling. The decision to rename the novel *Invisible Man* from *"The" Invisible Man*, was no mere marketing ploy; it captured the universality of the black freedom struggle

Ellison alluded to in his opening battle royal scene. Invisibility, while a peculiarly black phenomenon in the United States, was not a condition unique to African Americans.

"Who Knows but That, on the Lower Frequencies, I Speak for You?"

The closing line of the novel echoes W. E. B. Du Bois and any number of other black writers and intellectuals who, over the years, sought to convey something at once distinctive and yet deeply American in the black experience.

Ellison had traveled much of the ideological and geographical terrain found within the African American experience of the twentieth century—even as he wanted to, in a sense, be liberated from complete identification with it. By the 1960s, Ellison was a celebrated author, one identified with writing perhaps the signature literary work by an African American author to that point. And yet, he was also proudly set apart from other, more radical black writers such as the historian John Henrik Clarke and the playwright LeRoi Jones (Amiri Baraka).[39] Both Ellison and Jackson had to contend with the great challenge of success, now that both had attained it by the 1950s. Visibility would produce its own form of alienation, ironically enough.

Visibility

For years the Federal Bureau of Investigation monitored American writers suspected of Communist Party affiliation or sympathies. Ralph Ellison earned his FBI file for "Un-American Activities" which included his work at *The Negro Quarterly*, among other dubious distinctions. One report listed him as "O.K.'d by the Communist Party, but not a member."[40] Yet, by 1965, as Watts burned and America seemed on the brink of wide-scale rebellion, if not revolution, Ellison was busy speaking at Henry Kissinger's summer conference in Cambridge, Massachusetts. "You were an enormous success, as always," Kissinger wrote to Ellison, having appeared three years in a row.[41] In 1965 Ellison was less the underground militant protagonist of *Invisible Man*, yearning to return to the surface to spark some new movement, than the face of the Chamber of Commerce.

With the extraordinary success of *Invisible Man*, Ellison had become part of the inner circle of elite artists and cultural movers he'd longed to join. Not everybody approved. He had black detractors like Amiri Baraka and white writers like Norman Mailer, who was ever a thorn in his side. At the prestigious Bread Loaf Writers' Conference in Middlebury, Vermont, Ellison delivered three public lectures—but they, and he, did not go unchallenged:

> An exchange with an admirer of Norman Mailer led to the public accusation that, unlike Mailer, Ralph was leading a self-deceiving life. Days later Ralph still smarted from the attack. "This same character told me that I was harming myself because I no longer lived with Negroes," Ralph reported to [Albert] Murray, and I hung around too many intellectuals." "You mean," Ralph had shot back, "that I've stepped out of my place?" He had given the fellow hell for "trying to tell me what my life was like and what Negro life was like. I'm damned sick of these 'white Negroes' trying to tell me what it is like to be a black Negro."[42]

Naturally, Shirley Jackson didn't have this problem of "authenticity" with her success (although she did have to face direct and indirect public musings about what it meant to be a "good" wife, and whether she qualified); nor did Hyman have this kind of conflict. Ellison's "double-ghetto" was not simply a metaphor. Battles over "true" blackness and its expression had, by the 1960s, become a far more prevalent feature of black artists' lives than in previous periods. It was this form of imbroglio that sparked an epistolary feud of sorts between Ellison and Hyman in 1970. Ellison refused to accept the kind of "box" many wished to put him in. The aversion explains some of the elusiveness of the main character's ideological commitments in *Invisible Man*. Ellison had experienced the limits of ideology in the 1940s when the Communist Party withdrew from the South. "Can you imagine, abolishing the 'vanguard of the working class' in the country's area now undergoing rapid industrialization? You say you sold in your friendship for [a] Bentley, but look at me, I was eating and drinking with the lynchers of my people."[43]

The pressure to perform authentic blackness wore on Ellison over the years, even as the demand to do so grew with his notoriety. Meanwhile, Jackson remained an ambiguously popular figure; her work was well received, if not deemed categorically great. She was prolific, yet remained outside of the celebrated circle of "America's greatest writers." And, despite having published a remarkably witty and alluring memoir, *Life Among the Savages* (1953), and three novels in the 1950s (*The Birds Nest* in 1954, *The Sundial* in 1958, and *The Haunting of Hill House* in 1959)—all after having become a household name after the breakout story, "The Lottery"—she was still receiving invitations to faculty cocktail parties as "Mrs. Hyman."[44]

The slights from the world of academia and publishing were only less wearing than those suffered by Jackson in her private life. Her novel *Hangsaman*, Ruth Franklin observes, "can be interpreted in many ways, but on one level it is unmistakably a document of Jackson's rage at her husband."[45] Ostensibly in an open marriage, Jackson nevertheless was episodically crushed by Hyman's numerous infidelities. Jackson likewise suffered from the emotional ups and downs of weight gain—and, more seldom, weight loss. The Stanley Hyman Papers contain a batch of meticulously kept notes of Jackson's meal plans. There are pages of it, complete with calorie counts. And there appear to be notes on her emotional state throughout, including "nightmares," "anxiety," "irritable."[46] I'm willing to bet there are few, if any, male diaries with calorie counts and meal plans in the vast literary trove in the Library of Congress.

Today, Jackson may as likely be known as the author of *The Haunting of Hill House* as the author of "The Lottery." The 2018 Netflix series based on her novel—one that earned Jackson a hefty payment for film rights after publication—has brought renewed interest in her work. Much of the credit for the Jackson revival is owed to Ruth Franklin's compelling biography (2016). Perhaps the times have grown darker, and the gothic tradition to which Jackson rightly belongs—along with Hawthorne and Poe—has found a home in our age. More than likely it is that more women are having a say about the "canon" of writers deemed great within the American literary tradition. Perhaps there is some small redemption in that rising chorus of voices, given that Jackson suffered in silence, letting her characters speak for her. Her lamentations were not those of Ellison, or other African Americans; but they were a terror—so thought Ellison, it seemed, "almost like my own."

By the time Ellison wrote his last letter to Stanley Hyman on May 29, 1970, much had changed in the lives of the two men. Shirley Jackson had been dead for five years, passing at forty-eight of a heart attack days before the Watts Rebellion in August 1965. Hyman was soon remarried—to one of his Bennington students—and was to be a father again. He never lived to see this child; Hyman died three months after Ellison's letter, at age 51. Ellison's last letter thus holds even greater weight. It was a testament to their relationship in many ways—and a calling-card of Ellison's intellectual independence. Not that any was needed—but Ellison's fierceness in this last epistle, even in friendship, signified a new direction in the relationship.

Hyman had recently published a piece for *The Atlantic Monthly* on Richard Wright that caught Ellison's eye, and more than a bit of his ire as well.[47] Ellison felt compelled to respond to Hyman's "Richard Wright Reappraised," in part, because when Ellison first broached the subject at a party, Ellison "was drinking faster than [Hyman] or [Hyman was] three sheets to the wind."[48] He wanted to double back to the conversation when both men were sober. Ellison's chief criticism was Hyman's generalizations about black opinion, a particularly egregious affront to Ellison, whose driving personal motivation was to be an individual:

> My objection was to such generalizations as "There can be no doubt that Negro hatred of whites is close to universal." For if Negro hatred of whites were so universal such black militant writers as [LeRoi] Jones wouldn't have to go to such frenzied lengths in their efforts to arouse that hatred. I also objected because I believe that you make our Negro American attitudes and emotions towards whites far too simple. You allow us no contempt—a quite different emotion than hate—no irony, no forbearance, no indifference, no charity, no mockery, no compassion, no condescension—not to mention that ambivalence of emotion and attitude that you so readily see in the Blues.

And that was just the opening salvo.

Part of Ellison's frustration was with Hyman's seeming to reinforce the stereotype that blacks were ruled by emotions rather than reason.

It was the type of rationale against racial equality made by Jefferson in *Notes on Virginia*. "[D]espite the prevalence of stereotyped notions of Negro spontaneity and instinctually, our lifestyle—at least as it has evolved in the South—has been shaped by a determined will to control violent emotion (we seldom run amuck) as a life-preserving measure against being provoked into retaliatory actions by those who desire to destroy us," Ellison protested. In one of the letter's more poignant and beautifully worded passages, Ellison wrote that black "emotional control springs from our will to humanize a hostile society in our terms and to convert that control into a source of pleasure and affirmation by transforming the threat of social existence into forms of self-definition and triumph."

The letter is really a tour-de-force as a defense of black intellectual capacity and humanity. Ellison defends black art, physical beauty, and indeed African Americans, as wholly American. "As you damn well know," Ellison wrote, "I view my people as American and not African, and while our experience differs in unique ways from that of white Americans, it is never absolutely at variance with the dominant American mode. Diversity within unity is the dominant American mode." This last line rings familiar to those who recall the end of *Invisible Man*, where Ellison wrote, "America is woven of many strands. I would recognize them and let it so remain."[49]

If Ellison hated anything, it was being pigeonholed on account of his race; this was a sentiment familiar to Hyman, who did not view himself as a "Jewish writer" any more than Ellison viewed himself as a "Negro" one. To wit, Ellison objected to Hyman's notion of a "'racial' line of continuity in fiction by Negro Americans." Ellison reminded his friend that *his* influences were "American"—in the same manner that the American experience, rather than some unique ethnic line of artistic inspiration, has influenced Jewish and Irish writers. "The point is that, like yourself," Ellison continued, "I existed in a <u>field</u> of influences, both personal and environmental; but despite this obvious fact you go on reducing the complex field to a single writer and implicitly to the <u>race</u> of that writer." In the end, Ellison, like the protagonist in *Invisible Man*, was still searching in his own life for the right "frequency" to communicate his humanity to those who saw him at times, through a glass darkly.

Conclusion

As he closed his letter, Ellison reiterated his fundamental point: "While my status and statistical identity is that of a black, I am also an individual with an individual destiny, and an individual past." He signed off to Hyman somewhat lightheartedly. "Well, I guess this is enough abuse from one who seldom writes this type of letter anymore." It was the only such letter written to Hyman, and it conveyed a longstanding and recurrent theme within the dimension of interracial fraternity: the pressing need for African Americans to assert their personhood above and beyond the construct of race.

The triumvirate of Ellison, Jackson, and Hyman represented progress in the capacity for interracial fraternity in America. Where Benjamin Banneker had to "prove" his intellectual abilities to a skeptical Thomas Jefferson, or W. E. B. Du Bois was somewhat condescendingly invited into the social circle of William James, Ellison's intellectual relationship with Jackson and Hyman never suffered from the type of paternalism so common to that point in these kinds of relationships. And while there was no overt political mission attached to this creative circle, the friendship shaped public discourse and fostered greater understanding about racial injustice and the repression of women, through the production of iconic works in American fiction.

It was a terrible loss for American literature and culture that Jackson and Hyman each died so young; it is quite possible that either of them had even greater works ahead of them by the time of their passing at forty-eight and fifty-one, respectively. Ellison lived on. While his novel *Juneteenth* has its share of admirers, the long-awaited work remains largely unheralded, and far less known. It was as if fate had marked out this post-war moment—when the Holocaust was fresh in the minds of all, and the civil rights movement's embers were just beginning to glow—for these thinkers to collaborate about the meaning of democracy for those locked outside of it. Indeed, Ellison believed in the mission of *Invisible Man*. As he told *The Paris Review* in 1955:

I feel that with my decision to devote myself to the novel I took on one of the responsibilities inherited by those who practice the craft in the U.S.: that of describing for all that fragment of the huge diverse American experience which I know best, and which offers me the possibility of contributing not only to the growth of the literature but to the shaping of the culture as I should like it to be. The American novel is in this sense a conquest of the frontier; as it describes our experience, it creates it.[50]

Ellison, Jackson, and Hyman's work and friendship did not end the need for such conquests. But they made the venture less trying for those who came after them—a responsibility much less fearsome, and all the more beautiful.

6

Scripts

James Baldwin and Marlon Brando

Introduction: "To Renew Our Friendship"

James Baldwin was desperate. At least that's what he was hoping to convey to his friend Marlon Brando. During the later period of his years living in Istanbul, the celebrated black radical writer wrote to the greatest actor of his generation—now in his wilderness years—to seek out a collaboration that would not only restore their friendship but perhaps forward the prospects for a different vision of racial justice in America. The letter's tone is one of urgency—with more than a hint of personal vulnerability. "Dear Marlon, You're a very hard man to reach," Baldwin begins. Their mutual friend, the filmmaker Elia Kazan, had encouraged Baldwin to write to Brando; "so," continues Baldwin in the letter, "if you didn't want to hear from me, be mad at me, not him." Baldwin then follows this with one of a number of other cryptic allusions whose significance is perhaps lost to history:

> I don't know if you got my wire, but that emergency, anyway, I've decided to ignore. It only seemed, for a moment to be graver than most and it's your misfortune to be the only man on earth whom I feel I can call on, and who may be able to do something when the water threatens to go over my head.[1]

While Baldwin may have engaged the stance of a supplicant here in an appeal to Brando's ego to get a response, the truth is that the two men had been close friends for over twenty years at this point in their lives—and they shared an uncommon bond, irrespective of their racial differences. Somehow, over the years, with all of the marches, the novels, the films, and the dark politics of the times, the two men had lost contact—and by Baldwin's account, had had a falling out. "I'm writing you now in the hope of being able to re-establish some kind of communication with you which won't be at the mercy of twenty-five thousand middle men." And then, a plea: "I'd like to talk to you about things I hope to do—but I'd like, if you would, to renew our friendship. I've got great respect for you. And I'd like to work with you."

As I'll discuss in this chapter, Baldwin and Brando's friendship reflected a new world of possibilities in mid-twentieth-century America. Theirs was a fraternity defined by deep personal affection and private, perhaps amorous, love; but it was also one intentionally crafted for public enlightenment. From the beginning, the two were artists seeking a political forum for their inner turmoil to shape the injustices of their world. Baldwin was now hoping to finally bring to fruition an artistic collaboration that would cement their bond for the ages. "I have a script I want to discuss with you," Baldwin teased, "but it demands a discussion, for it's still in the works." Baldwin then became tantalizingly vague:

> And when I say discussion, I'm afraid I mean: a no-holds barred breakdown of <u>why</u> this script, <u>what</u> I'm trying to do, <u>why</u> I think it's important, and <u>why</u> I'm bugging you with it. The script may not survive this, but we will, and besides, I'll then be marvelously equipped to write you, as I have every intention of doing, one of the roles of your lifetime.

Baldwin clearly wanted to put the entirety of their friendship on the line in an effort to get a response from his old friend. He also wanted to assure Brando that the script had nothing to do with his new project with the film director Kazan—a long chewed-on, never-fulfilled effort to bring the life of Malcolm X to the screen. That would take another twenty-five years, when Spike Lee and Denzel Washington revisited the project for a new audience and a new time.

What was this "role of a lifetime" for Brando? The two had previously discussed working together to bring Baldwin's novel *Giovanni's Room* first to Broadway, and then to Hollywood. There were other discussions of collaborations over the years, including Brando starring in "Blues for Mr. Charlie"—a play loosely based on the horrific murder of Emmitt Till.[2] Baldwin had long sought Brando's star power for his work. Ironically, one of the greatest writers of his time had been perennially enchanted by the siren's call of Hollywood. Indeed, the lure of acting was how Baldwin had met Brando, back in the world of post-war New York, with Baldwin dipping into Brando's Dramatic Workshop at the New School for Social Research. Afterward, the two would be respectively engaged as private citizens in the black freedom struggle. In fact, it was Brando who would go on to introduce Bobby Seale of the Black Panthers to Baldwin, and not the other way around.[3] Photographs from the March on Washington capture their exuberance at bringing their celebrity to bear on America's racial sickness. In one, Brando is proud, arm draped around Baldwin, his massive hand gripping Baldwin's right shoulder. Baldwin is equally satisfied, in aviator glasses, his toothy trademark grin betraying the significance of the moment.

The artists-activists-lovers were invariably paired in a number of photographs from that day. The images endure as a symbol of how their relationship embodied what the Rev. Dr. Martin Luther King Jr. called for all Americans to be. For Baldwin and Brando, the March on Washington was but a piece of a decades-long journey—but in a sense, August 28, 1963, was the apex of their powers of collaboration. Was it enough—for either of them? For the country? What was accomplished that day—and how much more remained to be achieved? As the decade wore on, Baldwin would suffer immense losses—and he would grow even fiercer in his prophetic vision of an America irredeemably committed to hatred and violence. But somehow, he remained ever hopeful. And he ended his letter to his friend on just such a note. "Please let me hear from you, Marlon, I think the time has come."

Artists as Friends: 1944–1963

The 1946 student handbook for the New School for Social Research's Dramatic Workshop class lists a dozen rules and regulations. These include the perhaps all-too-well understood notification, "No promise is made regarding professional placement. Any aid of this kind furnished students must be regarded as a favor, not an obligation of the faculty." Further down the list, students are instructed that "no visitors are allowed at any time at lectures or rehearsals."[4] This commandment was apparently violated by James Baldwin, whom The New School today claims as a veritable passerby—someone who found his way into a workshop without formally attending class or graduating the school.[5] It was there, on 12th Street and Fifth Avenue, that James Baldwin and Marlon Brando began their friendship. Brando was in fact enrolled in a workshop taught by Erwin Piscator; Baldwin was, in his own words, someone who "spent a lot of time hanging around Manhattan's New School for Social Research."[6] The two men met in 1944.

Baldwin was considering a career as an actor at the time. Brando was far more serious. The New School, a haven for "new" thinking in the arts and social sciences, established a "University in Exile" in the 1930s for Jews and intellectuals escaping Nazi Germany and occupied Europe. Fiercely challenging the artistic and academic norms of the time, the institution was a logical draw for both men, although their first meeting was not on campus but in a less august place— Hector's Cafeteria in Greenwich Village.[7] The story is that Brando entered the diner and was drawn into a conversation between the novelist Norman Mailer and Baldwin, who were seated at the counter, an open seat between them. At some point, Brando, taking the open seat, began querying Mailer about what sounded like a Texas accent. Mailer told Brando he'd adopted it as a defense against anti-Semitism in the army. "It was a protective coloration," Mailer said.[8] Somehow this tight corner of Manhattan was hosting one of the greatest chance encounters of artistic force of its time—but Baldwin was, by far, more drawn to Brando.[9]

Baldwin's friend and biographer, David Leeming, describes Brando as a "man whom Baldwin loved but did not approach as a lover." This was owing to Brando's "toughness, a steadiness of emotions, and an ability to demonstrate love in spite of evident 'manliness.' This was an ability that made sex less necessary somehow than with the 'butch' but frightened and desperate lovers with whom he so hopelessly sought peace of body and mind."[10]

On the other hand, Darwin Porter's salacious telling of Brando's life claims the two men were in fact lovers, with Baldwin possibly taking Brando to the Mount Morris Baths in Harlem for their first sexual encounter.[11] And Quincy Jones's 2018 carnivalesque interview with David Marchese provides some, albeit rather untethered, confirmation of a sexual relationship between the two.[12] In the context of their era—the late 1940s to early 1970s in which they were both at their artistic and cultural peak of influence—their sexuality would necessarily remain private (or closeted, to be more accurate). The boundaries of interracial friendship were opening; those that defied the norms of heterosexuality remained firmly closed.

For Baldwin, there was also a political dimension to his reticence to embrace an openly gay identity. "Homosexual, bisexual, heterosexual are twentieth-century terms which, for me, really have very little meaning," Baldwin argued in an interview in 1965.[13] As the political scientist Lawrie Balfour explained, Baldwin was "most suspicious of any political stance that reduces human relationships to a formula."[14] In any case, Baldwin and Brando fell into a friendship of lasting importance to both men. The late tendency to draw substantive meaning to what both Brando and Baldwin considered secondary aspects of their identity, let alone their sexuality, suggests more about our era than theirs. As Brando told the author James Grissom in a telephone interview in 1990:

> If you wish to ask me what I cared about most now—if you ask me to state what was important or lasting—it would have to be that I walked and sat and dreamed next to a man named James Baldwin. James—or Jimmy—knew how to analyze, place, describe, repair, and destroy things—all in the right way and for the right reasons. Baldwin, as I liked to call him, taught me to think in a piercing way about things far more important than scripts or contracts or poems—he taught me to look into and understand people and their motives and their identities. And I didn't always like what I saw, but it led me toward something that might be called freedom.[15]

Brando and Baldwin's differences were self-evident. Brando was born white in Omaha, Nebraska, in 1924. Baldwin was born black in

Harlem, New York, the same year, four months later. Their families were ostensibly very different—with Brando coming from a middle-class background and Baldwin born into poverty. But they shared a common estrangement from their fathers, and this proved decisive in bringing them together as people. Brando biographer Susan Mizruchi paints the scene well, with Brando and Baldwin cooling "off in the open-air tops of buses" in New York, taking the ferry to Staten Island, discussing "race and the value of suffering, and the impact of violent, uncomprehending fathers."[16]

Baldwin never knew his biological father. His stepfather was an austere and cruel man who ridiculed his stepson over his appearance. It was the Rev. David Baldwin who instructed Jimmy in his "ugliness"—who tormented him over his presumed shortcomings.[17] Brando's father was no less harsh. "Most of my childhood memories of my father are of being ignored," Brando would recall. "I was his namesake, but nothing I did ever pleased or even interested him. . . . I loved and hated him at the same time. He was a frightening, silent, brooding, angry, hard-drinking, rude man, a bully who loved to give orders and issue ultimatums—and he was just as tough as he talked."[18] Brando biographer William Mann has written that the two were connected by what Brando referred to as "a shared history of not belonging."[19]

While Baldwin was drawn to Brando's ability to see beyond race, his connection to him was not premised on some cheap or imagined form of post-racialism. Brando's personal connection to disconnection, longing, and rejection gave him a level of depth remarkable for anyone—and certainly someone newly immersed in the social setting of post-war New York at such an early age. "I had never met any white man like Marlon," Baldwin would later say. "He was immensely talented—a real creative force—and totally unconventional and independent, a beautiful cat."[20]

New York was still a very segregated city in its own right, but it did have its oases of racially progressive enclaves—at least by the standards of the 1940s. Greenwich Village's The New School was among them, along with the Calypso restaurant where Baldwin worked as a waiter for a time. A veritable hangout for artists, intellectuals, and musicians, the Calypso drew an array of personalities—of all races; and it afforded Baldwin the first real opportunity for "extended face to face access to a person of 'the opposite race' and the same generation."[21] Baldwin and Brando's relationship was forged in this social milieu, with the world of theater serving as an initial point of focus for what would become a friendship whose political significance was sustained by the push to make art out of pain. Brando did this quite literally in his earliest Broadway performance. Baldwin recalled Brando's impact years later:

> I finally saw Marlon for the first time on the professional stage in Maxwell Anderson's *Truckline Café*. The play was pretty bad, but Marlon's performance was a great revelation to me and gave me my first real intimation of what acting was all about. He played a kind of shriveled, psychoneurotic war veteran who eventually murders his faithless wife. He was so shriveled, so lame and stricken that, after the curtain, I was vastly relieved and somewhat surprised to find him backstage looking perfectly able and healthy and with that crooked grin on his face.[22]

Both Baldwin and Brando would recall these early years of friendship as marked by the absence of race's significance in their personal relationship. "It just never came up," Baldwin said.[23] "Race truly meant nothing to him—he [Brando] was contemptuous of anyone who discriminated in any way."[24] For his part, Brando described theirs as "a special relationship, and one of its hallmarks was an absence of any sense of racial differences between us, something I have seldom experienced with other black friends. Our relationship was simply that of two human beings with no barriers between us, and we could tell each other anything about ourselves with frankness."[25]

Baldwin and Brando shouldn't be read too literally here. It wasn't so much that race was not discussed by either man, it is more that neither felt some racial "essence" guided their understanding of the other, or their common humanity. To be sure, Baldwin was instrumental in shaping Brando's ideas of race—of, in a word, helping radicalize his perspective on American racism—the chief subject of his most ardent political activism over the decades. As Brando biographer Susan L. Mizruchi has written, "Baldwin was pivotal to Brando's enlightenment."[26] Many years after their first meeting, Brando was underlining passages from Baldwin's classic work on America's racial calamity, *The*

Fire Next Time. "You were born into a society which spelled out with brutal clarity, and in as many ways as possible, that you were a worthless human being."[27] Whether it was Brando's revulsion at his father's psychological cruelty, or purely deep social awareness, Brando came to see a connectivity between himself and the historic struggles of blacks, indigenous people, and the oppressed.

The careers of both men rose steadily after the early post-war years. But Brando's was more of a meteoric rise. Three years after their meeting, Brando was staring in Tennessee Williams's *A Streetcar Named Desire.* It changed his life, making him an instant matinee idol—a position of fame he'd spend the rest of his life rejecting. Three years after *Streetcar,* he was in his first film, giving a highly praised performance in *The Men* (1950). Baldwin, for his part, had published a book review, and an essay; his early great work, *Go Tell It on the Mountain,* was published in 1953. He had been working on it for some time, ultimately completing it in Paris. But before its publication, Brando had a role in helping Baldwin get it published.

Sort of.

Baldwin was in Paris when he got word that the publisher Alfred A. Knopf "was interested in the novel and would like to meet with him if possible."[28] This was Baldwin's breakout moment. But he was flat broke and had no means of getting to New York. In at least one biography of Baldwin, what happened next is described as a "hustle," with Baldwin and his friend, the author Themistocles Hoetis, setting up a ruse where Baldwin met with Brando to tell him he needed money to start up a new magazine to highlight young writers. Perhaps it was— but there is no reason to believe Brando would have denied Baldwin the $500 he needed to return to the States under any circumstance.[29] Their friendship was well established at this point, but the episode did reflect the dynamic that would play out over the ensuing decades between the two, with Baldwin often in pursuit of Brando'ss help. There was always a new script, a new project, a new creative enterprise that Baldwin had Brando in mind for.

Despite Knopf's offer of a $1,000 advance for *Go Tell It on the Mountain,* the novel's subject (homosexuality) proved too risky for the publisher to support. The novel's ending, with the young character John proclaiming "I want a man," was too much. Knopf asked

Baldwin for a rewrite.[30] "I learned a great deal that afternoon; learned, to put it far too briefly, what I was up against," Baldwin would go on to say about the experience.[31] In the end, Knopf would publish the revised version, and James Baldwin was on his way. As it happens, the civil rights movement was about to take a turn—and with it, Baldwin and Brando would find themselves on the stage for its most enduring moment.

The March

"Five years later," Baldwin would write of the March on Washington, "it seemed clear that we had postponed, and not at all to our advantage, the hour of dreadful reckoning."[32] This was Baldwin in his memoir and micro-history of America's recent past. First published in 1972, it offered a searing critique of America's racial condition. Much had happened since Baldwin arrived in New York's harbor from Paris, his first manuscript in tow. There was the *Brown* decision, the Montgomery Bus Boycott, the murder of Emmett Till, and the freedom rides had begun. The civil rights years were passing with Baldwin as more of an onlooker than participant. Yet, Baldwin observed these events with characteristic insight and painfully prophetic writing. Was his estimation of the 1963 March simply a part of a psyche that would never accept honey when vinegar would do? Of course, the other side was that Baldwin, contrary to some contemporary musings, hardly abandoned all hope in his thoughts of his country, one he nevertheless had to contemplate in writing most effectively from "Another Country"—that country being Turkey.[33]

The short answer is that Baldwin came around to Malcolm X's view of the March on Washington—it was perhaps not quite a "farce," as Malcolm had described it, but it was something approximating it:

> The original plans for the March on Washington had been far from polite: the original plan had been to lie down on airport runways, to block the street and offices, to immobilize the city completely, and to remain as long as we had to, to force the government to recognize the urgency and the justice of our demands. Malcolm was very caustic about the March on Washington, which he described as a sell-out. I think he was right.[34]

Despite his criticisms of the march—foremost among them being that radicals like Baldwin were not allowed to speak, Malcolm X attended, albeit as more of an observer than a supporter. "When James Baldwin came in from Paris," Malcolm would recount in his famous "Message to the Grassroots" speech, "they wouldn't let him talk, because they couldn't make him go by the script." Indeed, Attorney General Bobby Kennedy had a switch installed at the speaker's podium to cut off any remarks deemed overly radical.[35] Malcolm never let his audience forget, whenever he recounted the march, that Burt Lancaster spoke in lieu of Baldwin. What were Baldwin and others in attendance hoping to achieve? Did the march amount to nothing more than a "liberal take-over" of a nascent black power movement, as some activists suspected?

There isn't an easy answer. Baldwin and Brando were, in a sense, scripted figures in a march tempered by liberal white support as much as it was aided by it. And their afternoon concluded with a government-organized and -supported roundtable to be broadcast around the world to demonstrate America's commitment to democracy. The march, in its own way, was to serve as a kind of puff piece for the United States Information Agency (USIA). America was going to promote the march to show the distinction between American democracy and Soviet-style authoritarianism. Brando and Baldwin were key players in that bit of propaganda. Indeed, as Baldwin would later recall, "The People's Republic of China had sent a telegram in our support, which was repudiated by Roy Wilkins, who said, in effect, that we would be glad to accept such a telegram on the day that the Chinese were allowed to petition their government for redress of grievances, as we were petitioning ours."[36] With these caveats, it is worth going back to the days leading up to the march and Dr. King's speech, the period when Marlon and Jimmy managed to come together to demonstrate the power of friendship—and the power to, in fact, go off script.

Aside from the friendship they shared at the time of the March on Washington, Baldwin and Brando also shared an outsider's status within the civil rights movement. Baldwin's was for less obvious reasons. It was a poorly kept secret that Baldwin was gay.

This meant that Baldwin—like men such as Bayard Rustin (not to mention nearly all African American women)—was kept at arm's length when it came to too public a level of participation or leadership within the movement.[37] In the heteronormative climate of the era, marginalization among the marginalized was a common practice. The fact is that Baldwin's sexuality (along with Martin Luther King's own sexual conduct) were potential weapons to be deployed by the American state against the claims of blacks seeking social and political equality. But some slights were bound to hurt more than others. As Baldwin friend and biographer James Campbell wrote, "He was neither a part of the rank-and-file of the civil rights movement . . . nor was he counted among its leadership, as he was later wont to claim."[38] The FBI actively sought to make this so, eavesdropping on leaders within the movement, including Baldwin, for information to damage their credibility. In a remark that apparently never made it back to Baldwin, King was recorded by the Bureau, saying of Baldwin that he was "better qualified to lead a homosexual movement than a civil rights movement."[39]

Before Baldwin left France for the march, he helped organize one in Paris. The goal was to demonstrate international support for the march in Washington. "Segregation is not now, nor has it ever been, a regional matter," Baldwin proclaimed at an overflow service at the American Church in Paris on the Left Bank, on August 19, 1963. "We in particular have an interest in turning America into the free country it has always claimed to be."[40] At this point in his life, Baldwin had become perhaps the most distinctive voice for black empowerment in America. His novels had made him a literary giant, and his two long essays that were to become *The Fire Next Time* had made him a household name. In May 1963, he was on the cover of *Time* magazine—the banner bearing the caption: "BIRMINGHAM AND BEYOND: The Negro's Push for Equality."

Baldwin was yet reduced to somewhat of a second-tier player during the march, his radicalism and sexual identity marking him out as potentially harmful. It is why he sided with the young John Lewis of the Student Nonviolent Coordinating Committee (SNCC) who had been asked to "tone down" his speech that day "in order not to alienate the white religious establishment involved in the march."[41] Some of Baldwin's fire would come out later in the day, after the march, while serving on the celebrity panel put together by USIA. He'd be cut off at the last moment, just as he was launching into one of his most profound and recurring lines about the true nature of racism in America.

Of course, Brando's outsider status at the march had to do with his whiteness. There was a fine line—one particularly monitored by the younger and more militant faction within the civil rights movement—of just how much white support amounted to a cooptation of the march's message. It wasn't Malcolm X who was critical of white financial and political control of the march ("It's just like when you've got some coffee when it's too black, which means it's too strong. What do you do? You integrate it with cream. You weaken it," he would famously say[42]). Others were raising these questions within the movement and it was posing all sorts of challenges to King's leadership. So Brando's presence, along with that of other famous whites, was on the one hand welcome, while simultaneously arousing suspicion of a takeover. Brando would understand this dynamic all of his life—but not without pain.

In the weeks leading up to the march, Brando used his clout as a celebrity to cajole some of his Hollywood friends to participate. He worked with his old and dear friend Harry Belafonte on this, reluctantly agreeing to bring along the actor Charlton Heston, a Republican, to round out the more left-leaning cadre of actors assembled.[43] It was a busy summer for Marlon as he worked to raise money for the widow and children of the slain civil rights leader Medgar Evers; he was also meeting with the "NAACP attorney Thomas Neusom to strategize the best ways he could help the cause."[44] The television coverage and photographs of an integrated march—one where the nation's most iconic stars could be seen protesting peacefully together—lent great credibility to the objectives of the movement.

The USIA, headed by Edward R. Murrow, was an active, behind-the-scenes player during the march, filming the event for later international release. It was a USIA photographer who captured the warm embrace of Brando and Baldwin among the historic photos taken that day. That photo is but one of a number showing the two men together smiling—on occasion holding each other's hands. Their warmth and personal closeness are evident. The intent of the USIA was purposeful—to show the virtues of American democratic society—that racial tensions in the United States were not beyond repair. For Brando and Baldwin, their reactions were spontaneous—although their presence was likewise purposeful. Their participation was not orchestrated to demonstrate support for American domestic policy. Rather, it was to draw attention to a crisis that demanded the attention of the nation's citizenry, especially those whites on the fence about civil rights. The desire on the part of America's mainstream media and institutions to show the nation's racial troubles in a more favorable light clashed with the desires of Baldwin and Brando to tell a far uglier truth. After the march, in the studio, a grim-faced Brando and equally somber Baldwin, old friends from New York, would offer a robust defense for radical racial change in America. Some of that defense would end up on the cutting room floor—a symptom of the very problem the two artists had been brought together to address.

The Roundtable

"What are you crying for, man?" Harry Belafonte said, looking at the actors assembled as Dr. King finished his speech. "Why don't you smile and join the dream? You're listening to the first Negro President of the United States!"[45] Years later, Brando would recall standing "a few steps behind Dr. King as he delivered his 'I Have a Dream' speech."[46] But other accounts have him with Belafonte and others assembled for the post-march roundtable put together by USIA. Those in the studio room included Belafonte, Brando, and Baldwin, the movie director Joseph Mankiewicz, actors Sidney Poitier and Charlton Heston, and the moderator, David Schoenbrun.

Schoenbrun, who worked for government news services during World War II, was recruited by Edward R. Murrow to work for CBS after the war. Murrow appointed him chief Paris correspondent in 1947.[47] The National Archives notes that USIA was created "on August 1, 1953, by the President's Reorganization Plan No. 8 and Executive Order 10477 as a consolidation of all foreign information activities of the US Government into one program."[48] There is little doubt that Baldwin and Brando had stepped into a government-sponsored propaganda film.

The Kennedy administration had been concerned about controlling the politics of the march nearly from its inception. But the panel of assembled guests from Hollywood had its share of wild cards. These included Brando, Baldwin, and Belafonte. It appears that some of Baldwin's comments were edited out of the broadcast—a censorship he would unlikely have agreed to had he known. As Joel Whitney has written, "In the end, only the more moderate of Baldwin's comments made it into the thirty-minute program segment."[49] That said, Baldwin had been promised by Sol Stein, the editor at Stein & Day, that his work would be purchased in bulk by the US government in its fight against radicalism abroad. It was the kind of development that prompted Langston Hughes to declare to Baldwin, "I fear you are becoming a NEGRO writer—and a propaganda one at that!"[50]

The USIA broadcast was not made available to the public at the time. It has since been made available online by the National Archives.[51] Schoenbrun opened the roundtable discussion by introducing Baldwin as "a very well-known novelist, one of our best writers." Baldwin responded to the question as to why he attended the march by stating pointedly that "I could say, the fact that I was born a Negro in this country," an acknowledgement of the perpetual problem of oppression of blacks in America from birth. Notably, the fact that no women were present on the panel went entirely unnoticed. This is a stark reminder of just how male-dominated political discourse was at the time—including within the civil rights movement. The panel's diversity was found in the multiracial makeup of its guests—including two Americans of West Indian ancestry, Poitier and Belafonte.[52]

Poitier told Schoenbrun he was in Washington to "appeal to the conscience of white supremacy." It was the beginning of an eloquent response about his belief in the potential of America—a country barely "scratching the surface" of its abilities, as he put it. Schoenbrun then pivoted to Brando, who was asked about the march "representing the greatest day of freedom in the nation's history." Brando then calmly gave a comprehensive response, seeking to tie America's racial injustice to a deeper human psychosis of hatred and violence. "Well, this is a revolution of course, that is sweeping our country now; if it ends up properly perhaps Indians will be given some of their land back that have claims based on treaties . . . all people will benefit." Brando then spoke to hatred on a global scale—including intra-racial hatred among blacks and whites alike. He emphasized the international struggle for peace, and asked Americans to contemplate the kind of hatred that led to "burning children with cattle prods," a reference to the assault on black children peacefully protesting in Birmingham in June of 1963.

The image clearly moved Brando, and he was seen throughout the March on Washington carrying an electric cattle prod to draw attention to this particularly heinous form of terror against African Americans.[53] The *Los Angeles Times* and AP photographer Larry Davis captured Brando holding the prod underneath his left arm, with his left hand clutching Baldwin's right hand. His right arm is draped around Baldwin's right shoulder. The men are beaming, standing directly in front of Lincoln's statue at the Memorial, with Heston and Belafonte in the background.[54]

It was always customary of Brando to see the myriad connections between human suffering. In his memoir, *Songs My Mother Taught Me*, when reflecting upon Gandhi's struggle to help end India's caste system, he wrote, "In the United States we've always had our own untouchables—American Indians, blacks, homosexuals. Who knows who will be next?"[55] Schoenbrun took Brando's effort to broaden the discussion of American racism as an opportunity to make the case for American exceptionalism:

> What strikes me is that almost all of the countries you've mentioned are countries in the Western world. . . . This is not a flag-waving question of mine. . . . It does occur to me that demonstrations of this kind could not be easily held elsewhere. . . . I have not seen any march on Moscow or march on Peking. . . . Wouldn't you agree it's fair that the hope of our country is that we can have demonstrations of this kind?

Mankiewicz agreed, noting that while America is the only Western country where this could happen, it is also the only one where it is necessary. Charlton Heston then came in to disagree with Mankiewicz and Brando, extolling the "virtues under which this country was founded," noting that "however tardy" the country had been in bringing about universal freedom, we were the nation that authored the concept.

Belafonte, unsatisfied with this, returned to the more critical themes discussed by Brando, arguing that "the bulk of . . . whether this thing is going to end successfully and joyously, or is going to end disastrously . . . lays very heavily with the white community, it lays very heavily with the profiteers, it lays very heavily with the vested interests, it lays very heavily with a great middle stream of this country of people who have refused to commit themselves or have even the slightest knowledge that these things have been going on." Schoenbrun, seeking to return to a more palliative theme, asked Baldwin about nonviolence and Dr. King's "great dream." Baldwin agreed that the dream of a democratic and free America could be achieved without violence—but not without cost.

Belafonte was less sure, placing the emphasis of a commitment to nonviolence on the part of whites. He also returned to Schoenbrun's reference to Moscow and Peking, suggesting that those societies could not be our standard. The two then got into a bit of an exchange—off script, it seemed—with Schoenbrun noting that over "100 countries" would be listening to the broadcast, and were not as informed as the panelists about America's commitment to democracy.

Before it was over, Baldwin got in something quite compelling just before the session ended, as Schoenbrun asked whether this was a white question or problem, or a Negro one. Brando, in effect, argued that Negroes had been instructing white Americans about democracy all along. Others went back and forth over whose responsibility it was to correct the nation's path toward racial destruction. Schoenbrun, sensing the conversation becoming too elliptical, chose to close out the program with a question for each panelist. He started with Baldwin— and perhaps owing to Baldwin's response, decided to end things there.

"If you had the right to say," Schoenbrun began, " 'I, James Baldwin, will tell people what to do and how to solve this thing,' what would you say?"

> My God . . . the nature of the problem as I see it, is so complex, one cannot simply say jobs . . . it's in the social fabric . . . at the risk of sounding mystical . . the first step probably has to be somewhere in the American conscience, the American white republic has to ask itself why it was necessary for them to invent the nigger. I am not a nigger. I have never called myself one. . . . It is very important, I think, for the American . . . that he face this question, that he needed the nigger for something.

"Please forgive me for interrupting," Schoenbrun stammered. "In fact, we have run out of time."

Baldwin had given a similar answer to the black psychologist and journalist Kenneth Clark, a little over three months before this response. It would become a critical and iconic refrain of his, lasting beyond his lifetime. The 2016 documentary on Baldwin, "I Am Not Your Negro," was the more polite expression of this sentiment—one designed to get whites to confront the deepest recesses of their need for black racial inferiority. At the roundtable discussion, Baldwin went as far as USIA was prepared to go—and the unbridled nature of the discussion may well have cost Edward R. Murrow his job. He was replaced by Carl T. Rowan, who had been appointed by President Kennedy as the nation's first African American undersecretary of state in 1961, as the director of USIA in 1964. As Joel Whitney's research bears out, Baldwin's "most pointed statements—that the FBI was working against black activists and civil rights—were scrubbed even from the transcript."[56]

Conclusion: "It Cannot Be Talked About"

As fate would have it, the March on Washington roundtable for the USIA was the only film James Baldwin managed to make with Marlon Brando. It is doubtful either of them saw it, although the film made it as far as Hong Kong, where it was shown to over 120,000 people.[57] Baldwin never managed to get Brando to star as one of the characters from his novels. He came close—Brando committed to playing the calculating café owner in *Giovanni's Room*. He even seemed to have Robert De Niro on board to join the cast. It fell through. Baldwin's penchant for brutal honesty hurt him. Apparently, he set Di Niro off after criticizing his performance in *The Deer Hunter*.[58] It was more Brando's talent to charm than it was Baldwin's.

Maybe it was for the best. What we have instead are the photos and interview footage from the March on Washington. The two would have other meetings, including stints in Paris and in Istanbul. But the remainder of their friendship was defined by attempts to get together, almost always met by near-misses and catch-you-laters. But the relationship continued to shape their work, as both men found themselves drawn to the Black Power movement that grew in the years after the March on Washington. Baldwin would be drawn closer to Malcolm, Brando to the Panthers. Ultimately, the journey for racial justice brought Brando in greater contact with the American Indian Movement. If you hadn't been watching his life over the previous three decades, you were likely to be among the bewildered members of the audience at the Academy Awards in 1973, when Brando had his Oscar rejected on his behalf by Shacheen Littlefeather, to dramatize the oppression of Native Americans by the US government.

In the span of a few days in April 1968, both men would be rocked by terrible news. Dr. King was assassinated in Memphis on April 4, and two days later, Bobby Hutton of the Panthers, all of seventeen years old and unarmed, was shot and killed by Oakland police. In a testament to his ability to draw national attention as well as the level of trust he engendered among black activists, Brando was asked to deliver Hutton's eulogy. Brando called his friend to join him, but Baldwin was still reeling from King's murder.[59]

A few months after Hutton's killing, Brando would face defamation charges from the Oakland police for placing the blame for his murder on "police," without specifying any officers in particular. He ultimately lost the defamation case, though he was not required to pay damages.[60] At Hutton's funeral, he chose to draw attention to his own personal struggle and responsibility with respect to race:

> That could have been *my* son lying there, and I'm going to do as much as I can, I'm going to start right now, to inform White people of what they don't know. The Reverend said, the White man can't cool it because he's never dug it. And I'm here to try to *dig* it. Because I myself as a White man have got a long way to go and a lot to learn. I haven't been in your place. I haven't suffered the way you've suffered. I'm just beginning to learn the nature of that experience. And somehow that has to be translated to the white community, *now!*[61]

Much of what Brando had learned of that experience was because of his friendship with Baldwin. His activism over the remainder of his life speaks to the sincerity of his commitment to working to help whites in America reflect on the nature of American racism. Many didn't want such help. Sacheen Littlefeather was booed during her speech at the Academy Awards—and Brando's effort to raise the nation's consciousness about the suffering of Native Americans at that moment was widely criticized.[62]

Whatever it is that produces the kind of confrontational honesty that allows one to challenge their society at the risk of losing their own personal success, Baldwin and Brando shared it. Perhaps it was the underlying bond to their friendship. Baldwin, for one, didn't care to talk about it. "[I]t is irrelevant for me to discuss Marlon as an actor; and I find it is quite beyond me to discuss him as a friend," he wrote of Brando. "What goes into the making of a friendship is very deep and quiet and it really cannot be talked about. In fact, I don't think it *should* be talked about."[63]

7

Mocambo
Ella Fitzgerald and Marilyn Monroe

Introduction: Myth and Memory

Mocambo is an African-derived word. It was used in Brazil as the name for the first settlement of fugitive slave communities.[1] Somehow, someone thought it a catchy name for a Latin-themed nightclub in Hollywood. That someone was former talent agent Charlie Morrison, who owned the Mocambo, an establishment that went on to run from January 3, 1941, through June 30, 1958. The Mocambo became a legendary joint—it was the model for *I Love Lucy*'s Tropicana Club, and it hosted the likes of Frank Sinatra, Perry Como, Edith Piaf, and Lana Turner, who reportedly "dropped $40,000 on a birthday party" there.[2] Today, a massive Equinox gym takes up much of the footprint where the club stood more than sixty years ago. It was an unusual setting for one of America's great interracial friendship narratives, one that continues to be mythologized.

Indeed, among the club's many fabled stories, one has persisted, and in recent years has managed to wind its way into the world of social media. It goes something like this: sometime in November of 1954, the legendary actress and national heartthrob Marilyn Monroe persuaded Morrison to book the equally legendary black singer Ella Fitzgerald at the Mocambo, a club that had been otherwise segregated since its opening. Morrison is said to have relented only when Monroe promised to show up every night for Fitzgerald's performances, thus guaranteeing a full house of fans eager to be seen in the same venue with America's leading female icon.

It worked like a charm. Fitzgerald sang; Monroe, with fellow celebrities in tow, sat in the front row; the place was packed. Most importantly, the Mocambo had now set the standard for other venues around the country. In one fell swoop, American nightclubs, great and small, began the process of integration, fearing to be left behind. Monroe was a veritable Pee Wee Reese to Fitzgerald's Jackie Robinson—a pair of interracial friends who worked together for the greater good to integrate their respective industries through courageous and demonstrative acts of solidarity. It's easy to see why the Mocambo story is the kind the internet can't get enough of, what with its cocktail of entertainment icons, racism, social justice message, and "secret" history—they're all there.

Most of these stories place Marilyn in the role of heroine:

"How Marilyn Monroe Changed Ella Fitzgerald's Life."
"How Marilyn Monroe Helped Break Ella Fitzgerald Into the Big Time."
"Ella Fitzgerald Was Actually Launched by Marilyn Monroe."
"The Time Marilyn Monroe Came to the Rescue of Ella Fitzgerald."
"Marilyn Monroe Surprisingly Risked Her Whole Career for Ella Fitzgerald"[3]

Taken most cynically, these renderings uphold the kind of white savior narrative so omnipresent in America's discourse on race.[4] *Changed*, *helped*, *launched*, *rescue*, and *risked*—these are verbs placing Monroe in the role of racial emancipator. The force of the idea is that without Monroe's help, Fitzgerald, however talented, would have remained an obscure singer, another black woman destined to play the Chitlin' Circuit.

But is it true? And what does the persistence of the story say about our collective memory when viewed through the prism of interracial friendship? Were Marilyn Monroe and Ella Fitzgerald engaged in the kind of democratic project involving personal friendship discussed in the preceding chapters? Or, when looking at the Mocambo story, are we more apt to see our own wants and shortcomings projected on a past that never was? A lot of it depends on which Mocambo story we are talking about.

Stories We Tell

The first place to start is with the photograph. Nearly all of the "Marilyn supports Ella" Mocambo stories on social media display the same photo. It is the one with Fitzgerald on the left, smiling in a light-colored silk dress. She's gesturing with her right arm extended and hand partially open—she seems to be making a point to Marilyn. She's wearing some killer earrings. Monroe is on the right, beaming at Ella, hands clasped, her neck encircled with what looks to be an equally impressive necklace. She's dressed in a black dress and a mink coat. A woman in the rear of the picture stares into the camera with an inquisitive look, photo-bombing the two stars. It's a great photo. But it's not the Mocambo.[5]

The people at Getty Images tell us it's the Tiffany Club in Hollywood. The night is November 19, 1954, and Monroe's escort for the evening was the Hollywood gossip columnist Sidney Skolsky.[6] This is the first sign of a problem. As Fitzgerald biographer Stuart Nicholson has written, "while recuperating from minor surgery in November 1954," Monroe "went to hear Ella at a club near her Hollywood home and became a devoted fan." Nicholson continues, noting, "Monroe put pressure on the Mocambo's owner Charlie Morrison to open the doors to one of America's most exclusive night clubs to a 'jazz singer.' "[7] Nicholson was only repeating Ella's story. In August of 1972, Fitzgerald told Gloria Steinem's *Ms.* magazine the following:

> I owe Marilyn Monroe a real debt. It was because of her that I played the Mocambo (an important Los Angeles club in the '50s). She personally called the owner of the Mocambo, and told him she wanted me booked immediately, and if he would do it, she'd take a front table every night. She told him—and it was true, due to Marilyn's superstar status—that the press would go wild. The owner said yes, and Marilyn was there every night. The press went overboard. . . . After that, I never had to play a small jazz club again. She was an unusual woman—a little ahead of her times. And she didn't know it.[8]

This recollection, like the Tiffany Club photograph, is but one of a series of "facts" that have been erroneously passed down over the years in service of the more heroic Mocambo story. For starters, Ella first played the Mocambo in March 1955. Marilyn was not in Los Angeles at that time.[9] Besides the fact that Monroe and Fitzgerald were not at the Mocambo together in November 1954, it has been argued that Monroe didn't have a hand in helping book Fitzgerald at the Mocambo. Of all things, a memo from Monroe's secretary, Inez Melson, recently auctioned off from the estate of Lee Strasberg for $1,152.00, tells a different story:[10]

> February 15, 1955
> Memo of conversation with Jo Brooks
> Jo Brooks is husband of Jules Fox who is a publicity agent, handling publicity for Ella Fitzgerald.
> A few months back, Miss Monroe visited the Tiffany Club on West 8th Street where Ella Fitzgerald was playing. Miss Fitzgerald talked of a possible future date at the Mocambo and Miss Monroe said when this happened, she would like to give a party for Miss Fitzgerald.
> Miss Fitzgerald will open at the Mocambo on March 15 and [Mr.] Brooks wanted to know if Miss Monroe was serious about giving a party. I told her that I did not think that Miss Monroe would be in town on that date but I would tell her about Miss Fitzgerald's opening.

Monroe wasn't in town for Fitzgerald's Mocambo gig and never threw a party for her. If she did intervene in the booking process on Fitzgerald's behalf, we can only know by conjecture, as the written record is circumstantial at best.

Monroe biographer Michelle Morgan argues that Marilyn did persuade the Mocambo's owner to book Ella—but the hurdle for Morrison wasn't Fitzgerald's race, it was that "he didn't see Ella Fitzgerald as glamorous enough to bring in the crowds."[11] The Mocambo was already integrated by 1954—black stars such as Dorothy Dandridge (1951) and Eartha Kitt (1953) had already played there. By this account, Fitzgerald was being discriminated against on the basis of her presumed lack of sex appeal, not her color.[12] But good salvific stories die hard—especially when race is involved. Fitzgerald biographer Geoffrey Mark not only holds up the Mocambo story but takes it further, arguing that Monroe once went to Colorado to hear Fitzgerald and, upon learning that Ella could not enter through the front door, is said to have exclaimed, "Marilyn Monroe and Ella Fitzgerald are entering through the front of this building, or Marilyn Monroe and Ella Fitzgerald are not entering at all!"[13] It may have even happened—though this author hasn't been able to find any other evidence beyond this claim. It's hard to parcel out the truth in an unreliable tale so widely agreed upon. In Mark's biography of Ella, the Mocambo isn't even the *Mocambo*; it's "The Moulin Rouge."[14]

What is it about the Monroe-Fitzgerald-Mocambo story that is so alluring—and even more—so prone to exaggeration? On the surface it is nothing more than a feel-good tale, a testament to the beginnings of racial progress in mid-twentieth-century America, a kind of harbinger of the civil rights movement. On the other hand, the Mocambo story combines three of America's greatest obsessions: sex, race, and celebrity. These elements work powerfully together in part because they satisfy different constitutive desires—those of the two protagonists involved and, for different reasons, both white and black Americans.

Take the most famous interracial relationship in early American history—that of Thomas Jefferson and Sally Hemings. When James Akin of Newburyport, Massachusetts, satirized then President Jefferson in his 1804 engraving (cheekily entitled "A Philosophic Cock") depicting Jefferson as a rooster and his slave, Hemings, as a hen, it signified the Federalist party's rejection of Jefferson on not only political but also moral grounds. Jefferson's sleeping with his black slave was seen as the worst kind of political slur. The rumors of Jefferson's relationship with Hemings—if the term *relationship* can hold meaning given the inherently compulsory nature of interracial sex in slavery—persisted for nearly two hundred years before they were confirmed through the work of historians such as Annette Gordon Reed and, ultimately, DNA testing.[15] What often goes unmentioned in this, and in so many cases like it during the history of American slavery, is the effect this ostensibly forbidden but widely practiced custom had on both black and white women. It was, of course, far more than a custom. It was rape.

While slavery insisted upon black inferiority in all forms—intellectual, cultural, and physical alike—it nevertheless countenanced the right of white men to have sex with their slaves. This right was undeniably a form of domination, but it was also a right to pleasure—an idea incompatible with the belief in black women's physical inferiority with respect to beauty. The accusations against Jefferson were thus often dismissed, down to recent historians, who deemed him incapable of sleeping with Hemings because of his "character."[16] As the *Atlantic Monthly* put it in its 1873 retrospective on the presidential Election of 1800, "'Mr. Jefferson's Congo harem' was a party cry." The *Atlantic* reassured its readers that such a charge against Jefferson was impossible based on the "pocket memorandum" or calendar he kept, recording his whereabouts, which did not square up with "the record of his slave's birth."[17] The slave, in this case, was Madison Jefferson, whom Jefferson fathered. It appears Jefferson didn't keep every coming or going in his pocket calendar.

White male sexual domination over black women was integral to the shaping of relationships between black and white women. Black women were subjected to rape and dehumanizing forms of eroticization; white women were put in the position of onlookers or deniers—positioned above black women, yet subordinated to their husbands. In the Jim Crow era, white women were made the objects of sexualized protection as the threat of miscegenation was deemed a threat to American civilization, which was linked to white social and political superiority. Projections of white femininity and beauty were shaped in this social context, and a heightened need for racial purity made whiteness a nearly unattainable abstraction. It became largely identified with a hierarchy of physical characteristics: white skin, blonde hair, blue eyes. White womanhood in America had long been erected upon the twin pedestals of racism and patriarchy.

Hollywood was soon exporting this ideal around the world. As Margaret L. Hunter has written, "As many people in other countries yearn for the good life offered in the United States, they also yearn for the aesthetic in the United States: light skin, blonde hair, and Anglo facial features."[18] Likewise, Richard Dyer points out in his study of race and American film, "blondeness is racially unambiguous. It keeps the white woman distinct from the black, brown, or yellow and at the same time it assures the viewer that the woman is the genuine article."[19] Indeed, when Malcolm X in his *Autobiography* describes his relationship with his blonde girlfriend Sophia from his wayward youth, he is highlighting his transformation to psychological and political blackness. The real Sophia was Bea Caragulian, a woman of Armenian descent. Like Monroe, her hair was bleached blonde. Even white "ethnic" beauty has historically run behind the allure of ultra-white blondeness. The Armenian-descended, dark-haired Kardashians are a recent phenomenon in American life, to be sure. Perhaps the Russian magazine *Nedyela* summarized America's exportation of blonde-haired white beauty best: "When you speak of the American way of life everybody thinks of chewing gum, Coca-Cola and Marilyn Monroe."[20]

The other side of Monroe's connection to beauty and hypersexuality was her presentation as a "dumb blonde." This aspect of her public persona made her sexual allure and power palatable, positioning white men and Anglo rationality, intelligence, and sophistication above the kind of raw carnality Monroe was asked to embody. For her part, Ella Fitzgerald's non-sexualized persona made her safe for both white male and female popular consumption. Part of the task in unlocking the persistence of the Mocambo story and its power is in getting at the authenticity of both Monroe and Fitzgerald as individuals. Their evolved status as cultural icons occludes critical features of why they did indeed establish a real friendship, even as it helps explain why their respective images made for a mystical pairing for a narrative of interracial friendship.

Sights and Sounds

Ella Fitzgerald and Marilyn Monroe represented two of America's defining attributes: optimism and beauty. I use the term *optimism* advisedly, because hope is the province of blues singers, and Fitzgerald, for all of her gifts, was not really a blues singer. Her voice carried the aspirational quality of America; the sense that not only would things *be* alright—they were *in fact* alright. In a sense, Monroe's presentation of beauty worked the same way. Her sexual energy and presentation were inviting, but they were cooled through a child-like and often comedic affect, one that diminished the danger of her sensuality. Like most artists, the truth of their lived experiences ran counter to Ella and Marilyn's presentation on stage and screen. Nevertheless, their individual stories made for a compelling friendship, however short-lived, one that has survived over generations—precisely because the mythos of the country was so bound up in what their relationship symbolized.

Ella Fitzgerald was born to William and Tempie Fitzgerald in Newport News, Virginia, on April 25, 1917. Her parents were unmarried, and within a year, Ella's father left the family. Tempie soon found companionship with Joseph Da Silva, a Portuguese immigrant, with whom she and Ella moved to Yonkers, New York, while Ella was still a baby.[21] While she never spoke of it publicly, there has been much speculation that Da Silva abused Fitzgerald after her mother's death in 1932. Her aunt apparently stepped in and took Fitzgerald in with her in Harlem.[22] Despite this early hardship, Fitzgerald was viewed by her friends and classmates as a very happy child.

The move to Harlem proved fortuitous. Two years later, in 1934, Fitzgerald made her Harlem debut at the Apollo Theater. It was the beginning of one of the most iconic careers in American music. Early in 1935, Fitzgerald made her first appearance in print, with the *New York Age* noting her Harlem Opera House audition win on February 9.[23] The *New York Times*, ever conservative, would take another eight years to cover her, recording her appearance, along with Dizzy Gillespie's, at Carnegie Hall. Fitzgerald was an afterthought in that review, with Gillespie getting the lion's share of coverage, almost all of it a positive assessment of what would be known as the be-bop sound. Still, the *Times* couldn't resist ending on a sour note, declaring "Mr. Gillespie's own technical deficiencies are many, however, and the lack of shape in his work pervades the whole impression."[24]

Fitzgerald experienced an extraordinary rise between her *New Age* and *Times* notices. She had become enough of a personality to perform two numbers in 1942's Abbott and Costello film "Ride 'Em Cowboy"; she had brought "scat singing to a new level of artistry"[25]; moreover, she was consistently listed as the top, or near the very top, of America's most talented female vocalists. In 1937 Fitzgerald "was voted Number One Female Vocalist in the first-ever Down Beat and Melody Maker readers' poll." It was the first of many such awards. Indeed, Fitzgerald won the Down Beat Female Vocalist of the Year eighteen consecutive years at one point before being bested by Roberta Flack in 1971. It was a nearly unbroken run going back to 1937.[26]

These successes, including the financial stability that came along with it, did not erase other, deeper, and more profound inner crises experienced by Fitzgerald. She developed an abiding sense of self-doubt, and perhaps self-loathing, owing to her appearance, and how people—whites especially—responded to both her weight and her color. In her early years, she was mocked on account of her shabby clothing; on occasion she was shunned because of her weight and personal hygiene—at one point in her teens she had run away and was essentially homeless. Chick Webb, the great black band leader Fitzgerald would work with at the beginning of her career, nearly didn't hire her. "Too ugly," he is purported to have said.[27] As the black cultural critic Margo Jefferson has written: "Thank God for the radio and the phonograph: they gave a singer like Ella Fitzgerald the same advantage—invisibility—that letters gave Cyrano de Bergerac. And thank God for jazz. It gave black women what film and theater gave white women: a well-lighted space where they could play with roles and styles, conduct esthetic experiments and win money and praise."[28]

Fitzgerald never shook her sense of non-belonging and self-consciousness. She tended to isolate herself on the road and developed a performance anxiety surprising for an artist of her level of success. Much of this was attributed to her perception of her appearance—and what others thought of it.[29] On top of all this, Fitzgerald, belittled on account of her looks, also had to contend with the criticism of being musically "white." Her 1938 recording of "A-Tisket, A-Tasket," although widely popular, came to symbolize an easy-going, "soulless" sound. Here was a black woman whose voice captured a kind of child-like sweetness, one filled with comforting notes and impeccable diction—simultaneously having to contend with being "too white" and "too black." Band leader Chick Webb "was focusing on white America, the constituency that could provide the biggest paychecks." He not only didn't mind that "Ella's voice sounded as if it could just as easily be from a white singer," he saw it as an unquestioned benefit.[30]

Nevertheless, by the time Fitzgerald met Monroe, she was wildly successful and an established star in her own right. She had already helped integrate lily-white spaces such as the Coconut Grove Park

Central Hotel in New York as early as 1939. She was likewise already winning acclaim, and on occasion rubbing elbows with the likes of Guy Lombardo, Benny Goodman, and Audrey Hepburn.[31] Fitzgerald's meteoric rise suggests that the Mocambo story, even if true, was not the pivotal event in "launching" her career. What it did do was link her to a star whose image was nearly the opposite of her own. That polarized connection—and why it matters—can best be understood when Monroe's own rise to fame is taken into account.

Like Fitzgerald, Monroe's childhood was anything but idyllic. Born Norma Jean Baker, she was, as one biographer succinctly put it, "the unwanted love child of a woman who had gone insane."[32] Monroe's mother, Gladys Pearl Monroe, gave birth to her in Los Angeles, California, on June 1, 1926. Gladys spent the first two weeks with her daughter before she handed over the infant to a stranger, Ida Bolender, as part of a pre-arranged agreement.[33] It was the beginning of a "childhood being passed from foster home to foster home, never knowing what it felt like to belong."[34] Monroe's father never recognized her, and she spent the better part of her childhood shuttling between five women caregivers: her mother Gladys, Gladys's friend Grace Atchison McKee, her grandmother, Della Monroe, and two of Norma Jean's foster mothers, Ida Bolender and Ana Atchison.

It was a period of great instability, one defined by the troubling fact that Marilyn's mother Gladys "was declared paranoid schizophrenic and admitted to a state mental hospital."[35] It was a devastating reality that would affect Monroe's relationship and public discourse about her mother, as well as her own sense of self-worth and mental well-being. One positive and lasting development during Monroe's childhood was "the egalitarian attitudes of the Bolenders toward race, her first foster parents."[36] Thus, despite projections of her "goddess"-like purity, almost always presented in scripts devoid of any black presence onscreen, Monroe would always have a strong African American fan base. Many blacks identified with her difficult childhood and her open embrace of black celebrities—including Fitzgerald.[37] James Baldwin, for one, is said to have "recognized the childhood abuse visited on [Monroe] and called her a 'slave' of the Hollywood system."[38] Employing the British scholar Diane Negra's work on representations of whiteness in film, Monroe biographer Lois Banner sees Monroe as fitting into Negra's category of a "white ethnic" figure, one whose poor childhood and marriages to ethnic outsiders such as Joe DiMaggio (Italian) and Arthur Miller (Jewish) make her a kind of "bridge between minorities."[39] While this was hardly the intent of Hollywood, Monroe's life circumstances ran counter to the "pristine" image of whiteness it almost invariably found itself selling.

Monroe would spend much of her adult life hiding the truth of her childhood, frequently describing herself as an orphan to the press.[40] While this served the purpose of shielding her from scrutiny into a difficult period in her life and troubled relationship with her mother, it had the added benefit of allowing the studios she worked for to preserve a wholesome image of her. The outsider status, or "imposter syndrome," experienced by Monroe which later connected her to Fitzgerald, was part of the vulnerability she conveyed on screen and in real life. That vulnerability was disguised by the persona of "Marilyn Monroe"—a construction of Hollywood, yes, but also of Norma Jean Baker—who had to, over the course of her life, summon the image of sexual allure at a moment's notice.

Part of what has made friendships among whites and blacks so difficult is the layered nature of masks worn by both parties; the masks that individuals often have to wear just to survive—and those superimposed on them by a society that asks them to play a role in the drama of white supremacy. Ralph Ellison's nameless protagonist is confronted with this very dilemma, presented by a white character named Emerson in *Invisible Man*:

> "Oh, damn! What I mean is, do you believe it possible for us, the two of us, to throw off the mask of custom and manners that insulate man from man, and converse in naked honesty and frankness?"[41]

It's notable that Ellison's character refers to a generic mask worn by individuals irrespective of race. The struggle of racial fraternity is not so much the adornment of masks among prospective friends; it is, rather, the tendency to tighten those already being worn. That Monroe and Fitzgerald could remove—or at least loosen—their respective masks when together was a crucial aspect of their connection to one another.

By the time of their purported first meeting at the Mocambo, Monroe was a certified star. Her hands were imprinted in the cement outside of Grauman's Chinese Theater in Hollywood. She had recently filmed her iconic subway-grate scene for *The Seven Year Itch*, had starred in *Gentleman Prefer Blondes*, and was several years removed from her first appearance on the cover of *Life*. Despite these successes, Monroe was in a period of intense personal difficulty. She had recently separated from the retired Yankees great Joe DiMaggio and was in divorce hearings; she was likewise struggling to be taken seriously as an actress—a point of great contention for her, as she was in constant pursuit of shedding her "dumb blonde" image that the studios couldn't seem to get enough of. As one historian and Monroe biographer has written:

> Monroe's politics were to the left. . . . In *My Story* Marilyn states that she read [the radical muckraking journalist] Lincoln Steffens's autobiography on the set of All About Eve and liked his discussion of oppression and resistance. When [director] Joe Mankiewicz heard she was reading Steffens, he told her she could get into trouble if studio executives found out. [The publicist] Harry Brand cautioned her: "We don't want anyone investigating our Marilyn." She hid the book under her bed in her apartment and read it at night by the light of a flashlight. She was observed reading other radical literature on the set of her films.[42]

For some time, Monroe had been coping with her personal anguish and anxieties—including the physical abuse she suffered from DiMaggio—through the increased consumption of alcohol, sleeping pills, and other mood-altering drugs. "There's little doubt that Marilyn was dependent on sleeping pills by this time—doled out to her without concern by the studio physicians—and had also become used to the idea of taking other drugs to calm herself during times of stress.[43] Fitzgerald's music was reportedly not only a salve for Marilyn's anxiety but was also an important part of her own development as a singer. Her vocal coach, Hal Schaefer, is purported to have told her to study the album *Ella Fitzgerald Sings George Gershwin*.[44] The introduction to Ella's technique is thought to have improved Marilyn's singing—and it was an important part of her desire to meet Ella.

By late 1954 Ella Fitzgerald and Marilyn Monroe were household names. In many ways, had either not lived beyond that year, they would have already established for themselves a place in American pop-culture history. Ironically, Fitzgerald would have been considered the more significant figure—and historically, in terms of influence in her field, she undoubtedly remains so. Which makes the Mocambo story a bit of an inverted tale of salvation. The truth of their meeting, and the complicated evolution of its story, is not so much missing as it is scattered—a byproduct of different memories, agendas, and temptations.

Truths

The Mocambo story endures online and in print some sixty-five years after Monroe is thought to have called Charlie Morrison on Fitzgerald's behalf. Two children's books were published about it in 2020 alone.[45] That's fairly astounding for stars whose meeting occurred during the Eisenhower years. In 2008, the American-British playwright Bonnie Greer's musical *Marilyn and Ella* premiered at the Theatre Royal in Stratford, London.[46] People can't get enough of this story—but do we know what their friendship was like, let alone if the Mocambo yarn is true?

We know that Fitzgerald was not the first black performer to integrate the legendary club. We can therefore surmise that if she had any issue with the club's owner, Morrison, it had less to do with race than with the fact that Fitzgerald didn't comport with his image of the kind of stars he wanted to showcase. Still, Ella did play the Mocambo— but when? *Billboard Magazine* reported that "Ella Fitzgerald will open March 15 [1955] at Mocambo, Los Angeles for two weeks while in town to work in the new Jack Webb flick."[47] The Associated Press and other outlets likewise reported on it, and we have that photo, however erroneously applied to the Mocambo over the years.

Ella played the Mocambo in March 1955—but Marilyn wasn't there. *Jet* magazine, the leading black publication in the nation, included a number of photos of celebrities attending Fitzgerald's performances, including Frank Sinatra, Judy Garland, and Eartha Kitt, who is seen with Fitzgerald and Charlie Morrison's wife.[48] There's no mention of Monroe, an implausible omission if she was there. Monroe biographer

J. Randy Taraborrelli's only mention of the Mocambo is a reference to Marilyn's visit to see the black singer Diahann Carroll perform there in 1959.[49] Fitzgerald biographer Stuart Nicholson's straightforward account is probably closest to the truth.

Nicholson notes that Ella played the Mocambo, "a big upper-crust nittery in Hollywood" in 1955.[50] He also rightly establishes that the club in which Marilyn saw Ella perform in November 1954 was *not* the Mocambo. And, most importantly, while he credits Monroe for helping book Fitzgerald into the Mocambo, he does not place her there, only mentioning, "On opening night Monroe ensured that the audience was liberally sprinkled with celebrities, including Judy Garland and Frank Sinatra."[51] He also credits the Mocambo performances for helping Fitzgerald land similarly impressive venues, including the Fairmount Hotel in San Francisco, "where she became the first-ever jazz performer to entertain in the hotel's Venetian Room."[52]

The truth of the matter is that Fitzgerald had not played the Mocambo—or other similar clubs—before meeting Monroe. That could be purely coincidental, except for the fact that Fitzgerald credited Monroe with helping book her Mocambo appearance. Fitzgerald's recollection is backed by many other accounts over the years—the only significant difference being that Monroe did not attend her performances there. She was, however, good for her word of ensuring that her top-line celebrity friends such as Sinatra and Garland would be in attendance. What is most ironic about the Mocambo story is that Monroe likely helped her friend not so much out of an interest in social justice, though Monroe clearly had one; she did it because she wanted to help someone whose art inspired her. She was helping a friend, not so much a cause.

Perhaps those who've looked to the Mocambo story of Fitzgerald and Monroe for inspiration over the years are not necessarily wrong, just slightly off the mark. While Morrison had booked the likes of Dorothy Dandridge and Eartha Kitt over the years, his reticence to host the less "glamorous" Fitzgerald fits within a certain paradigm of objectifying black women's bodies. Shorn of their sexual appeal and erotic allure, black women like Fitzgerald who have not fit the Western world's personification of beauty have been triply disadvantaged. Their blackness is only acceptable in the context of their ability to titillate—and preferably for commercial consumption; their womanhood, already a second strike against them, is only of value under these limited circumstances.

It is in this sense that Marilyn Monroe and Ella Fitzgerald's friendship, such as it was, gathers sociopolitical significance. Their connection was about a mutual desire to assert their talent and creativity beyond the perceived value of their bodies—and what it could do for male onlookers. Their bond, perhaps forged by mutual appreciation of troubled childhoods—much as was the case with James Baldwin and Marlon Brando—was further deepened by the need to be taken seriously. The "A-Tisket, A-Tasket" box of musical conformity Fitzgerald found herself fighting to get out of was not altogether different from Monroe's efforts to shed the "cooing" dumb blonde image she longed to eviscerate.

Whether knowingly or not, Monroe's intervention on Fitzgerald's behalf was an effort to move the identification of black womanhood beyond the purely libidinous or primitive erotic.[53] That this project could only succeed through a promise of financial gain through guaranteed celebrity appearances says much about the relationship between racial progress and economic necessity. Certainly, Monroe understood her appeal better than anyone; promising to attend each of Fitzgerald's performances at the Mocambo was part and parcel of ensuring the presence of other big names, and thus a full house. Despite never making it for those March 1955 dates, social media and a number of authors over the years have placed her there, in the front row, making good on her promise. The version of the Mocambo story with Marilyn cheering her friend on has proven irresistible. Sadly, that very need to place her there, particularly by her admirers seeking to substantiate Monroe's racial benevolence, is in itself an example of the kind of white savior narrative that reinforces racist tropes. In fairness, there has been much confusion about the episode over the years. Either way, Monroe was indeed ahead of her time, as Fitzgerald herself suggested.

Conclusion: Interracial Longings

It's hard to pin down how many more times Monroe and Fitzgerald met after Ella's Tiffany Club performance. Various biographers suggest other similar meet-ups at Ella's shows in Denver and San Francisco. Their friendship was largely kept at a distance, in part because of their mutually hectic schedules, but also, apparently, because Ella was leery of Marilyn's drug habit.[54] In any case, given the number of allusions to their friendship over the years in print and online, it's safe to say the friendship has been somewhat exaggerated. But that tends to be the case in any number of interracial friendships that are linked to larger political projects in American history. Oftentimes, the protagonists themselves have tended to embellish the relationship—but not without cause. The crafting of an interracial friendship has often been about an effort to mold public understanding of democratic possibilities—about not only what is acceptable practice for Americans, but what is essential in making our society whole.

And of course we, the spectators of such friendships, have our own reasons to exaggerate the depth of these friendships. In doing so, we can establish our own racially progressive bona fides; we likewise get to simplify what are often complex relationships to fit within our paradigm of what we would like to see—even if it may run counter to what really was. "Stars and shadows ain't good to see by," Huck Finn warned us. But sometimes it is the only light we have to go by.

Marilyn Monroe's career continued to rise over the remaining years of her life, even if unevenly. In her last days she had signed a new and lucrative one-million-dollar contract with Fox for two pictures.[55] She was every bit the star she had dreamed of becoming. But her personal demons were ever present—and her institutionalization, failed marriages, drug use, and psychic trauma from her childhood rendered every success temporary and uncertain. Monroe was an Icarus figure whose rise to the world of Kennedys, Arthur Millers, and Sinatras demonstrated the limits of American stardom as much as it did its potentialities. Her call to Charlie Morrison, made on Ella's behalf, reflected her deep humanity and self-understanding. Perhaps too much has been made of it, except for the fact that over six decades later we seem to need reassurance that white privilege can indeed be conscious enough to recognize injustice when it sees it—and to act.

Marilyn Monroe's apparent suicide in August 1962 marked the beginning of her legend. Ella Fitzgerald would go on to live another thirty-four years. As Fitzgerald biographer Stuart Nicholson has written, "Ella's odyssey has taken her from dire poverty to the luxury of Beverly Hills via dance halls, dingy nightclubs, and segregated accommodations in a country that still totters on the racial divide."[56] Fitzgerald got to experience the fullness of her legend as it grew over the years, even as she held her insecurities deep within her to the end. It makes sense that these two extraordinary figures, tinged with self-doubt and insecurity, would spark such interest over a moment of intersection in their lives.

In fact, a number of more recent internet postings have engaged in correcting some of the myth of the Mocambo. It is a sign that perhaps the Ella and Marilyn friendship can survive on truthful terms, that we have matured beyond the need for white saviors—even when their efforts have been laudable. The Mocambo closed its doors for good on June 30, 1958. Perhaps it is well time we let it rest in peace.

8

Riverside

Rev. Dr. Martin Luther King Jr. and
Rabbi Abraham Joshua Heschel

Introduction: A Transcendent Friendship

Somewhere in Selma, Alabama, probably in 1965—Dr. Clarence B. Jones can't recall the precise date—Dr. Martin Luther King Jr. was listening intently in someone's home to Rabbi Abraham Joshua Heschel hold forth. It was a small gathering of maybe five or six people. The details of such conversations fade over time, but one remark made a lasting impression on Jones, who had become one of King's closest advisors. After listening intently to Heschel for some time, King interjected jokingly, "Joshua Heschel, are you sure you weren't on one of those slave ships?"[1]

Friendship transcends difference. Faith transcends friendship. But prophetic faith transcends ordinary faith. King's wry aside to his friend and compatriot in the struggle for racial justice helps explain, at least in part, how these two otherwise very different men became as close as they did. As Jones explained it, King and Heschel—the Preacher and the Rabbi—were connected by a profound moral understanding of human catastrophe. It was at the heart of the bond the two men shared and strove to address in their spiritual work. Certainly, Heschel and his kin were not on any middle passage journey, but King's playful rejoinder was on the mark. He was letting his friend know he recognized a fellow traveler in the vessel of human oppression.

Of course, this anecdote only goes some way in explaining how one of the world's leading Orthodox Jewish theologians and scholars—an otherwise conservative figure—joined personal and spiritual forces with one of the world's most renowned—and, it must be remembered, misunderstood—Christian thinkers and activists. Not every Jewish rabbinical scholar found themselves on the frontlines of the black freedom struggle in America. Nor was every black minister seeking direct action with American racial injustice—let alone opposition to the nation's increasingly divisive actions in Vietnam. Heschel and King were odd political bedfellows, and not just on the surface. They were outliers within their own faiths—men who took the scriptures seriously, if not literally. "How could you as a good Jew prosecute a war like this?" Heschel is reported to have upbraided a sheepish Henry Kissinger in the White House about Vietnam in 1969. You don't address the new national security adviser in such terms with paper-thin faith.[2]

King and Heschel met for the first time in January 1963 at the Chicago Conference on Religion and Race. It was, as Taylor Branch describes it, "an unprecedented gathering of nearly one thousand delegates including world renowned theologians such as Paul Tillich and the established leaders of nearly every religious body in America."[3] Heschel's speech was an unequivocal bromide against racism and its cozy acceptance within mainstream religious denominations at the time. In his talk titled "Religion and Race," he noted that the "first conference on religion and race" was between Pharaoh and Moses. Cheekily, he added, "it was easier for the children of Israel to cross the Red Sea than for a Negro to cross certain university campuses." And then, he went to the heart of the matter:

> Religion and race. How can the two be uttered together? To act in the spirit of religion is to unite what lies apart, to remember that humanity as a whole is God's beloved child. To act in the spirit of race is to sunder, to slash, to dismember the flesh of living humanity. Is this the way to honor a father: to torture his child? How can we hear the word "race" and feel no self-reproach?

Referencing the author of the Declaration of Independence while reminding his audience of God's prophetic justice, Heschel quoted

Thomas Jefferson's warning: "I tremble for my country when I reflect that God is just."

It was not the centrist, safe message one might have expected from a gathering of fairly conservative religious leaders. But Heschel was hardly an ordinary religious figure. His closing remarks to the gathering offered the kind of unconditional choice so often presented in the prophetic tradition—one Dr. King was deeply familiar with. As Rev. Richard Fernandez would share with me on this point, "Dr. King would refer to the Old Testament prophets five times for every time he'd reference Jesus."[4] Fernandez would prove instrumental in organizing the Riverside Address by Dr. King on April 4, 1967, one that signaled his break with President Lyndon B. Johnson and most civil rights organizations over his opposition to the war in Vietnam. The Riverside speech would mark a fateful, and yet morally unambiguous, choice—an American Rubicon of sorts—in the life of Dr. King, and the nation. Standing in the prophetic tradition came with a price. "We are all Pharaohs or slaves of Pharaohs," Heschel warned as he neared the close of his Chicago address. "It is sad to be a slave of Pharaoh," he said. "It is horrible to be a Pharaoh."[5]

As Taylor Branch notes, both Heschel and King quoted from the prophet Amos and the American theologian Reinhold Niebuhr in their remarks in Chicago.[6] Branch saw the combination of prophetic witness along with pragmatic faith as well suited to the politics of the time, when either cynicism or moral avoidance by religious leaders was the order of the day. Reflecting on the four-day conference held at Chicago's Edgewater Hotel, King remarked: "It is my sincere hope that this confrontation with our own ineptness as it relates to race will give us the courage to take up the prophetic task of seeing to it that 'justice rolls down like waters and righteousness as a mighty stream.'"[7] At a minimum, the conference brought together two prophetic voices, marking the beginning of a five-year friendship that would help shape the purposes and meaning of the greatest movement for democratic freedom in America in over one hundred years.

Warsaw and Atlanta

The great German-American political philosopher Leo Strauss famously wrote of the cities of Jerusalem and Athens as emblematic of deeply embedded traditions in Western civilization. The two ancient cities represented dichotomies of faith and reason; biblical wisdom as opposed to Greek wisdom; two ever-present and yet contradictory impulses that have shaped, and continue to shape, Western society.[8] In a sense, Warsaw and Atlanta, the respective birthplaces of Abraham Joshua Heschel and Martin Luther King Jr., reflect similar dichotomies—though those founded more along racial lines and limitations.

Mid-twentieth-century Warsaw and Atlanta embodied the cruel hoax produced by Western optimism. Both cities represented the potentialities of material wealth and status—for Jews and African Americans, respectively. Both groups did comparatively well for a time in these cities. Yet, each city had to be brutally conquered to restore any semblance of antiracist fair play—one by the Red Army, the other by General Sherman. Neither "liberation" led to longstanding freedom; each was followed by decades of deep authoritarian oppression. Heschel and King's cities, like the people they produced, were marked by occupations and the false hopes of modernity.

Heschel was born in Warsaw, Poland, in 1907 to Rabbi Moshe Mordecai Heschel and Rivka Reizel Perlow. As Heschel biographer Edward K. Kaplan has noted, "By 1917, when Heschel was ten years old, Jews comprised 41 percent of the city's population," one of the "largest and most influential" Jewish communities in all of Europe.[9] Heschel's daughter, Dr. Susannah Heschel, Professor of Jewish Studies at Dartmouth College, has written, "My father was born into one of the most distinguished families of Hasidic rebbes, royalty to the world of Jewish piety."[10] This illustrious line of Jewish scholars would be cut down like so many of their brethren during the savage years of Nazi-occupied Europe. Heschel was a "brand plucked from the fire of an altar to Satan in which millions of lives were exterminated," he himself would write.[11] He had arrived in New York City in 1940 with little more than his faith and understanding of moral truth. Heschel's identification with a "brand" saved from fire was no mere hyperbole. The Jewish population of Warsaw—as was true throughout much of Europe—would be reduced to almost nothing by the war's end.

Rabbi Heschel would personally lose one sister to German bombing, two other sisters to concentration camps, and his mother, who was murdered by the Nazis. The reality of evil in the world deeply informed Heschel's theology—and the moral commitments he made in the political world. As he wrote in *God in Search of Man*:

> The essential predicament of man has assumed a peculiar urgency in our time, living as we do in a civilization where factories were established in order to exterminate millions of men, women, and children; where soap was made of human flesh. What have we done to make such crimes possible? What are we doing to make such crimes impossible?[12]

The only path to an answer for Heschel was redemption. One's life had to be informed by atonement and a commitment to act. "Actions teach" may best sum up, however simply, Heschel's moral philosophy, as he wrote in *God in Search of Man*.[13] More often than not, moral instruction has had it the other way. Teach, and *then* act. When he arrived in America in 1940, Heschel elected to act in a world where the scourge of racism and hatred persisted, and where the work of atonement was engaged in by very few.

In a sense, Heschel's life was a counter to Greek rationalism. As was observed in the *New York Times'* obituary of him, "Rabbi Fritz A. Rothschild, who has written essays on Rabbi Heschel and an introduction to one of his books, observed some years ago that 'where Aristotle saw God as the unmoved mover, Professor Heschel sees Him as the most moved mover.'"[14] If God was in "search of man," then that meant human suffering had the deepest meaning and could not be relegated to arbitrariness or meaninglessness. That the depth of Heschel's scholarship was met with such passionate theological understanding goes some way toward explaining his close relationship with King. Both men's education came during periods of profound societal upheaval. Heschel's doctorate was completed in 1933, the year Hitler became German Chancellor. King completed his doctorate in 1955, the year of Emmett Till's murder and the beginning of the Montgomery Bus Boycott. Heschel would join King in Montgomery in 1965, completing the March from Selma, Alabama, that would mark another turning point in the civil rights movement. Heschel would offer a profound expression of the unity between faith and action in that moment. "For many of us the march from Selma to Montgomery was about protest and prayer. Legs are not lips and walking is not kneeling," Heschel explained. "And yet our legs uttered songs. Even without words, our march was worship. I felt my legs were praying."[15]

King's personal journey to that first meeting with Heschel in Chicago in 1963 was among the greatest and most significant ascents to influence in American history. King turned thirty-four on the first day of the Conference on Race and Religion. Over the previous decade, he had been in an unrelenting struggle to rewrite the history of the American South, and ultimately the United States. Growing up, the paradoxes of what counted as middle-class black life in Atlanta taught King the possibilities and limitations of racial justice in America. As Taylor Branch has written, King "had been born into a most unusual family, which had risen from the anonymity of slavery to the top of Atlanta's Negro elite within the short span of three generations, attached to a church named Ebenezer."[16]

As numerous King biographers have recorded, he gained the nickname "Tweed" or "Tweedie" as a young man, for his penchant for tweed suits.[17] Young Martin—often called "Mike" after his given name, which was famously changed at age five along with his father's—was the picture of what the sociologist E. Franklin Frazier would call "the black bourgeoisie."[18] King was a very talented, if not always hard-working, student. He skipped grades, entering Booker T. High School at age thirteen, and Morehouse College at fifteen. Unlike many African Americans, he was able to muse about a variety of career paths, including medicine and the law. Had he wished, he could have chosen a quieter, albeit far more conciliatory path, one that allowed him to comfortably live within the acceptable confines of second-class citizenry, yet one that conferred its share of benefits on those blacks who "knew their place."

King would ultimately choose the life of a Christian minister, like his father, Martin Luther King Sr. He was ordained at nineteen, the year he graduated from Morehouse College. From Morehouse, King would go on to attend Crozer Theological Seminary in Pennsylvania. His recommendations to Crozer were hardly stellar. "I am informed that he is a little above the average in scholarship," one read. "In personality and ability he shows promise for the ministry. Mr. King comes from a fine family." Another letter, endorsing King and another student for entry, read "You will see from their records that they are not brilliant students, but both have good minds." No matter that these were from an era when grade inflation and universally stellar letters of recommendation were far less common; these were not glowing endorsements. Granted, King entered Morehouse at fifteen, but his early career as a student did not mark him out for greatness. "The academic record of Martin Luther King, Jr. at Morehouse is short of what may be called 'good': but I recommend that you give his application serious consideration."[19]

Despite these less-than-superlative recommendations, King would finish at the top of his Crozer class.[20] His next stop was Boston University's School of Theology, where he would complete his doctorate in theology from 1951 to 1955. It had to have satisfied King to know that he had performed exceptionally well at Boston. His adviser, Harold DeWolf, would rank King "as one of the five or six best graduate students he had taught in his thirty-one years at Boston University."[21]

In a sign that he would mark out his own career path, King elected to move to the Dexter Avenue Baptist Church in Montgomery, Alabama, after finishing up at Boston. Leaving Atlanta and his father's ministerial presence was the beginning of King's life as a public figure. For it was in Montgomery that his leadership would come to the fore during the Montgomery Bus Boycott. Given his less-than-impressive early academic career and an otherwise unremarkable stature—Richard Fernandez would be struck upon meeting King in 1961 at how "slight the man approaching" him was coming down the hallway—it would have been easy to underestimate him.[22] Until he spoke. The combination of King's intelligence, conviction, and power coming from that small body was instantly remarkable, and set him apart from nearly every other preacher—and most every speaker people had encountered in their lives. Indeed, "in the first few minutes of his first political address, a power of communion emerged from him that would speak inexorably to strangers who would both love and revile him, like all prophets."[23]

That address, coming in the aftermath of Rosa Parks's arrest, was King's passing of the temptation of the safe and prosperous life. W. E. B. Du Bois had warned of that temptation—typified by the classical story of Atlanta—that maiden for whom "greed of gold has led to defile the temple of Love."[24] Modern "Atlanta," Du Bois cautioned, "must not lead the South to dream of material prosperity as the touchstone of all success." This was an affliction of a city where even blacks were subject to the enticements of material comfort over moral clarity. "In the Black World," Du Bois wrote in 1903, "the Preacher and Teacher embodied once the ideals of this people—the strife for another and a juster world, the vague dream of righteousness, the mystery of knowing; but to-day the danger is that these ideals, with their simple beauty and weird inspiration, will suddenly sink to a question of cash and a lust for gold."[25] Presaging the prophetic journey he would undertake, one that would bring him to condemn not only America's treatment of its own black population but also of those whom it victimized around the world, King would utter these lines on December 5, 1955, at a gathering of the Montgomery Improvement Association at the Holt Street Baptist Church:

> The Almighty God himself is not the only, not the, not the God just standing out saying through Hosea, "I love you, Israel." He's also the God that stands up before the nations and said: "Be still and know that I'm God, that if you don't obey me I will break the backbone of your power and slap you out of the orbits of your international and national relationships."[26]

From the very beginning, King made what appeared to some to be a localized struggle among Negroes to ride buses without segregated seating an enthralling question as to whether or not the United States of America was fit, in the eyes of God, to enjoy the comforts and standing of its long-held power.

A Summons to Selma

Heschel had declared, "Racism is Satanism," in Chicago.[27] His unequivocal stance on racism and other anti-democratic practices in America would eventually place him on the FBI's watch list in 1965. Heschel's opposition to the McCarran Act (1950), which "required that Communists and other suspected 'subversives' register with the Attorney General," earned him that distinction.[28] Rabbi Heschel's political activism was decades old at that point, with him having been one of four hundred rabbis to march on Washington in October 1943 to protest America's abandonment of European Jews during the war. The protesters, organized by Agudat Israel, an ultra-orthodox organization, sought a meeting with President Roosevelt, but they were denied, having to be satisfied with a short outdoor appearance by FDR's vice president, Henry Wallace, on the Capitol steps.[29]

Heschel's activism and friendship with Martin Luther King Jr. would only intensify his position as a presumed threat to American stability and order. Not long after their Chicago meeting, Heschel would become involved in the March on Washington to be held in August 1963. Ever out in front of political volatility, the attorney general Robert F. Kennedy invited Rabbi Heschel and some four hundred Christian and Jewish clergy to the East Room of the White House to meet with him and President John F. Kennedy on June 17, 1963. June 1963 seemed to have marked a change in President Kennedy's attention to civil rights and matters of world peace. On June 10, he delivered an extraordinary speech at American University. "What kind of peace do I mean?" Kennedy asked. "What kind of peace do we seek? Not a Pax Americana enforced on the world by American weapons of war. Not the peace of the grave or the security of the slave. I am talking about genuine peace, the kind of peace that makes life on earth worth living, the kind that enables men and nations to grow and to hope and to build a better life for their children—not merely peace for Americans but peace for all men and women—not merely peace in our time but peace for all time."[30]

That statement about a possible path out of Cold War relations with the Soviet Union was followed by an equally impressive one about the connection between America's actions at home and around the world. "Finally, my fellow Americans," Kennedy concluded, "let us examine our attitude toward peace and freedom here at home. The quality and spirit of our own society must justify and support our efforts abroad."[31] The following evening, Kennedy went on television, finally taking a morally unambiguous stand against racism in America. With the recent horrible repression of peacefully protesting African Americans, and fresh defiance from the Governor of Alabama over the rights of blacks to attend the state university, at the epicenter of national convulsion, Kennedy declared, "We are confronted primarily with a moral issue. It is as old as the scriptures and is as clear as the American Constitution." In a speech that would be the basis for what would become the Civil Rights Act of 1964, Kennedy reiterated his American University statement linking American foreign and domestic policy. "We preach freedom around the world, and we mean it, and we cherish our freedom at home," Kennedy stated, "but are we to say to the world, and much more importantly, to each other that this is the land of the free except for Negroes; that we have no second-class citizens except Negroes; that we have no caste system, no ghettoes, no master race except with respect to Negroes?"[32]

However eloquent and hopeful his twin speeches of June 10 and 11 were, Heschel wanted to press the president on his stated commitments. In a telegram sent to President Kennedy the day before the East Room gathering, Heschel wrote the following:

I look forward to privilege of being present at meeting tomorrow. Likelihood exists that Negro problem will be like the weather. Everybody talks about it but nobody does anything about it. Please demand of religious leaders personal involvement not just solemn declaration. We forfeit the right to worship God as long as we continue to humiliate Negroes. Church synagogue have failed. They must repent. Ask of religious leaders to call for national repentance and personal sacrifice. Let religious leaders donate one month's salary toward fund for Negro housing and education. I propose that you Mr. President declare state of moral emergency. A Marshall plan for aid to Negroes is becoming a necessity. The hour calls for moral grandeur and spiritual audacity.[33]

Kennedy's American University speech and televised address to the nation on June 11 were to be his strongest statements on world peace and civil rights. Tragically, he had just over five months to live. It would be left to President Johnson to tackle the unfinished work of the Kennedy administration on civil rights.

For whatever reason, Heschel did not attend the historic March on Washington that summer. Many years later, his daughter, Dr. Susannah Heschel, could not recall his having been invited. Perhaps Heschel's earlier opposition to the McCarran Act and subsequent monitoring by the FBI made him too "hot" to have on board for a march where organizers were already concerned about the perception that it was filled with radicals and anti-American dissidents. Even better known and committed personages such as James Baldwin were politely disinvited from speaking.[34] If this was the case, the fear was soon overcome. When I asked King's speech writer and confidante Clarence Jones about Heschel's later involvement in the Selma March of 1965, he became quite adamant. "Listen carefully," he began, "at that time it is unlikely that Dr. King would be *anywhere* speaking or marching where Abraham Joshua Heschel wouldn't be there."[35]

The pace of events picked up momentously, and quite tragically, after the March on Washington. As Dr. Susannah Heschel has written, "Just weeks later, on September 15, 1963, a church in Birmingham was bombed, killing four young black girls. That same day, James Bevel and Diane Nash launched the Alabama Project that ultimately led to the famous march from Selma to Montgomery in 1965."[36] Several days later, on September 19, Kennedy met with King and other civil rights leaders in the White House over Birmingham. It did not go well, with Kennedy unmoved by pleadings to take a stronger stand protecting Negroes in Alabama and elsewhere. He seemed to be more impressed with the white leaders from Birmingham he met with days later, who warned him about the Student Nonviolent Coordinating Committee (SNCC) and its young chairman, John Lewis.

> "Who is heading up SNCC?" asked [one] telephone executive.
> "Well, this fellow Lewis," replied Kennedy.
> "They're sons of bitches, I'll tell you that," said another Birmingham guest.
> "Oh, they are," agreed Kennedy. "They're gonna get tougher. They're gonna be tough."[37]

With his 1964 re-election campaign set to begin in the fall, Kennedy was unwilling to take decisive action in the South and upend the delicate electoral balance that had made Democrats the dominant power in Washington since FDR's election in 1932. The president's assassination and King's subsequent working relationship with Lyndon B. Johnson changed those dynamics.

By 1964, LBJ and King were beginning a historic relationship between black leadership and the White House, one not seen since Abraham Lincoln and Frederick Douglass. Indeed, just three days after Kennedy's death, LBJ was on the telephone with King, pledging to support a new civil rights bill. "I'm going to support them all, and you can count on that," he told King. "And I'm going to do my best to get other men to do likewise, and I'll have to have y'all's help."[38] Johnson proved to be good for his word, working with King to pass the 1964 Civil Rights Act, and then publicly supporting the Selma marches for black voting rights, which would culminate in the passage of the 1965 Voting Rights Act.[39]

Heschel became involved in the Selma campaign after watching on television as John Lewis and others were beaten by state troopers on what would become known as "Bloody Sunday," in their march across the Edmund Pettis Bridge. Days after the March 7, 1965, assault, Heschel co-led a demonstration in New York City to protest the attack. On Friday, March 19, two days before the Selma march was scheduled to begin, Heschel received a telegram from King, inviting him to join the marchers.[40]

Heschel would fly down to Atlanta to meet with Andrew Young to be driven from Atlanta to the Selma.[41] Meeting with King and others at a Sunday worship service at Brown's Chapel, Heschel would read from the Book of Psalms. As Heschel biographer Edward Kaplan has written, "King ended the service with a sermon on the Israelites' long wandering in the wilderness after the Exodus from Egypt."[42] The prophetic narrative binding Heschel and King, the black sojourn in America and the Hebrew scriptures, had come full circle.

Among the indelible images from the Selma-to-Montgomery March is that of Heschel walking with King, at the front of the march, each adorned in leis provided to the marchers by a delegation from Hawaii. The line of marchers included John Lewis, an unidentified nun, Ralph Abernathy, King, Ralph Bunche, Heschel, and Rev. Fred Shuttlesworth. Despite the presence of the US Army, including the Third Army's 142nd Ordinance Detachment, all of the three thousand marchers understood they were risking their lives. As Taylor Branch has written, "Bill Moyers notified President Johnson from the White House that Army demolition teams had disarmed a total of four large bombs at Negro sites in Birmingham."[43] Heschel's later immortalized comment, "I felt my legs were praying," was beautiful in its literary sensibility. But it was also indicative of the less-than-eloquent truth that, given the very real possibility of violence, prayers were needed.

Reflecting on Heschel's presence at Selma, Andrew Young said, "It lent a tremendous degree of credibility to have him join."[44] It was not the conventional kind of credibility, however. Few Americans knew who Heschel was. He had no official political power or standing. But with his white beard, yarmulke, glasses, and grave demeanor, he had the look of a sage and intrinsically good man. His presence highlighted the racially diverse quest for racial justice, as well as its relation to a moral objective that knew no religious bounds. It was, moreover, the kind of credibility conferred by someone whose moral fervor and virtue was without question. King's friendship with Heschel also had the added benefit of giving King great comfort and increased solace. I asked Richard Fernandez about King and Heschel's friendship. He mentioned how King would show up at a few board meetings on occasion. And then, his voice trailing off, he said, "He would leave with Heschel. I didn't know where they were going. But they were spiritually connected."

Riverside

"What is this?" Dr. King asked. He was none too pleased with his speechwriter. "I'm trying to protect your ass," came the response.[45] Clarence Jones had proven himself a more-than-reliable speechwriter for King, having been tasked by King with drafting the "I Have a Dream" speech five years earlier. Jones had been surprised at how closely his friend hewed to the written text that August afternoon. "Perhaps after all the years together," Jones would later write, "I had been lucky enough to tap into his psyche this one time."[46] This would not be the case with King's speech at Riverside Church in New York, delivered on April 4, 1967.

In 1963, King's speech before the nation was centered on the "promissory note" of equal citizenship. From beginning to end, the subject was the plight of the American Negro, the one hundred years since Emancipation that had failed to provide racial justice and economic equality. But this was different. When King asked, "Clarence, why don't you try your hand and write a speech about what I should say about Vietnam?" Jones understood that this undertaking would be a powder keg for King and the movement. Despite his own opposition to the war, Jones decided if King was going to take a public stand against the war in Vietnam, a grave prospect over which even his closest advisers were divided, he'd have to do it himself. Jones drafted a speech and sent it to King via a midnight Western Union telegram. As he shared with me:

> I'm trying to protect the brother. I had written something to the effect: "There are those who contend that *blah, blah, blah*. On the other hand others say [about Vietnam] *blah, blah, blah.*" It went like that. I was trying to have him succinctly and carefully speak on the issue without coming down hard on either side. He said to me: "No, no, no, no. You above all people ought to know the Vietnam War is either morally right or morally wrong. Clarence, you should know better!" I told him, "I'm not a preacher. I'm a lawyer. I'm trying to protect [you]." He got in touch after that with Vincent Harding to write what became "Time to Break the Silence." I read the speech. I called him up. I said to him: "Hold up. Are you sure you really want to say this?"[47]

Jones was understandably upset by what he read. Vietnam was American foreign policy—and foreign policy was the mother's milk of American empire. There's a reason why civil rights leaders from Booker T. Washington to W. E. B. Du Bois to A. Philip Randolph found themselves supporting America's wars. There was always a kind of unwritten rule, understood by all but the most radical black organizations and leaders, that African Americans had to display outsized loyalty to the United States to justify an always elusive equal citizenship status. It had always been a Faustian bargain, and like most such bargains, the lines were always clearly delineated. As Jones put it flatly, "Most leaders, either they kept their mouth shut, or they supported the [Vietnam] war."[48]

In 1963, the year of the March on Washington, 122 Americans were killed in Vietnam. At the end of 1968, more than a year after King delivered his Riverside Church address, 16,899 Americans were killed fighting in the war. That year's total represents nearly 30 percent of all US deaths in Vietnam.[49] Rev. Richard Fernandez, the executive secretary of the Clergy and Laity Concerned about Vietnam (CALCAV) who organized the Riverside speech, put the numbers in stark perspective. "Edison High School in Philadelphia lost 56 young men to the War in Vietnam," Fernandez told me. "Dr. King's attitude was, 'Don't tell me these things are not related.' Our black friends paid a heavy price."[50]

Vietnam was sinking the resources and lives that were purposed for the beloved community that King had so often preached about—the Great Society promised by President Johnson. Moreover, more than one million Vietnamese children were reported to have been "killed or wounded or burned" during the war. "No food would taste good, King told [SCLC member] Bernard Lee, until he discovered his part to end the war."[51]

Taylor Branch has written that Fernandez "brashly informed" Union Theological Seminary President John Bennett, Heschel, and peace activist Rev. William Coffin "that they would never turn public opinion against the war with theological pedigree and seminars. Within a year, he raised the number of active CALCAV chapters from eight to sixty-eight by goading clergy into systematic outreach beyond the comfort of friends."[52] Fernandez's leadership notwithstanding, the Vietnam War, seemingly outside the purview of the civil rights movement, was making many movement activists uncomfortable—and it would prove an incredibly divisive issue from 1965 on.

The war did not try the friendship between King and Heschel, however. In 1965 Heschel called for an immediate withdrawal of US forces from Vietnam. Expressing his disenchantment with America's moral apathy, in his recently released book *The Prophets*, Heschel wrote: "In regard to the cruelties committed in the name of a free society, some are guilty, all are responsible."[53] It was a moral clarity King valued. But he was not ready to publicly declare himself to be against the war. His decision to do so was carefully considered. Before the Riverside address, King had been weighing what to say about Vietnam and "talked to a lot of people over a five month period before his speech," Fernandez recalled.[54] Despite his opposition to the war, Susannah Heschel recalled her father fretting over whether King should take such a stance. Rabbi Heschel, like Clarence Jones, Stanley Levison, and other advisers, worried that "such a sharp criticism of U.S. policy [might] affect the support of Congress and the president for the civil rights movement."[55]

Levison was like "an older uncle [King] didn't have," Clarence Jones recalled. "I think it's fair to say Stanley and I were first among equals among his advisers. He loved Stanley Levison." Jones noted that Levison could not bear to hear King's address at Riverside, mindful of the ruptures in the movement likely to ensue—and the personal political damage that his friend would suffer.[56] Heschel, who introduced King, stayed for the speech, and spoke after King. Heschel and Levison were representative, on that April night, of the very split that would mark King's call to end the war in Vietnam.

Unlike Levison and Jones, who opposed the war but were motivated by the understandable desire to protect King's political standing, Heschel's opposition to the war, as a spiritual teacher, was unfettered from such restrictions. In his 1967 essay "The Moral Outrage of Vietnam," Heschel placed America's involvement in the starkest terms. "Militarism is whoredom, voluptuous and vicious, first disliked and then relished," he wrote. "To paraphrase the prophet's words 'For the spirit of harlotry is within them and they know not the Lord' (Hosea 5:4)."[57] King's task at Riverside was to make the same kind of unambiguous moral statement, while simultaneously addressing the very present and real political concerns, principally the question of America's opposition to communism in the Cold War era. "I lost," Levison would say regarding his efforts to persuade King to take a more moderate stance, "and we'll just have to live with it."[58]

After Jones's effort to moderate King's speech failed, the task of drafting the Riverside address was turned over to Vincent Harding. Weeks later, King would tease Harding, his Atlanta neighbor and Spelman College professor, about the speech, saying it caused him "a month of ceaseless trouble."[59] Many have speculated, over the years, that it caused King much more than that. I raised the delicate question with Dr. Jones over the phone. We had spoken for nearly an hour and this was the only time he became truly animated. "Coming one year to the date of his assassination," I asked him, "are you among those who feel the Riverside speech contributed to Dr. King's death?" Jones was unequivocal. "Without question! Without question! Without question!"[60]

I was not surprised by Jones's belief as much as I was by the ferocity of his conviction. Driving to Oberlin, Ohio, that Friday after our interview, I decided to listen to the speech again. The words alone, like so many of Dr. King's speeches, don't quite do it justice. When King took to the podium, he was flanked by Heschel on his far right, followed by the historian Henry Steele Commager, and then Union Theological Seminary President Dr. John Bennett on his left. It was Bennett who suggested Riverside Church, when Union's chapel was deemed too small.[61] King's cadence and delivery were slow and methodical. Moments before he rose to speak, Fernandez observed King. "He took out a little pen, and went from page to page, making little notes. He spoke without a teleprompter. He delivered it as if from memory. This was not to be a short statement, it was to cover the waterfront."[62]

Copies of the speech had been delivered to the press days before the address. The hope was to cushion the blow of the anticipated criticism. The plan backfired. "Every newspaper had a copy twenty-four hours ahead of the speech," Fernandez recalled. "Their editorials were already written by the time he delivered it. That's what prompted an immediate response. Hardly anyone supported it, except for Stokely Carmichael."[63] After his usual introductory remarks about the majesty of the church and thanking those on the dais with him, including Rabbi Heschel, King asked the question everyone wanted an answer to: "Why are *you* speaking about the war?" King asked rhetorically. "Why are *you* joining the voices of dissent? Peace and civil rights don't mix, they say. Aren't you hurting the cause of your people, they ask?"[64]

Much of the "waterfront" King covered was a deliberate recounting of Vietnam's history since 1945. But when he arrived at the nexus between the Cold War struggle over Vietnam and the civil rights movement, he arrived at the answer to his critics' questions.

There is at the outset a very obvious and almost facile connection between the war in Vietnam and the struggle I, and others, have been waging in America. A few years ago there was a shining moment in that struggle. It seemed as there was a real promise of hope for the poor—both black and white—through the Poverty Program. There were experiments, hopes, new beginnings. Then came the build-up in Vietnam and I watched the program broken and eviscerated as if it were some idle political plaything of a society gone mad on war, and I knew that America would never invest the necessary funds or energies in rehabilitation of its poor so long as adventures like Vietnam continued to draw men and skills and money like some demoniacal destructive suction tube. So I was increasingly compelled to see the war as an enemy of the poor and to attack it as such.[65]

The grim zero-sum game of guns versus butter had played itself out, redirecting resources for racial uplift and the poor, toward the making of war. But King was only beginning. Reading over Harding's draft, Clarence Jones feared for his friend. Jones had studied the art of speechmaking, and his training drew him to perhaps the most powerful and provocative line in King's text. "I read that line 'The United States is the greatest purveyor of violence in the world,' " Jones recalled. "It was the topic sentence of a paragraph. I said to him, 'Why don't you [bury] it in the text?' "[66] Of course, there was no way of hiding that line any more than there was of getting King to strike a middle-ground position. When King offered his theoretical response to America's black youth languishing in ghettoes by responding, "I knew that I could never again raise my voice against the violence of the oppressed in the ghettoes without having first spoken clearly to the greatest purveyor of violence in the world today—my own government," he positioned himself not only against America's war in Vietnam, but indeed, its militarism around the world.

The Riverside speech opposing the war in Vietnam was really a righteous assault on the immorality of American foreign policy. Noting that "Vietnam is but a symptom of a far deeper malady within the American spirit," King predicted future protests against US involvement in Guatemala, Peru, Thailand, Cambodia, Mozambique, South Africa, and Venezuela if the nation did not undergo "a radical revolution of values."[67] As he moved toward his recommendations for ending the war, the audience at Riverside began to punctuate King's remarks with thunderous applause. Nevertheless, the atmosphere was closer to that of a lecture than a sermon. Even the usually soaring close from Amos ("If we will but make the right choice, we will be able to speed up the day, all over America and all over the world, when justice will roll down like waters, and righteousness like a mighty stream") was delivered more with melancholy than inspiration. It was as if King understood: he had made his choice—a time to break silence, as the speech was called—and America had made its own. The old line borrowed by King from the poet James Russell Lowell, of the "scaffold and the throne," was once again employed at Riverside.

> Though the cause of evil prosper, yet 'tis truth alone is strong
> Though her portions be the scaffold, and upon the throne be wrong
> Yet that scaffold sways the future, and beyond the dim unknown
> Standeth God within the shadow, keeping watch above His own.[68]

King's crossing at Riverside was his decision to stand on the scaffold. Few of his friends and supporters understood; even fewer remained at his side in the difficult days and weeks ahead. On the stage, readying to make his own remarks that evening as King took his seat, was Abraham Joshua Heschel, who, from Chicago to Selma, and now at Riverside, stood witness to the prophetic voice within.

Conclusion: Legacies

Speaking after King at Riverside, Heschel likewise condemned the war in Vietnam, asking, "Has our conscience become a fossil? Is all mercy gone? If mercy, the mother of humility, is still alive as a demand, how can we say 'yes' to our bringing agony to that tormented country?"[69] Criticism against Heschel's stance against the war was not solely a result of the divisive politics of Vietnam, which he anticipated; it also had to do with his support for the Arab-Israeli War of 1967. The split stance provoked a divide within CALCAV, as some questioned how one war could be supported and the other condemned.[70] Despite the close relationship between Jewish organizations and the American civil rights movement, Israel represented a new line of fracture in the history of liberalism with respect to Jews and the political left.

This was but another kind of fracture within the progressive history of the United States, as the relationship between blacks and Jews had long been one mixed with mutual support, unrest, and suspicion. That King and Heschel were able to supersede these historic strains was a testament to their friendship, but also to their mutual focus on advancing the cause of racial justice in America.

Susannah Heschel has written about her father's legacy and the rich relationship he had with Dr. King, while also tackling the complicated nature of the larger historical dynamic between African Americans and Jews:

> Heschel was hardly the only Jew or rabbi to participate in the Selma march. On the contrary, Jews flocked to the South to participate as Freedom Riders and in efforts to register Black voters. Indeed, Andrew Goodman and Michael Schwerner were two Jews murdered by the KKK along with James Cheney in Philadelphia, Mississippi during Freedom Summer in 1964. On the other hand, [one] Selma photograph also shows the other side. In the background is a large billboard advertising Tepper's, a department store owned by Sol Tepper, a member of Selma's Jewish community and an outspoken proponent of segregation. A member of the White Citizens Council and a friend of the notorious Sheriff Jim Clark, Tepper's active opposition to the Civil Rights movement was shared by nearly all members of Selma's small Jewish community.[71]

Whether it has been questions over support for Israel, Jewish racism, black anti-Semitism, or the long-contested folly of comparison over whose epic suffering is greater, Black–Jewish relations remained mixed in their at-once strained and symbiotic character. I recall not that long ago conducting research on the UK's history of racism while in London, and listening as one of the white activists lamented over the "falling out over Zionism" with a leading American scholar on the left. James Baldwin's pithy and, by some lights, troubling comment that "Negroes don't hate Jews because they're anti-Semitic—they hate them because they are anti-white"—is revelatory in its staying power as an expression of one segment of black thought in America.[72] By the same token, black opposition to Israel's policies toward the Palestinians, and more general antipathy at times toward Jews that crosses the line into anti-Semitism, likewise mark a complicated impasse in mutual understanding and, indeed, love in the post–civil rights era. Heschel and King's meetings in Chicago, Selma, and ultimately Riverside represent a high-water mark of sorts, in this relationship. Their bond, one directed toward a great democratic project, elevated the nation's attention to moral courage in the face of deep injustice. It did not end altogether debates over what constitutes the nature of right or justice—even among friends and people with shared political visions.

Martin Luther King Jr. died on April 4, 1968, one year to the day after his Riverside speech. Abraham Joshua Heschel died on Christmas Eve, 1972. Neither lived to see a formal end to hostilities in Vietnam, though both lived to see crucial legislation pass in the United States conferring historic rights on African Americans that had long been denied. Their shared prophetic visions and commitment to justice made for one of the extraordinary friendships of the twentieth century. Fernandez reflected on the insanity and yet power of those times. Recalling how Clarence Jones warned him to get out of Birmingham during one of his visits, Fernandez spoke of being interrogated briefly by the FBI. "Are you a member of the NAACP, the Communist Party, or do you write for the *New York Times*?" he was asked.[73] Relative to the stature of Dr. King, Fernandez and Jones were ostensibly minor figures at the time. And yet, their impulse toward racial justice marked them out as threats to the United States and its international standing all the same.

Perhaps one anecdote shared by Fernandez puts the depth of King and Heschel's friendship and moral standing in greatest relief. "During our conversation I used the term 'white trash' a few times," Fernandez recalled in recounting his first meeting with King at his office in Atlanta. "Dr. King interrupted me at one point. He said, 'When we use the word 'white trash' we alienate the people we are trying to convert.'" Somehow that stood out to Fernandez over these many years. It speaks to King's rejection of the "I-It" impulse to turn our enemies into "others." Somehow, the cause of justice had to implore us to destroy a certain way of thinking in the world, while preserving, as best we could, the humanity of those who held those very thoughts dear to them. In the theology of Rabbi Heschel and Rev. King, friendship's spiritual dimension can know of no "other."

9

Icons and Intersectionalities
Angela Davis and Gloria Steinem

Introduction: Converging Movements

Angela Davis first came into the public eye when California Governor Ronald Reagan fired her from the faculty of the University of California–Los Angeles in 1969 for belonging to the Communist Party. One year later, she became one of the most recognized faces in America, and one of only three women to be named on the FBI's "Ten Most Wanted Fugitives" list. Davis was alleged to have assisted in the kidnapping and murder of Judge Harold Haley, a charge she was later acquitted of. Conversely, Gloria Steinem first gained notoriety for her exposé of the Playboy Club in New York, going undercover as a waitress for three months, for *Show* magazine. Later that year, she appeared in the *New York Times* for her publication of *The Beach Book*, described by the *Times* as "a newly published work" which "includes some fantasies to be indulged in while lying in the sand."[1] The book came with an insert of aluminum foil in the inside flap, to assist in tanning.

How did these divergent beginnings lead to a shared status as two of the most iconic personalities representing feminism and social justice? Today, Angela Davis is more wanted on the speaker's circuit than by federal authorities. Steinem, on the other hand, is perhaps the most recognized feminist in the United States, if not the world—hardly the anticipated path of a Camelot-era "pretty" graduate of Smith College.

Their paths have crossed many times over the years, the product of a friendship that can be said to have begun in 1971, when Steinem took on the role of treasurer of Davis's legal defense fund. This answer, if one is to be had, provides insights into how the objectives, struggles, and histories of black and white women activists have served contradictory, and at times mutually beneficial, ends.

For different reasons, Davis and Steinem have been uniquely lauded, and at times pilloried, figures—both within and outside of their respective movements. While Davis's radical black politics has subjected her to both praise and criticism for her Marxist critique of American racism and sexism, Steinem's more conventional politics has made her the face of second-wave feminism—an image that has brought her scorn for insufficient revolutionary commitment, or, by other measures, for posing a danger to the conservative foundations of American life. Examining the friendship between Davis and Steinem thus presents a unique opportunity to understand what has come to be known as intersectional theory, in an era where the politics of interracial friendship are as open as they have ever been. Indeed, their friendship, begun during a period of open social relations between blacks and whites, has been far less about their racial differences as it has been about their political ideologies and shared status as feminist icons.

The divisions inherent in their connection have been intense and varied: the Black-Jewish civil rights alliance and its skeptics, the charged relationship between black and white women feminists, the class divide within the women's movement—not to mention the more recent critiques of mainstream feminism by members of the LGBTQ community and its allies. Somehow, Davis and Steinem's relationship—one thin on shared time but rich in symbolism—has managed to survive the onslaught of both time and politics over the decades.

The Meaning of Birmingham

Angela Davis grew up in Birmingham, Alabama. Her neighborhood was subjected to so many bombings by whites opposed to integration that it was known as "Dynamite Hill."[2]

Davis was thus familiarized with terrorism at an early age, a presence she could not shield herself from despite her family's relatively stable economic position. By the time of the infamous bombing of the 16th Street Baptist Church that killed four black girls, Davis was a second-year student at Brandeis University. She learned of the murders while studying abroad, in the seaside town of Biarritz, France. "I kept staring at the names" in the paper, Davis would later write. "Carole Robertson. Cynthia Wesley. Addie Mae Collins. Denise McNair." With the exception of Addie Mae, Davis knew each one intimately, and would describe her family's relationship with them in her autobiography.

The bombing was not the beginning of Davis's politicization, but it heightened her sense of the deeply embedded impediments to racial equality in the United States. "This act was not an aberration," Davis wrote. "It was not something sparked by a few extremists gone mad. On the contrary, it was logical, inevitable. The people who planted the bomb in the girls' restroom in the basement of 16th Street Baptist Church were not pathological, but rather the normal products of their surroundings."[3]

The meaning of the 16th Street bombings has been revisited over the decades, not the least of which because Condoleezza Rice, who would go on to become America's first woman to serve as National Security Adviser, and later, first black woman as Secretary of State, was eight years old at the time of the bombing and, like Davis, knew the girls—one of them quite well. Ironically, one of the lessons of Birmingham Rice would write about in her memoir was its roots to her present support for the Second Amendment. As Rice would explain, her father kept armed watch on the porch of their home the night of the bombings. Rice notes her father did not join in the Birmingham movement led by Rev. Martin Luther King Jr. because, among other reasons, he did not believe in nonviolence.[4]

Conversely, Davis was not drawn to a career in government. Where Rice drew inspiration from President Kennedy, and the eventual passage of the Civil Rights Act, Davis never shook her deep skepticism of Kennedy or America, nor did she believe the nation was prepared to uphold its founding ideals. The bombing was designed to incite terror in the face of efforts to integrate the City of Birmingham. Coming weeks after the March on Washington, the horrific episode marked a pivotal moment in the black freedom struggle in America; and it was a pivotal moment in Davis's life.

By 1963 Davis had already been moved by James Baldwin during a speech at an antiwar rally at Brandeis, as news of the Cuban Missile Crisis was announced; in 1962, she attended the Communist Youth Festival in Helsinki ("Don't you know how we feel about Communists? Don't you know what we do to Communists?" an FBI agent asked her upon her return to the United States).[5] Davis was also by that time familiar with Malcolm X, who likewise visited Brandeis while she was an undergraduate. Most importantly, during her second year on campus, she attended Herbert Marcuse's lecture series on European political thought since the French Revolution. Coupled with her experiences with Cubans and Algerians living in Paris, while studying abroad, Davis found a path into revolutionary politics. By the end of her senior year she had "made up [her] mind to apply for a scholarship to study philosophy at the university of Frankfurt" under Marcuse. Thus began Davis's journey into Critical Theory.[6]

At the University of Frankfurt, and later at the University of California, San Diego, where she was Marcuse's graduate student, Davis cultivated a comprehensive, anticapitalist critique of American politics. Decades later, she would reflect upon her time with the legendary theorist of the Frankfurt School of philosophy:

Marcuse counseled us always to acknowledge the important differences between the realms of philosophy and political activism, as well as the complex relation between theory and radical social transformation. At the same time, he never failed to remind us that the most meaningful dimension of philosophy was its utopian element. "When truth cannot be realized within the established social order, it always appears to the latter as mere utopia."[7]

As influential as Marcuse was to the emergent New Left and others in America at the time, his political thought was largely outside of the experience of black politics or black political thought in the mid-1960s. Indeed, after Davis's acquittal in 1971, *Ebony* magazine ran a long profile of Davis, complete with some information on Marcuse and a photograph of him in his San Diego office, as if to explain to its upwardly mobile black readership just who this white man was, and why he was so important to Davis.[8]

Davis's decision to return to America was not one based on her academic pursuits. "While I was reading philosophy in Frankfurt," Davis would recount, "there were young Black men in Oakland, California, who had decided that they had to wield arms in order to protect the residents of Oakland's Black community from the indiscriminate police brutality ravaging the area. Huey Newton, Bobby Seale, l'il Bobby Hutton—they were some of the names that reached me. One day in Frankfurt I read about their entrance into the California Legislature in Sacramento with their weapons in order to safeguard their right (a right given to all whites) to carry them as instruments of self-defense. The name of this organization was the Black Panther Party for Self-Defense."[9]

Marcuse agreed to take over Davis's dissertation oversight from Theodore Adorno, as he had already agreed to a position at University of California, San Diego. Davis's return to the United States would transform her life and put Condoleezza ("Condi") Rice's theory of Black Second Amendment rights to the test—and usher in a period of radical black politics with a woman's face at the fore, for one of the few times in American history. Although she would only briefly join the Panthers, Davis immersed herself in the organization's local politics and programs. Her admiration for the party's work did not inhibit her criticism of the organization's often open misogyny. She was also critical of some of the strains of Black Nationalism she encountered. Indeed, on her return to the United States from Europe, a departure that would begin her activism in California, it was Stokely Carmichael who provided her with a false contact to reach out to upon her return. Carmichael, who put race before class in his political ideology at the time, was suspicions of Davis—especially her Marxist critique of America's racial problems. "Black Power" was proving, even in its earliest inceptions, to mean different things to different people.[10]

Davis's return to the United States and subsequent activism and arrest made her an iconic figure. But her symbolism—the prodigious afro, the raised fist—has carried a multiplicity of meanings, ones that belie a straight path out of segregated Birmingham. As Joy James has written, "Davis's political impact would reside partly in her evolving status as a cultural icon. In symbolic representations, she signifies victorious opposition to state repression. Later her stature grew as an intellectual due to her antiracist feminist writings and lectures. Angela Davis's representational status and freedom from incarceration gave currency to the tenets of American democracy."[11]

The Glorias

Angela Davis and Gloria Steinem were born ten years and worlds apart. Steinem was born and raised in Toledo, Ohio—a place she would reference later in life as a symbol of her unpretentious tastes, despite her worldliness. Her father, Leo, was a German Jew, who worked and lived as a traveling salesman. Her mother, Ruth, was the daughter of Protestant working-class parents, who gave up her budding career as a journalist to raise Gloria and her sister, Susanne. Steinem's parents separated when Gloria was ten, and by "the time they divorced, Ruth was addicted to sodium pentothal—'the same drug they fed to Virginia Woolf and Sylvia Plath,' Steinem says—and Leo was living out of a car in California, visiting once a year."[12]

The deterioration in Ruth's mental health after the divorce had a profound effect on Steinem's worldview. In time, she learned of how her mother supported "her husband's impractical dreams and debts, suffering a miscarriage and then a stillbirth, and falling in love with a man at work: perhaps the man she would have married. All of this ended in so much self-blame and guilt that she suffered what was then called a nervous breakdown, spent two years in a sanatorium and emerged with an even greater feeling of guilt for having left my sister in her father's care."[13] The addiction to sedatives would follow, along with the diminution of the light that had once been in Ruth. "It was only much later," Steinem would say, "when I began to understand how unjust the position of women was in this country, that I knew my mother had never been 'ill,' as the doctors claimed. It was that her spirit had been broken."[14]

At seventeen, Steinem gained a sense of freedom for the first time. She moved to Washington, DC, to live with her sister, then twenty-six, and her roommates in Georgetown. It marked an end to a life of scraping by, and brought her into a cosmopolitan, albeit nearly all-white setting. As Steinem biographer Patricia Cronin Marcello would note, Georgetown was the first place Steinem would claim to have learned "that people ate regular meals around a table, rather than while standing in front of the refrigerator. Her high school in Georgetown was also the first place she went to that was an upscale school. . . . The student body included children of congressmen, diplomats, and military personnel."[15] It was an all-white school, a marked change from her education in Toledo.

Despite attending a racially mixed admissions tea held for prospective Smith College students while in Washington, Steinem was shocked to learn there were no black women in her class at Smith. "There aren't enough Negro college men to go around," was the answer she was given by administrators, for Smith's lily white campus.[16] To counter her lack of exposure to African Americans, Steinem worked in two segregated swimming pools in Washington during her college years. As Steinem biographer Carolyn G. Heilbrun has written, "These early encounters with black people would make even sharper than it might otherwise have been the barrenness Steinem later felt returning from India to find herself in a world of only whites and the uniform culture of the 1950s."[17]

It was after graduating Smith in 1956 that Steinem embarked on a two-year period abroad where she lived in India. The decision was a departure from the 1950s-era prescription for women fortunate enough to graduate college: pursue marriage and a family. Before India, Steinem presumed this would be her path in life as well. "Not even in a movie had I seen a wife with a journey of her own," she would recall.[18] It was in India that Steinem began to connect the struggles of American women, such as her mother's, with women of color and those in developing countries. But she also was able to learn of different forms of women's empowerment that had escaped her awareness in America. "It was the first time I witnessed the ancient and modern magic of groups in which anyone may speak in turn, everyone must listen, and consensus is more important than time," she would write in her memoir, *My Life On the Road*. "I had no idea that such talking circles had been a common form of governance for most of human history. . . . I didn't even know, as we sat in Ramnad, that a wave of talking circles and 'testifying' was going on in black churches of my own country and igniting the civil rights movement."[19]

Steinem's trip to India had been delayed in London, where she awaited a visa. The front end of her two-year stint abroad was also deeply impactful. It was in London that she broke off an engagement, and also learned she was pregnant. The revelation led her to choose an abortion, a decision that further heightened her growing sense of the need for women's empowerment. She would later dedicate her memoir to the physician who performed the surgery:

THIS BOOK IS DEDICATED TO: Dr. John Sharpe of London, who in 1957, a decade before physicians in England could legally perform an abortion for any reason other than the health of the woman, took the considerable risk of referring for an abortion a twenty-two-year-old American on her way to India.[20]

Upon her return from India, Steinem embarked upon what she thought would be a career in journalism. In 1960, she began writing for *Help!* magazine, a satirical publication. She would later write pieces for *Esquire*, the *New York Times Sunday Magazine*, and *Glamour*, among others. It would not be until 1968 that Steinem would get a position writing political commentary at *New York* magazine, which she helped found. But it was her 1963 undercover piece for *Show* magazine that brought her national attention. Her exposé was a deeply political piece in its own way, though it was pitched more for its voyeuristic quality than Steinem's hard-hitting account of how an all-male world of powerful men lorded over a sexualized female staff hired to display compliant femininity. Indeed, *Show's* introduction of Steinem that preceded the article was its own kind of tone-deaf sexism, emphasizing Steinem's "hidden qualities of a Phi Beta Kappa, *magna cum laude* graduate of Smith College with the more obvious ones of an ex-dancer and beauty queen."[21]

The article remains an extraordinary piece of journalism—and a time capsule of the kind of acceptable degradation women experienced in the age of Camelot. Steinem uncovered a world where women's appearances were hyper-sexualized and their intelligence, experiences, and professional pursuits were irrelevant. "We don't like our girls to have any background," she was told when hired.[22] In truth, the Playboy Club was a more intense version of what many women were experiencing in a corporate world where women were still relative newcomers, and presumed to be *in loco parentis* to the men for whom they worked.

Given her "good looks," as she was often reminded, Steinem didn't have to become a feminist; she was already one step ahead of other women in an era premised on beauty and quiescence. Yet, as she told the *New Yorker* in 2015, "Other women in the movement helped me enormously, but there was one old woman in particular. I was giving a talk and the 'looks' thing came up. Before I could answer, she stood up and said, 'It's important for someone who could play the game, and win, to say, The game isn't worth shit!' I was so grateful to her for understanding that I could use who *I* was to say who *we* were and what we represent."[23]

The *Show* article was provocative and highly memorable. Steinem laced the piece with humor, to be sure, but also with detailed accounts of routine assaults on both the psyche and the bodies of the women employed at the club. Yet, the article that would perhaps best capture the direction of her future, and the type of feminism she was interested in, would appear at the end of the decade. The publication of "After Black Power, Women's Liberation" in the April 7, 1969, edition of *New York* magazine was most telling. And it would provide insights into how Gloria Steinem's and Angela Davis's paths would cross—and why their friendship would come to matter.

Indeed, this moment would prove to be another transformative one in the life of Steinem—a life most recently turned into a biographical film in director Julie Taymor's *The Glorias* (2020). The film brings together four "Glorias" from different periods in Steinem's life. The device works well, in part, because Steinem's life was marked by these evident transitions, ones that "speak" to her past incarnations as markers of personal and intellectual growth. And none proved more germane to her connection to what would become known as intersectional feminism, than her 1969 *New York* article.

WLM to BLM

"If the WLM [Women's Liberation Movement] can feel solidarity with the hated middle class, and vice versa," Steinem mused, "then an alliance with the second mass movement—poor women of all colors—should be no problem. They are already organized around welfare problems, free daycare centers, for mothers who must work, and food prices."[24] At the heart of Steinem's *New York* magazine article's analysis was a critique of capitalism and patriarchy—attached to a less obvious admiration for the Black Power movement (as opposed to the more respected and mainstream civil rights movement). Steinem drew several connections to this movement's conclusions: women and blacks had been deemed intellectually inferior; structural changes to the system were required to improve their respective conditions; and group solidarity had to be affirmed before real change would come. "[A]s black militants kept explaining to white liberals," she wrote, " 'You don't get radicalized fighting other people's battles.' "[25]

This was some distance from Steinem's reportage from the Playboy Club in 1963. While that reporting was groundbreaking in its own way, "After Black Power, Women's Liberation," turned Steinem into a feminist leader. Her concluding statement in the article, "Because the idea is, in the long run, that women's liberation will be men's liberation too," however, hopeful and unifying, did not shield her from an enormous backlash among men and the many conservative publications and news outlets they controlled. Nevertheless, the piece holds up as an early example of what, twenty years later, the black legal scholar Kimberlé Crenshaw would term "intersectionality." "Because the intersectional experience is greater than the sum of racism and sexism," Crenshaw would write, "any analysis that does not take intersectionality into account cannot sufficiently address the particular manner in which Black women are subordinated."[26] If Steinem's feminism was different than the likes of Betty Friedan's from the previous generation, it was because it adhered to this basic premise.

Steinem's commitment to intersectional feminism explains the risk she took in raising money for Angela Davis's legal defense in 1971. Years later she would tell the story of her second cousin's Christmas letter to the family, repudiating her for her support of Davis. "Gloria is the first of our name to depart from the American principles as to help our sworn enemies, so we must repudiate her pronouncements and disclaim the cousinship. Love and kisses."[27] On a more practical level, it marked Steinem for potentially far greater consequences. An initial loss was the $5,000 contract Steinem had to consult for *Seventeen* magazine.[28] As Bettina Aptheker would recount, the conservative writer William Buckley would devote his nationally syndicated column to condemning Steinem for her support of Davis.[29] Steinem thus became a symbol of feminism's "unpatriotic" values for the right. Steinem was initially approached by longtime friend and aide to Dr. Martin Luther King Jr., Stanley Levison, to serve as treasurer of Davis's legal defense fund, which ultimately raised over $50,000.[30] Levison had been linked to the Communist Party in America, reducing his visibility, if not his significance, within the civil rights movement for years. King could ill afford to be associated with communists, and thus the relationship between him and Levison became less public, and necessarily at arm's length. With Davis, who was openly communist, Levison had little to fear, beyond what was already known about his earlier associations. Ironically, Steinem, who had been making her own connections between racism, sexism, and consumerism, had, earlier in her career, been linked with the Central Intelligence Agency (CIA). She was hired by the agency to help infiltrate the very Helsinki Festival in which Davis had participated in 1962.[31] This initial "intersection" between the lives of Davis and Steinem was thus rooted in opposing sides of Cold War politics. The *Journal of Scandinavian History* would later publish an account of Steinem's ties to the agency:

> [I]n Helsinki the anti-festival leader Gloria Steinem and Angela Davis, then an 18-year-old student, who leaned towards communism, demonstrated the divisions in American society. . . . In Helsinki, Davis was enthusiastic about the Cuban national concert, which combined Latin rhythms with revolutionary energy. From Steinem's perspective, the Cuban delegation represented the enemy that had humiliated the mighty Americans at the Bay of Pigs in 1961. Denigrating news stories about the Cubans were frequently published in Steinem's anti-festival newspaper *Helsinki Youth News*. Later in the 1960s Steinem too became an American feminist icon, and a person whose CIA-contacts and manoeuvres in Helsinki were sensationally revealed in 1967.[32]

Steinem would later defend the revelation that she had worked for the CIA for a time. When the *New York Times* reported on her involvement ("CIA Subsidized Festival Trips") in 1967, Steinem said, "I was never asked to report on other Americans or assess foreign nationals

I had met." Unlike other students, who expressed regret for their involvement, Steinem said that "far from being shocked by this involvement I was happy to see some liberals in government in those days who were far-sighted enough to get Americans of all political views to the festival."[33] With respect to the agents she met, she explained to the *Washington Post* regarding her work with the Independent Research Service, a front for the CIA sponsoring American students, "They wanted to do what we wanted to do—present a healthy, diverse view of the United States."[34]

And yet, as feminist scholar Joy James has pointed out, at a time when white women feminists refused to participate in the Free Angela Davis campaign, Gloria Steinem "agreed to chair the fund-raising committee of the National United Committee to Free Angela Davis."[35] The decision was not made lightly. Davis had been charged in the 1970 killing of a Marin County judge in California. The guns used by Jonathan Jackson and three other escaped convicts in the murder were tied to Davis, and she took flight before being captured in New York City. It was the beginning of one of the more sensational trials of the civil rights era. Davis was ultimately acquitted of all charges by an all-white jury on June 4, 1972.[36] The "Free Angela Davis" movement made Davis a symbol of black resistance and made her an uneasy hero for others.

Noting Steinem's involvement with the CIA—and her role in the Free Angela Davis movement—James's insights into the politics of black and white feminisms is profound in its nuance and for what it reveals about the layered nature of intersectionality:

> Within US feminism and civil rights advocacy, anticommunism is such a cultural pillar that progressives who embrace this ideology find expedient alliances with corporate-state power and funds tenable. White feminists such as Steinem (who with hundreds of other prominent people signed a 1998 *New York Times* ad calling for a new trial for death-row intellectual and black activist Mumia Abu-Jamal; and who with the Ms. Foundation raised funds for "anti-prison-industrial-complex conferences") have no monopoly on conflictual political personas that offer contradictory images of resistance and allegiance to the state.[37]

As Davis would recount in a 1988 interview, the vast majority of white feminists did not see her relevance to their struggle. "[T]he response was, 'Well Angela Davis is not associated with the women's movement, she's associated with the Black movement,' as if one had to make a choice between the two, as if one was either a feminist or an antiracist. In all fairness, I should also point out that white feminists were active around my case. Gloria Steinem, for example, was the treasurer of my legal defense fund."[38] In effect, where the claims of the second-wave feminist movement had been staked along primarily white middle-class lines, Steinem had, through her writings, charisma, and sense of racial justice, broadened the horizons of what had been a fairly conventional and quite limited women's movement. The ideological boxes that so often separated Davis from Black Nationalists and Steinem from white radicals (her marriage to the conservative publisher Mort Zuckerman would further link her to establishment politics), had broken down in the Free Angela Davis moment. The subsequent decades would only heighten the respective statures of Davis and Steinem—and their friendship would serve practical and symbolic purposes for the mass mobilization of women of all backgrounds.

Icons

Over the ensuing decades, Steinem and Davis would occasionally cross paths, but it was Steinem's work with other notable black women that would be most relevant to her work in the women's liberation movement. Her work with Dorothy Pitman Hughes in the early 1970s, for example, was an early sign that Steinem recognized that women of color were integral not only to the work of feminism but to the expansion of democratic politics overall. Inspired by Hughes's work running a community child care center, the two began public speaking tours together across the country, speaking to audiences about feminism and racial justice. "Right away we discovered that a white woman and a black woman speaking together attracted far more diverse audiences than either of us would have done on our own," Steinem would later say.[39]

The tours helped the two fashion an important connection between feminism and antiracism. The National Portrait Gallery in Washington memorializes Steinem's friendship with Hughes with a 1971 photograph. Both women are in light-colored turtlenecks, their right fists raised in the air, symbolizing solidarity with the Black Power movement. The exhibition label for Dan Wynn's iconic photograph references Steinem's 1969 article "After Black Power, Women's Liberation," signifying the article's success in raising the public perception of intersectional feminism.[40] Decades later, in 2014, the photo was recreated for another museum exhibition. "The symbolism of a black and white woman standing together, demonstrating the black power salute," Hughes noted, "is as important now as it was in the 70s." The exhibit was an important reminder that "A hundred years of the suffrage movement has not eliminated racism, classism and sexism. Black women and white women can make this change together, but not until we acknowledge and resolve the racism problem that stands between us."[41]

How the politics of interracial friendship is conveyed is often revelatory. The same children's book that celebrates the friendship between Marilyn Monroe and Ella Fitzgerald includes a chapter on Steinem and Hughes' friendship. The author, Violet Zhang, notes that the photo was re-created in the same year "Gloria won the Presidential Medal of Freedom." Zhang also points out that "At the Women's March on Washington, DC," held in the aftermath of Donald Trump's election, "Gloria's mere presence served as a reminder that while there's still so much progress to be made, if we're willing to put in the work, we can do it, because look how far we've already come."[42] While Zhang's work also includes a chapter on Davis's friendship with Toni Morrison, it would be Davis and Steinem who would serve as honorary co-chairs of the 2017 Women's March on Washington, widely hailed as the largest protest gathering in American history. Despite their less celebrated friendship—Davis and Steinem have not been as close to one another as to others in their lives—the impetus to bring them together as symbols of resistance for the looming Trump era was powerful.

Upon reflection, Steinem's work with Hughes was the beginning of a lifetime of work with black women activists and political figures. In 1972, Steinem wrote Shirley Chisholm's only televised speech during her presidential campaign. Steinem would call the moment "the still unmatched moment of pride in my life."[43] While appreciative, Chisholm was also frustrated with Steinem's support for George McGovern's candidacy. As Chisholm biographer Barbara Winslow has written:

For Chisholm, the support she got from mainstream feminists was problematic. Many offered lukewarm support, either because they had their own political ambitions or because they assumed a Chisholm victory was impossible. Bella Abzug, one of the most prominent feminists in Congress, was present at Chisholm's second announcement of her candidacy . . . but would not endorse her. . . . Steinem would qualify her political support. She ran as a Chisholm delegate in the New York State primary, but had stated publicly, "I'm for Shirley Chisholm—but I think George McGovern is the best of the *male* candidates."[44]

Intersectional feminism, like interracial friendship in America, has always been fraught with as many dividing lines as there are points of commonality and possibilities for mutual uplift. The nature of power dynamics, often dictated by race, has proven to be a difficult, if not insurmountable, obstacle over the years. Steinem's consciousness of these challenges has been noteworthy—and her honest reflection on these matters has been part of her legacy. As Winslow notes, "Thirty-eight years later, at a tribute to Chisholm at Brooklyn College, Steinem expressed regret that she had never sought Chisholm out to explain her position and heal the rift."[45]

While Steinem was very much engaged in American politics in the 1970s, leveraging her persona as her generation's most well-known feminist, Davis spent the decade traveling, writing, and leveraging her credentials as one of America's better known Marxists to work for women's rights and racial justice around the world. It's hard to imagine how the woman who received the Lenin Peace Prize in Moscow in 1979 would one day co-chair the largest protest march in American history almost forty years later. But this is precisely what Davis's journey to a broader public acceptance in American life encompassed. As Steinem's past involvement with the CIA would remain a thorn in her reputation among more radical feminists, so would Davis's ties to communism tinge her legacy with opprobrium in more moderate feminist circles. The two moved steadily closer over the years—mainly in terms of reputation and their symbolic power as figures from a bygone era who had much to teach a new generation of women activists.

Though Davis would run on the Communist Party ticket in 1980 for vice president, she would leave the party a decade later. By 1995, she became the Presidential Chair in African American Studies at the University of California, Santa Cruz. Much of her work was focused on the prison-industrial complex—work that did not get much political acknowledgment, let alone support, until recent years. Davis was an early advocate and leader of the decarceration movement, sometimes referred to as the new abolition—the end of America's draconian system of locking away members of society whose social, economic, and psychological needs it has neglected to meet. As she told a Kennedy School of Government audience at Harvard University in 2003, "This is a measure of how difficult it is to envision a social order that does not rely on the threat of sequestering people in dreadful places designed to separate them from their communities and their families," said Davis. "The prison is considered so natural and so normal that it is extremely hard to imagine life without them."[46]

It has been an issue Steinem and Davis have found common ground on over the years. As Steinem has written in her memoir, "Nothing has quite prepared me for the impact of the profit motive on the prison system. It's been many years since Angela Davis warned us about 'the prison-industrial-complex,' an echo of President Eisenhower's warning about the 'military-industrial-complex.'"[47] Steinem's early support to stay the execution for the former Black Panther Mumia Abu-Jamal, who was convicted of killing a Philadelphia police officer, was but one example of her commitment to linking her status as a feminist icon with issues of racial justice over the years. Abu-Jamal's case became internationally known—in part because of activists' work on the ground for many years, but also because people like Steinem lent their names and credibility to a cause that remains deeply divisive among the American public.[48]

The Women's March

"I don't think you know how much you've been part of our lives," Gloria Steinem began. She and Angela Davis were on stage for the Sackler Center First Awards in Brooklyn in 2016. Davis was there to receive the Sackler award for women first in their fields, and to be interviewed by Steinem after a screening of Shola Lynch's film, "Free

Angela and All Political Prisoners." "It's really great to see you, Gloria. It's been awhile—a few years since we've seen each other," said Davis. The event was one of the few moments captured on film where both Davis and Steinem were together. Steinem was effusive throughout, as Davis displayed characteristic humility in sharing her experiences in the struggle for women's liberation and racial justice over the years. Steinem would ask Davis what she thought of the growing Black Lives Matter movement:

> "Black Lives Matter, this is what we've been waiting for," Davis said about the urgent needs the movement fulfills among civil rights advocates. "This is a historical conjuncture where all the ingredients came together in an amazing way and Opal, Patrisse and Alicia (the co-founders of the movement) were able to read the times and understand that this is what we need at this moment."[49]

The tone of the evening was optimistic, and one cannot help but imagine what those in attendance were thinking as the country appeared to be a mere five months away from electing the first woman to the presidency in American history. Davis reflected on her acquittal; Steinem reminisced about losing that second cousin as a relative after her support for Davis back in 1971. There was evident warmth between the two, and the audience was highly attentive, as the power of the historic moment unfolded. Yet, there was a sense of foreboding, as Donald Trump's candidacy appeared to be more than a laughing matter, as some had imagined. By October 2016, Davis was voicing those concerns. "If poor white people are suffering, if they're seeing that their children will be even poorer than they are, Donald Trump is now saying: 'Yes you are suffering, I feel your pain . . . it is because of immigrants, it is because of Mexicans, it is because of black people in the inner cities, it is because of Muslims," she said. "He's creating an enemy on which they can project their own suffering and pain. And this is very scary because this can certainly be interpreted as the making of a fascist movement."[50]

Davis voted for the first time for a member of one of the two major US parties in 2008, when she cast her vote for Barack Obama. While both she and Steinem shared misgivings about Hillary Clinton as a candidate in 2016, neither was willing to countenance the alternative of a Trump presidency. While Steinem upset some feminists for her 1998 *New York Times* op-ed defending Bill Clinton in the light of revelations of his sexual affair with Monica Lewinsky, others have been disappointed in her support for Hillary Clinton's candidacy in 2016. In both instances, Steinem was reflecting a more conventional politics—eschewing the demand that Bill Clinton resign over what she called a consensual relationship with Lewinsky, and "clumsy" passes made by him on other occasions.[51] With regard to Hillary Clinton, her support over Bernie Sanders in the 2016 Democratic primaries had more to do with her validation of Clinton's experience than all of her policy views. In a sense, both Davis and Steinem had, by 2008, moved toward a common ground, at least with respect to electoral politics. Donald Trump's election in 2016 only solidified that sense of shared space.

Within two weeks after Trump's election to the White House, the call for a Women's March on Washington was national news. One of the early points of emphasis of the organizers was that the march would represent a cross-section of women, with racial diversity a chief hallmark of the participants. The fact that exit polls initially showed that 53 percent of white women had voted for Trump was a critical point that had to be addressed.[52] Indeed, in the wake of the election, political scientists tried to provide context to Trump's victory, reminding the public that the tendency to lump all women with progressive politics is a chimera. As Jane Junn wrote the week after the election:

> The elephant in the room is white and female, and she has been standing there since 1952. This result has been hiding in plain sight, obscured by a normative bias that women are more Democratic than men. They are, and it is also true that white women are more supportive today of Democratic Party candidates than white men. But this does not mean that white women are more Democratic overall. They are not.[53]

One way of addressing the need to pull together a diverse coalition of marchers was to recruit two of the most recognizable figures from the women's liberation movement and Black Freedom Struggle to serve as the faces of the march. As Amanda Hess wrote for the *New York Times*, days after the march, "The organizers had stumbled into a conflict that has dogged women's organizing from the very beginning: Of all the tensions that have coursed through the women's movement, none has ever been quite so pronounced as the one between white and black women." The historic nature of the challenge—namely, that there has never been one single women's movement in American history—had to be recognized. Hence, the march "put Angela Davis on the same stage as Scarlett Johansson."[54]

The Facebook call for the march was made by the retired attorney Teresa Shook and fashion designer Bob Bland (née Mari Lynn Foulger). Soon, Vanessa Wruble, a white producer, got involved and quickly brought on Carmen Perez, Linda Sarsour, and Tamika Mallory. "The three women—one Chicana Latina, one Palestinian-American, one black—met through their involvement in Justice League NYC, a juvenile-justice initiative. In 2015, they organized a nine-day march from New York to Washington, ending in a rally at the Capitol that drew a small crowd."[55] Explaining the expansion of organizers for the march, Bland said, "These women are not tokens; they are dynamic and powerful leaders who have been organizing intersectional mobilizations for their entire careers." Bland would also implore white women participating in the march to "understand their privilege, and acknowledge the struggle that women of color face."[56]

The organizers of the march selected Davis and Steinem as honorary co-chairs, along with longtime activists Harry Belafonte, LaDonna Harris, and Dolores Huerta. It was fair to say that the Steinem and Davis pairing drew the most attention—and was an important element in reconciling the history of an at-times contentious relationship between black and white women's activists.[57] Davis and Steinem would be among the speakers at the march—and each, in her own way, would address the historic divisions within the women's movement—while focusing attention on the most recent prospects of a new administration not only indifferent to the concerns of women, but considered by many women activists to be actively dedicated to dismantling their progress.

Conclusion

Gloria Steinem and Angela Davis's remarks at the Women's March were reflective of their respective activist careers, and political beliefs.

Steinem began forty minutes into the program by offering thanks to "friends, sisters and brothers, all of you who are before me today and in 370 marches in every state in this country and on six continents and those who will be communing with us in one at 1 [p.m.] in a silent minute for equality in offices, in kitchens, in factories, in prisons, all over the world." She drew her loudest applause from the audience for her praise for Barack and Michelle Obama. She also praised Hillary Clinton, who made women's rights a "human rights issue." And she displayed her characteristic intersectional approach to feminism, imploring continued opposition to Islamophobia, drawing loud shouts of support from the massive gathering, when she inveighed against Donald Trump, who had been sworn in the day before. "So don't try to divide us," she said. "Do not try to divide us. If you force Muslims to register, we will all register as Muslims."[58]

Steinem invoked the slain heroes of her generation—Dr. Martin Luther King Jr., John and Robert Kennedy, and Malcolm X. Her speech was a reminder of how far women around the world have come, and how much work needed to be done. In contrast, Davis, speaking some four hours into the program, agreed with Steinem's human rights connection—while offering a different, and undoubtedly more controversial, list of heroes. "Women's rights are human rights all over the planet and that is why we say freedom and justice for Palestine," Davis said. "We celebrate the impending release of Chelsea Manning. And Oscar López Rivera. But we also say free Leonard Peltier. Free Mumia Abu-Jamal. Free Assata Shakur." It was the kind of litany of names and issues that led to the stripping, and then reinstating, of the Birmingham Civil Rights Institute's Fred Shuttlesworth Human Rights Award, given to Davis in 2019.[59]

In her close, Davis promised, "The next 1,459 days of the Trump administration will be 1,459 days of resistance: Resistance on the ground, resistance in the classrooms, resistance on the job, resistance in our art and in our music." While Trump's defeat in 2020 marked a clear victory for those who organized and attended the march, it remains a somewhat daunting probability, that it was white men, among all groups, who shifted their votes toward the Democratic candidate—while Trump showed modest gains among all others. If the exit polls are to be believed, it appears that the work of intersectional feminism, like all social movements, continues an uphill climb, to achieve the ideal features of a truly antisexist and antiracist democratic society.

Many feminists have taken solace in the fact that, along with Joe Biden, the United States elected its first black woman to the vice presidency. Kamala Harris, born in the year the Civil Rights Act became law, and one year after the bombing of Birmingham's 16th Street Church, is an heir to the legacy left by Davis and Steinem and the millions of other women who labored for racial and women's justice. As Steinem has said, "I thought [black women] invented the feminist movement. I've learned feminism disproportionately from black women."[60]

That education informed Steinem's support for Davis in her darkest hour—and has led her to take stances that have proven controversial over the years. Her past work with organizations and men who have been the antithesis of that movement may complicate her contribution, even as it undoubtedly complicates the trajectory of her friendship with Davis. Nevertheless, the path from Helsinki, to the Free Angela Davis Defense Fund, to the Women's March on Washington demonstrates that the performative art of interracial friendship needn't be uniformly straight, or without its stumbles. For as this history has shown us again and again, the paths of racial justice and interracial friendship are lit not by the bright lights of our reality, but only by the dim, yet hopeful light of stars and shadows.

IO

A Bestowal
Barack Obama and Joe Biden

OVER THE COURSE of writing this book, I've often returned to W. E. B. Du Bois's argument from *The Souls of Black Folk* (1903) about social interaction—tea and cigars among friends—as a prerequisite for ending, or at least destabilizing, racism in America. Was this a rare instance of the great sage of race being sophomoric? Certainly, this idea has not gone without challenge in black political thought. Four years after Du Bois's death in 1963, Charles V. Hamilton and Stokely Carmichael published their germinal work, *Black Power* (1967). Among the myths of racial progress to be made through interracial alliances, the authors underscored this one:

> The [final] myth proceeds from the premise that political coalitions can be sustained on a moral, friendly or sentimental basis, or on appeals to conscience. We view this as a myth because we believe that political relations are based on self-interest: benefits to be gained and losses to be avoided. For the most part, man's politics is determined by his evaluation of material good and evil. Politics results from a conflict of interests, not of consciences.[1]

As I've attempted to take Du Bois's theory of interracial fraternity seriously in my examination of friendships throughout this book, I want to give Carmichael (Kwame Touré) and Hamilton, and other critics of

Du Bois's perspective, their due in this closing chapter. For if nothing else, the friendship between Barack Obama and Joe Biden is perhaps most instructive of the possibilities—and limitations—of the politics of interracial friendship in America. Its instruction is owed to its historical timing, but also the quality of their relationship. The latter either serves to erode or to uphold the assessment of those within the Black Power camp on this premise offered by Du Bois. I hope to show why shortly.

* * *

Obama and Biden's friendship is probably best considered within the context of the past forty-five years of presidential politics, when the dynamics of interracial friendship began to play out in an era less defined by the acquisition of civil rights for African Americans than that of economic equality and "social uplift." Moreover, there has been a different kind of racial signaling in this period, one where black representation in presidential politics has been important not only for the black community but for America's position in the world. This re-prioritization was evident when Jimmy Carter brought former civil rights icon Andrew Young into his administration to help America's image in the "Third World" as UN Ambassador. When Young was forced to resign in 1979, after a number of controversial statements and stumbles over American foreign policy, it reflected the challenges of interracial friendship's ability to preserve moderate political objectives in the presence of more radical black politics.

On the other hand, when Bill Clinton brought another civil rights veteran into the White House fold, as an aide to the president, it exemplified race's "declining significance." Vernon Jordan was ubiquitous—whether golfing with Clinton, or confiding with him about appointments, policymaking, or just there for counsel and solace. Jordan was often described as a Washington "fixer"—but he was Clinton's fixer, more than he was the representative of black interests, broadly understood. This fact was brought home by Clinton's impeachment crisis, one where Jordan was purported to have made the kind of closed door arrangements for Monica Lewinsky—a position with Revlon, it was reported—that signified not only his status as Clinton's friend and consigliere, but the changing face of power in Washington.[2]

Part of the shifting dynamic in race relations in Washington in the years since Andrew Young's resignation was the fact that the presence of black power brokers was less of a surprise. The nation was clearly out of the era of shadow "black cabinets" or purely symbolic racial gestures. As the *New York Times* reported during Clinton's scandal, "The Jordans, in many ways, have been the Clintons' bridge to the Washington establishment."[3] That marked a form of progress in its own right, even as the relationship reflected some of the limitations and misuses of interracial friendship's democratic significance. Indeed, public perceptions of racial progress underwent a shift in the 1990s, as the percentage point difference between all adults saying race relations are "generally good" and those saying "generally bad" underwent a 70 percent upward swing between the lowest point in the decade, marked by the acquittal of Los Angeles police officers who had been filmed beating Rodney King in 1992, and Clinton's last year in office in 2000. Race had hardly diminished as an issue in American life—but it appeared that blacks and whites were closer to seeing the issue through the same eyes than they had been in recent memory.[4] Thus, the emphasis in presidential politics with respect to interracial friendships began to move from questions of black power and advocacy to a focus on national interest and personal politics.

When Clinton's successor, George W. Bush, appointed a number of high-profile African Americans to consequential positions in his administration, it was a notable departure from prior Republican administrations. Indeed, the appointments of Colin Powell to secretary of state and Condoleezza Rice as national security adviser were historic by any measure. Powell became the first African American secretary of state, as Rice became the first to lead the National Security Agency. When Bush appointed Rice secretary of state at the start of his second term, she became the highest ranking black woman to ever serve in a presidential administration. The days of Mary McLeod Bethune having to call up the first lady to procure hospital beds for African Americans suffering from a tuberculosis outbreak from an indifferent White House were gone, it seemed.

Nevertheless, Rice's portfolio was outside the purview of the economic or political needs of African Americans. Her foreign policy expertise was in Russia, not Africa or the developing world. She evinced little interest in the political issues or causes favored by strong majorities of the black community. Along these lines, Bush's appointments were suggestive of a "color-blind" era in American life, one where merit, service, and credentials, rather than identity politics, were to dictate the parameters of public service. Moreover, Rice and Bush were friends—and quite public ones at that. There was evident admiration and bonhomie between the two, and as Clinton and Jordan shared a great deal of social time together, so did Bush and Rice—perhaps more so. As Rice biographer Elisabeth Bumiller has written, "Rice made Bush feel sharper, particularly when she complimented him on his questions. Bush did not know many black people well, and it made him feel good about himself that he got along so well with Rice. It was also hard not to see that she was also attractive, athletic, and competitive, and like him, underestimated for much of her life."[5] In the end, Bush and Rice were good friends, but their relationship inspired little more than salacious rumor-mongering with respect to its larger socio-political significance.[6] This, in itself, was touted as a kind of racial progress, or its transcendence.

Yet, when Barack Obama was inaugurated as the first black president in America's history in 2009, the question of how the performance dynamic in interracial politics might change was looming. How would racial politics shape the new and groundbreaking administration with a black president? What dangers and potential opportunities might present themselves to a leader whose very person called to mind cosmopolitanism? And, could this historic dance of interracial fraternity, publicly performed, even play out when the chief protagonist himself entering the White House famously insisted there would be "no new friends"—black or otherwise?[7] Oddly enough, many of the answers could be found in the background and personal makeup of the new vice president, Joseph R. Biden.

Friendship and Loss

Evan Osnos's biography of Joe Biden begins with a searing episode in Biden's life that would be a defining moment for most people. It is the moment in 1988, at the end of his first presidential run, where Biden found himself awake in Rochester, New York, "on the floor of his hotel room" at the age of 45, in a near paralytic state. He had suffered a cranial aneurysm, and were it not for the quick thinking of an aide who flew Biden to Delaware, and the work of surgeons over a three-month period, he might have died. Indeed, Biden was administered the last rites by a priest upon arrival at the hospital.[8] Yet, as anyone remotely familiar with Biden's story knows, this was hardly his most trying moment.

As Biden tells it in his memoir, a week before Christmas in 1972, after being newly elected to the United States Senate, his sister Val took a call from their brother Jimmy. "When she hung up the phone, she looked white," Biden recounts. " 'There's been a slight accident,' she said. Nothing to worry about. But we ought to go home.' " Somehow, Biden instinctively knew the worst had happened. " 'She's dead,' I said, 'Isn't she?' "[9]

While the night of December 18, 1972, irrevocably and most cruelly altered Biden's life, a night in which he lost his wife Neilia, age thirty, and their thirteen-month-old daughter, Naomi, in a horrific auto collision, over the ensuing decades, Biden has been more defined by his resilience than his suffering. It is that resilience and deep empathy that has given him a powerful connection to those who've befriended him over the decades, and in recent years, to the American people. Among American presidents perhaps only Theodore Roosevelt experienced the kind of loss Biden did, when on Valentine's Day in 1884, Roosevelt lost both his wife and his mother. Somehow, he gathered himself, and seventeen years later, became president of the United States. It would take Biden forty-nine years after that fateful night to do so.

Yet, for Biden, more, if not greater, loss was to come. As vice president in 2015, Biden lost his son Beau, still in the prime of his life at forty-six, to brain cancer. It was this tragedy that would seal his friendship with Barack Obama, often and not unreasonably depicted as an insular if not aloof man, one who nevertheless feels deeply and is moved by his own connection with human suffering. To return to the beginning of this concluding chapter, if Carmichael and Hamilton are right, that "man's politics is determined by his evaluation of material good and evil," that it "results from a conflict of interests, not of consciences," none of this should be of consequence to interracial politics—or the relative state of racial hierarchy and discrimination in America.

* * *

As he frequently reminds his audiences, Joe Biden grew up in Scranton, Pennsylvania, the eldest of four children, before his family moved to Delaware after his father lost his job. The reason recalls the scene in Ralph Ellison's *Invisible Man*, where a group of young black men are forced to scurry for loose change in a boxing ring whose mat is electrified. As Osnos tells it in his biography of Biden, "Once at an office Christmas party, the boss tossed a bucket of silver dollars onto the dance floor and watched the salesmen scramble to pick them up."

> "Dad sat frozen for a second, he stood up, took my mom's hand, and walked out of the party, losing his job in the process."[10]

That affront to Joe Biden Sr.'s dignity, and his protection of it, stayed with Biden, and it has become the underpinning to a mantra he repeats in his speeches: "The dignity of work." Indeed, at the start of the 2019 campaign for the presidency, at least one journalist had grown tired of Biden's phrase. "Americans don't need further grandstanding about the purported dignity of work," Sarah Jones wrote. "They need policy reforms that reflect the innate dignity of human life, and Joe Biden isn't the candidate to deliver them."[11]

In addition to the economic uncertainty that defined this period of his life, Biden also was a stutterer, and he was the target of frequent bullying. That Biden would become identified as one of those politicians who never knew a pause in conversation he didn't disdain, is testament to his will and deep resolve. It begs the question as to whether or not Biden would have ascended as far in life if his father had taught him a different lesson, stooped his shoulders, and kept that job in Scranton.

By the time he was enrolled at the University of Delaware, Biden had become a popular, but middling, student. Wilmington, Delaware, was where Biden had his first significant experiences with race, "playing bit parts in protests against segregation, including walking out of a

Wilmington diner that refused to serve a Black classmate in 1961 and picketing the segregated Rialto movie theater the following year."[12] A significant part of Biden's call to public service—beyond the requirement of an outsized ego common to politicians—was his Catholic faith. As Massimo Faggioli recounts in his book on Biden's religious faith, "In a videotaped message that he prepared for the funeral of George Floyd, killed during a June 2020 police arrest in Minneapolis that sparked a summer of deep unrest in the country, Biden said, 'I grew up with Catholic social doctrine, which taught me that faith without works is dead, and you will know us by what we do.'"[13]

In a sense, Biden's experience as a middle-class Irish Catholic male navigating life in the early 1960s was fairly common. By 1966 he was confident enough to tell Neilia, not long after meeting her, that he intended not only to marry her but to become a senator by thirty, and to one day be elected president. The post-war generation of white Americans was particularly privileged, and while the recognition of racial inequality was growing, there was an equal sense of invulnerability for many, not punctured until the dark shadow of the war in Vietnam began to grow. Remarkably, Biden was good for his word, as he was elected to the Senate in 1972 at the age of twenty-nine.[14] That Biden's life was thrown into utter despair shortly thereafter—and his phoenix-like rise in the decades since—is what has come to define his character. And, it is the fortitude and authenticity derived from those trials that made an otherwise improbable friendship with Barack Obama possible.

Over the years the US Senate became a refuge and an extended family for Biden, as his colleagues rallied around him after his devastating loss. He lost himself in his work, making up for the intellectual deficits he felt burdened him since his youth. He crossed the line with allegations of plagiarism that were sustained during his first run for the White House in 1988, though these were not the first such allegations to bedevil him. He would apologize for these missteps over the years, and upon reflecting on the 1988 episode would conclude, "I didn't deserve to be president."[15] Perhaps he was trying too hard, as Biden biographer Evan Osnos has concluded. But the efforts produced illuminating moments of intellectual curiosity. In 1975, he wrote to the political theorist Hannah Arendt:

Dear Miss Arendt,
    I read in a recent article by Tom Wicker of a paper
that you read at the Boston Bicentennial Forum.
    As a Member of the Foreign Relations Committee
of the Senate, I am most interested in receiving a copy of your paper.
    Thank you.
            Sincerely,
            Joseph R. Biden Jr.
            United States Senator[16]

Aside from winning over the hearts of every political scientist who comes across this letter, Biden's willingness to push his limits has endeared him to the general public. Not because he has often succeeded but because he has often failed. Conversely, Barack Obama's academic and intellectual successes have provided the credentials that white candidates for high office like Biden have never quite needed in the same way as candidates of color. But those credentials and intellectual sensibilities of Obama have, ironically enough, often burdened him. The emergent and powerful connection between Biden and Obama, therefore, has had far less to do with discussions over Arendt. It is deeper, less obvious, and ultimately more meaningful to the story of interracial politics' significance to multiracial democracy's possibilities in America.

Dreams and Phantoms of Barack Obama

Statistically speaking, black fathers in the United States spend, on average, more time with their children than their white counterparts.[17] But it is the absence of black fathers in married households that has often become the explanation for nearly every ill associated with blackness, including violent crime, drug addiction, and poverty. In his 2008 Fathers' Day address, then presidential candidate Barack Obama returned to this theme, one for whom, as a man who grew up without a father present in the home, had shaped his early life, and arguably much of his racial politics.

"[M]ore than half of all black children live in single-parent households . . . children who grow up without a father are five times more likely to live in poverty and commit crime," Obama told the largely black congregation at the Apostolic Church of God in Chicago. He continued with the statistic that black children are "nine times more likely to drop out of schools and 20 times more likely to end up in prison. They are more likely to have behavioral problems, or run away from home or become teenage parents themselves. And the foundation of our community is weaker because of it," he said.[18] That message of racial responsibility (indeed, Obama's inauguration speech, "A New Era of Responsibility," suggests how significant the theme is to him) represents a form of social conservatism that at once links Obama to the African American community, as a familiar trope often employed by black nationalists and black conservatives alike, while also endearing him to white conservatives, who ever since the Moynihan Report of 1965 have lamented the scourge of "broken" black families.[19]

Yet, the title of Obama's memoir, *Dreams from My Father*, emphasizes his African lineage and connection to a man whom he admittedly came to know only apocryphally.[20] The story of "Barry"—the chubby, introspective, and fatherless boy that was Barack Obama—has become familiar to many Americans. That of his white mother, the anthropologist Ann Dunham, who died tragically at fifty-two of cancer, is now equally, if not better, known than the story of Obama's father. The choice to reflect upon "my father" as opposed to "my mother" is but one example of how Obama's racial bildungsroman has involved personal, as well as political, choices as he positioned himself as a candidate whose racial bona fides as a black man were unquestioned, yet one whose ability to connect with whites was equally secure. Highlighting his phantom father was a political act for Obama.

Indeed, by his own admission, Obama's interracial romances before his marriage to Michelle Robinson were subjected to his own political scrutiny, a fact that underscores his awareness of how his biracial background translated to a public otherwise familiarized with "tragic mulatto" narratives. In this sense, Obama's romantic life was little different than that of W. E. B Du Bois's, discussed earlier in this book, as Du Bois's prospective marriage to a white German woman died on the vine of white supremacy nearly seventy years before Obama was born. According to David Garrow, whose biography of Obama covered his relationship as a graduate student with Sheila Miyoshi Jaeger, a biracial woman of Dutch and Japanese ancestry, Obama ended their relationship out of deference to his political ambitions, which he presumed required marriage to a black woman if he were to ever become president. Despite proposing to Jager in 1986, Obama painfully broke off the relationship. The "resolution of his black identity was directly linked to his decision to pursue a political career," Jager told Garrow.[21] Obama's numerous romantic relationships with white women—he would later admit to "consolidating" them into one composite figure in *Dreams from My Father*—proved to be too much of a burden given his ambitions, which fundamentally called for him to assert his blackness. Barry had become Barack.[22]

* * *

Barack Obama Sr. died at age forty-six in a car crash in Kenya in 1982. He had left Obama and his mother in Hawaii when Obama was two. Obama would never see his father again after he turned ten. Obama describes knowing his father mostly as "a myth to me, both more and less than a man."[23] Obama does not describe the loss of his father as devastating, but his absence stirred, at least to some, the insular, reflective, and at times isolating character that would form Obama's personality. The death of his mother, however, was far more searing. Indeed, in the preface to the 2004 edition of his memoir, Obama wrote: "I think sometimes that had I known she would not survive her illness, I might have written a different book—less a mediation on the absent parent, more a celebration of the one who was the single constant in my life. . . . I won't try to describe how deeply I mourn her passing still. I know that she was the kindest, most generous spirit I have ever known, and that what is best in me I owe her."[24] Stanley Ann Dunham died on November 7, 1995. *Dreams from My Father* was released in July of that year.

Obama's construction of his personal history, not unlike those in this book, embraces a certain form of memorialization, one that implicates race in ways unique to the times and the author. For Obama, his African and American heritages served to imbue him with a post-partisan ("neither a Red America, nor a Blue America"), if not post-racial, sensibility. Most significantly, the pain of losing two parents has served to shape an inner life for Obama that, despite whatever truth there may be to his "aloofness," gives him a wellspring of compassion and deep emotional connectivity. Obama feels, and, as any number of his public displays of grief have shown over the years, he feels deeply.

This familiarity with familial loss and esteem for the connectivity engendered by family is ultimately what fostered the emotional ties Obama shares with Biden. As Steven Levingston wrote, "Barack and Joe shared a fierce devotion to their families, and Barack felt Joe's palpable adoration of his children."[25] Whatever differences and fissures were present in their personal and political relationship, it was the mutual respect and admiration felt over family that made the bond between these two historic figures, and unlikely friends, possible. With that prefatory understanding, neither Biden nor Obama was oblivious to the politics of interracial friendship. Indeed, Obama's most important political speech during the 2008 presidential campaign was an object lesson in his ability to illustrate for the American people the connection between civic and social life that bridges racial divisions.

In what has often been described as his most important, if not best known, address, Obama's March 2008 speech came in the midst of a firestorm of criticism for Obama having befriended his pastor, Jeremiah Wright, whose criticism of the United States over the years was deemed by many whites to be hateful. With Wright's condemnations of American foreign policy and racism at home being broadcast in a near loop on cable television ("God damn, America," Wright intoned in the widely replayed excerpt from a sermon), Obama chose to address the issue head on with a speech in Philadelphia. Nothing less than his candidacy for the presidency was at stake.

Wrapping himself in the nostalgia of great American founding moments at the Constitution Center that day, Obama ended his speech by telling the story of a young white woman named Ashley, who spoke at an Obama campaign rally in South Carolina. When asked why she was there, supporting Obama, Ashley explained that she had grown up so poor that she often lied to her mother about her love for mustard and relish sandwiches, so as to not burden her with the grief of not being able to satisfy her daughter's hunger. It was a powerful story in and of itself. But Obama went further than simply illustrating Ashley's sacrifices—he introduced another story, that of an older, and unnamed black man who was asked the same question at the gathering. When posed the question as to why *he* was at the event supporting Obama, the man gave a simple response, Obama recalled.

"I'm here because of Ashley," he said.

The line resonated throughout the audience, and undoubtedly throughout much of the country. Obama had little to do after that but close. "By itself, that single moment of recognition between that young white girl and that old black man is not enough," Obama told his audience. "It is not enough to give health care to the sick, or jobs to the jobless, or education to our children. But it is where we start."[26] That start, akin to Du Bois's call for the removal of the veil that separated blacks and whites from social interaction, was rooted in something deeper than politics. It was Obama's greatest effort to that point, to model the necessity of interracial friendship, as highly consequential to improving the nation's politics. In Obama's construction, "Ashley" and "this elderly black man" became stand-ins for the rest of us—the broad swath of Americans who, day by day, engage with one another across racial lines, doing so, often with great care for the consequences. In this regard, Obama's speech was but the latest in a long tradition of American political lives, speeches, and acts attempting to elevate racial fraternity into a type of performance art. The moment would only be surpassed by Obama's own friendship with his vice president, one that would serve as an unfolding study in how even the most genuine of transracial bonds have played a distinctive role in shadowing, and at times illuminating, the political history of America.

First Black President

There was a moment during the 2008 presidential campaign when Barack Obama began employing a faux presidential seal on his podium during speeches. The seal contained the words "Vero Possumus"—*Yes We Can*—an oblique latinesque nod to "E Pluribus Unum."[27] The McCain campaign cried foul, charging Obama with prematurely measuring the drapes for the Oval Office. The Obama team sheepishly took down the seal, but the incident suggested a campaign anxious to prepare the American public for what a black man standing in front of the presidential seal looked like. Whether or not the seal was connected with that anxiety, the concern was real. Were the American people, in fact, "ready" for a black president?

Obama's political rise gained national attention at the Democratic National Convention in 2004, where he delivered the keynote address for the nominee, Senator John Kerry. The speech highlighted Obama's ability to transcend party politics, and for some, race itself. Yet, in the wake of the Wright affair during the 2008 campaign, Obama's black-ness—and the radical turn in American politics it suggested—became an unavoidable topic of conversation for the Obama team. While there was never any serious consideration for choosing anyone other than a white (and most likely male) running mate, Obama's selection of Biden provided a kind of reassurance that an older, more moderate influence would be close at hand. These considerations were not unlike John F. Kennedy's selection of Lyndon Johnson—a pick designed to offset the regional, political, and religious concerns of nominating a north-eastern Catholic liberal. But Obama's blackness represented a greater historic hurdle than Kennedy's Catholicism. By way of comparison, Biden had the far heavier lift in providing political "cover" for a presi-dent unlike any other in the nation's history.

In the words of Steven Levingston, "The friendship was radical. It epitomized the revolution of Obama's presidency. In practice and in symbolism, Barack and Joe reversed more than two hundred years of American black-white interaction."[28] There is no denying the lit-eral truth of this observation. Americans, black and white alike, had never experienced the highest office of the land occupied by an African American, one whose word and power carried greater weight than his white second. The symbolism of black power eclipsing white power was mostly that—symbolism; but, as political scientists began to discover, a great deal of the backlash experienced by the Obama administration in its early years had more to do with race than conservative Tea Party outrage over public policy.[29]

Though the friendship of Biden and Obama carries great symbolic weight, its authenticity remains unquestioned. Part of the reason is that the relationship developed from real missteps along with personal and idiosyncratic differences. Biden, the elder statesman, cautioned Obama to "go slow when [you] get in the Senate." He talked far too much and was far too emotive for the cerebral and cool Obama. "Shoot. Me. Now.," Obama famously scribbled to one of his aides, Robert Gibbs, as Biden droned on in the Senate during one hearing.[30] And then there was the infamous comment Biden made during the 2008 Democratic primaries about Obama being "the first sort of mainstream African American [candidate] who is articulate and bright and clean and a nice-looking guy. I mean, that's a storybook, man."[31] As Obama strategist David Axelrod described their early relationship: "I would not describe them as close in any way."[32]

Yet, impressed with his debate skills during the primaries, his knowledge of foreign policy, and his preparedness for the office, Obama selected Biden to be his vice president. Over time, Biden demonstrated a loyalty to Obama that belied their occasional, and at times significant, policy differences, such as when Biden opposed the raid that ultimately led to the killing of Osama bin Laden. Demonstrative examples of Biden's loyalty came in public at times, such as when he stood with Obama during his confrontation with General Stanley McChrystal, who was undermining Obama's foreign policy objectives in Iraq in an interview that bordered on ridiculing the president and vice president. "It's fucking outrageous," Obama recalled Biden sharing at the time.[33] As Obama deputy national security adviser Ben Rhodes noted, Obama "came to love [Biden] with the almost protective sense of devotion to an older family member."[34]

But it was what Obama heard secondhand about Biden's loyalty that truly made a lasting impression on him. As Evan Osnos recalls it in his biography of Biden:

> At a Democratic Caucus lunch, after the party had lost the House of Representatives, the then congressman Anthony Weiner criticized Obama for making a deal with the Republicans on tax cuts. Biden erupted, saying, "There's no goddamn way I'm going to stand here and talk about the president like that." A short while later, he unleashed a similar blast at Israeli prime minister Benjamin Netanyahu, who had found fault with Obama's Middle East policy. . . . The stories reached Obama. . . . "He knows the vice president has his back," [said Rhodes].[35]

Ever the Chicago politician, the displays of loyalty meant a great deal to Obama. Moreover, they reflected well upon Biden with the Democratic base, particularly the African American community. In a country where black leadership in the corporate or political world remains noteworthy, and where supervision over white colleagues is historically fraught with tension and the fragility of being undermined from below, Biden's earnest friendship and loyalty were incalculable to his relationship with the president and his own future political success. As James Clyburn would say in South Carolina in 2020, as he endorsed Biden to the dismay of many progressives, including younger African American voters: "We know Joe. But more importantly, Joe knows us."[36]

* * *

Over the eight years of the Obama presidency, countless images and memes emerged touting the extraordinary bond between Biden and Obama. Whether it was the two men jogging to a meeting in their ties and shirtsleeves, or sharing a hearty laugh seated in the Oval Office, many Americans took great enjoyment out of a friendship that seemed truly heartfelt. In a sense, the fraternity witnessed between the two was less consciously performative than any other interracial bond in presidential history. Yet, both Biden and Obama were undoubtedly aware of what their friendship meant not only to each other but for the nation.

When on January 12, 2017, Obama bestowed the Presidential Medal of Freedom upon a surprised and tearful Biden, the symbolic value of the politics of interracial friendship had come full circle. Here were Obama and Biden, in the same White House as Lincoln and Douglass, only this time with the black man in the role as president, and with a gift for posterity. As presidential staffer, Liz Allen recounted, "[W]e knew it was so important to Obama to give this moment to Biden. People moved mountains to make all this work logistically because it was about Obama and Biden and their relationship, which everyone had such reverence for."[37]

Steven Levingston devoted an entire chapter to the episode in his book on Biden and Obama's friendship. That the love and affection between the two most powerful political leaders in the nation could be the subject of such popular and scholarly attention speaks to the novelty of interracial friendship's ability to shape public discourse and suggest something deeper about the status of our republic. No, this historic friendship did not change the material reality of black life in America and the persistence of racism or white supremacy. That would be magic, not an accounting of history. But what occurred during the Obama presidency between the president and vice president was quite significant. It was the radical but reassuring notion that the face of black power was not to be feared; that the nation could live on, and do so, without malice.

Reversal of Fortune

Many white Americans did not see it that way, of course. For some, the Obama years represented the loss of white privilege, and the decaying of "traditional values." That Donald Trump, a virulent and unapologetic white nationalist, xenophobe, and misogynist, eked out a most improbable victory over Hillary Clinton in the 2016 presidential election underscored the "boomerang" quality of American political development Ralph Ellison wrote about in *Invisible Man*. The comity and bonhomie of interracial friendship had been replaced in an eye-blink, by the most caustic and atavistic constructions of racial hierarchy found in American history, in the new administration.

Indeed, Donald Trump's relationship to race was well known before he became president of the United States. He and his father had been sued for racial discrimination in housing in New York City; he was, and remains, unapologetic for calling for the deaths of the Central Park Five—a group of young black males wrongfully accused of raping a white jogger in 1989. Indeed, Trump took out an ad in four New York City papers calling for their deaths ("Bring Back the Death Penalty! Bring Back Our Police!"); and, he had been famously willing to opine about his belief in the racial inferiority of African Americans and others, over many years, to friends and confidantes.[38] His presidency would not be much different, with references to "shit-hole" countries, Mexican "rapists," and Muslim American citizens made nearly indistinguishable from "terrorists." Indeed, the very foundation of Trump's ascent to the presidency had been premised on the lie that Barack Obama was not an American citizen.

Nevertheless, ever the student of American politics, Trump cultivated rhetorical and visual evidence of his indifference to race as an issue for him. "I am the least racist person in this room," he said during his first debate with Joe Biden.[39] Months earlier, he had claimed to have done more for the black community than any president with the "possible exception of Abraham Lincoln."[40] These absurd claims were accompanied by staged presentations of racial fraternity over the course of his campaign and presidency. Prayer meetings with black ministers; calling out black attendees at his rallies. "Look at my African American over here!" Trump exclaimed gleefully, on one occasion.[41] Despite having the least diverse cabinet in recent history, Trump nevertheless promoted his relationship with black supporters, such as when he hired "The Apprentice" star Omarosa Manigault as his "public liaison." Every such attempt at performing interracial friendship seemed to confirm the temporal as well as moral distance between the Trump presidency and others. Despite Trump's claims, his actions and example were far removed from the well-considered grandeur of Lincoln calling out in the White House, "There is my friend, Douglass!"

Indeed, Trump's verbal tick of referring to African Americans as "the Blacks" suggests a kind of colonial mindset with respect to race. As Kathleen Parker has written, the usage amounts to a "separatist term," one that creates an unnecessary and perhaps unconscious "other."[42] It is the kind of language more common to nineteenth-century America—one often used when white officials would reference indigenous peoples in the United States. "The Indians," or "the Blacks," or later "the Jews" (see Richard Nixon)—all have the familiar ring of establishing a kind of knowing sense of what this alien group is all about. It is perhaps the most telling sign of the absence of fraternity—the utter disconnection from intergroup affinity and affection.

It was into this political context that Biden launched his 2020 presidential campaign. It was a run for the White House to "restore the soul of our nation," as he put it.[43] Despite the high-mindedness of his campaign, Biden languished early in the polls, and there was no endorsement from his friend as Obama stayed out of the fray. As former Obama secretary of defense Leon Panetta told Politico in a wide-ranging piece on the Biden-Obama friendship, "[Biden] was loyal, I think, to Obama in every way in terms of defending and standing by him, even probably when he disagreed with what Obama was doing," Panetta said. "To some extent, [Biden] oftentimes felt that loyalty was not being rewarded."[44]

Biden's loyalty would indeed be rewarded, however—but from a different source. It was the black congressman Jim Clyburn's endorsement on February 26, 2020, just three days before the South Carolina primary, that catapulted Biden back into the race for the Democratic party nomination. As the political scientist Marc Hetherington put it, it was "the most important day of the election year."[45] Biden never looked back, besting Bernie Sanders, Pete Buttigieg, Kamala Harris, and a long field of Democratic contenders. Despite a mixed record on issues of race, having been opposed to busing and supporting the 1994 crime bill that many black and younger progressives have come to abhor in recent years, Biden's history of support for civil rights and his deep experience with the black political elite, and with African American voters in general, gave him a leg up on his competitors. More importantly, it was the sense among older black voters that Biden would be best positioned to defeat Trump, rather than a democratic socialist, a black woman, or a gay white man, that fueled Biden's victory in South Carolina and later primaries. If there is a fundamental source of political acumen cultivated over many decades among black voters, it is their sense of how white voters will respond to the choices before them that ask more from their spirit of political benevolence than is possible. Few doubted Biden could win over white voters better than the rest of the field. As it turned out, white males were the only constituency to vote more for Biden in 2020 than Donald Trump in 2020. But it was enough.[46]

Biden's loyalty to Obama and their very public and sincere friendship were crucial components of Biden's ascendancy to the White House. But what did it mean for race relations and the endemic scourge of racism in America more broadly? Were Clyburn's nod to Biden and subsequent black support a refutation of Carmichael and Hamilton's "material" understanding of Black Power? While it is clear that black political power in 2020 dwarfed that which resided in the political landscape in 1967, Biden's victory—much like Obama's—did not portend the erasure of white supremacy, nor did it effectively reconfigure the status of racial hierarchy in the nation's politics. What was new, however, was that the employment of racial symbolism, anchored to interracial fraternity, had changed as the level of political standing among the protagonists had become equal. How and why this departure from centuries of practice in the performative art of interracial friendship might matter going forward remains to be seen.

Conclusion: Stars and Shadows

As the United States moves toward becoming a "majority-minority" nation, one might presume that the need or value for political displays of interracial friendship may be behind us. Yet, the movement toward a more democratic and inclusive America has always been fraught with violent moments of backlash and disavowals of progress. If the political history of interracial friendship teaches us anything, it is that the symbolic value of demonstrating moral commitments to not only legislative acts but also those of the heart matter a great deal. At the very least, they are instructive of the overarching state of affairs—and where the nation might be headed. This is especially true during moments of perceived vulnerability among whites: the Haitian Revolution; the Nat Turner Rebellion; Reconstruction; the Civil Rights Act; and now, our period of profound demographic change, one that has made the votes of whites no longer uniquely decisive.

The assault on the nation's Capital on January 6, 2021, by white nationalists, Trump supporters, and insurrectionists, revealed, oddly enough, the deep connection between democracy and communal bonds. When those bonds fray, as they have throughout American history, they are suggestive of authoritarianism's appeal. If those whom I deem to be inferior, or otherwise illegitimately disposed to govern *themselves*, let alone *me*, share in political power, then I am less likely to turn toward democratic forms. I am, on the contrary, more likely to reject them. For, in a large, diverse republic such as ours, we must make common ground in recognizing not only the rules of democratic society, but also its virtues. And there can be no meaningful acceptance of rules with those whom you fear, absent an inward psychological—and, dare I say, spiritual—shift in how one sees their fellow citizens. Lincoln understood this as well as anyone. This is the "new birth of freedom" he declared at Gettysburg. It goes deeper than voting, canvassing, marching, or even elections, as sacred as they are. For democratic life requires bonds of affection—an abiding trust that you may not like the decisions made by democratic majorities constituted by those who may look, believe, and feel differently than you do—but you nevertheless prefer those decisions to those won by violence, out of respect for them. Perhaps even love. And, if one can implore such a thing, in light of recent days revealing democracy's tragic vulnerability, one could say: *must* love.

* * *

Would any of this be necessary in a world free of racial animus and, more significantly, white supremacy? Certainly not. But the human condition is rife with a multitude of forms of oppression, each guilty of erecting novel and exquisite forms of repression. Dismantling racism and other endemic inequalities cannot be achieved through scientific, economic, or self-empowering acts alone. For in the end, we live in communities, with other people. Our nationalisms, racial, ethnic, or religious encampments, may provide self-regarding value—and they are not to be underestimated, particularly in a society such as ours, that has sought to denigrate the personhood of people who do not conform to the racialized standards of belonging established from the nation's founding. But these encampments, psychological bulwarks though they are, ultimately do not resolve the problem of deep group marginalization in a racist society. Even forms of economic or political empowerment have proven temporal and vulnerable to decimation. We are a nation of untold and innumerable "Black Wall Streets"—models like the Tulsa, Oklahoma, community of the 1920s—that nevertheless proved susceptible to racist violence and destruction.

In the end, the ten cases presented in this book, representing over two hundred years of interracial friendship's centrality to shaping public notions of what a healthy, multiracial republic might look like, suggest that we cannot disavow friendship's role in making over our democratic republic. It may be an insufficient element of the comprehensive work we must all undertake, but without it, all the work we engage in may well be in vain. So, it is the talking to strangers, the politics of conviviality, the abandonment of our caves, and the rough travel by stars and shadows, or nothing at all. We must make ourselves vulnerable, even as vulnerability is our inherited condition.

NOTES

———

Introduction

1. W. E. B. Du Bois, *The Souls of Black Folk* (Oxford: Oxford University Press, 2007), 87.
2. Danielle S. Allen, *Talking to Strangers: Anxieties of Citizenship Since Brown v. Board of Education* (Chicago: University of Chicago Press, 2004), xiv.
3. Wilson Carey McWilliams, *The Idea of Fraternity in America* (Berkeley: University of California Press, 1973), 28.
4. Angel Puyol, *Political Fraternity: Democracy beyond Freedom and Equality* (New York: Routledge, 2019), 5.
5. McWilliams, *The Idea of Fraternity*, 621.
6. Ibid., 623.
7. Allen, *Talking to Strangers*, 167.
8. Desmond S. King and Rogers M. Smith, "Racial Orders in American Political Development," *The American Political Science Review* 99, no. 1 (2005): 75–92.
9. Randall Kennedy, *Interracial Intimacies: Sex, Marriage, Identity, and Adoption* (New York: Vintage, 2003).
10. See King and Smith, "Racial Orders," 77–78.
11. See Seyla Benhabib, "Toward a Deliberative Model of Democratic Legitimacy," in her *Democracy and Difference: Contesting the Boundaries of the Political* (Princeton: Princeton University Press, 1996), 67.
12. Ibid., 69.
13. Allen, *Talking to Strangers*, 138.
14. Paul Gilroy, *Postcolonial Melancholia* (New York: Columbia University Press, 2005), xv.

15. Ibid., 131.

16. Mona Chalabi, "What's Behind the Rise of Interracial Marriage in the US," *The Guardian*, February 21, 2018, https://www.theguardian.com/lifeandstyle/2018/feb/21/whats-behind-the-rise-of-interracial-marriage-in-the-us.

17. Annie Karni, Maggie Haberman, and Sydney Ember, "Trump Plays on Racist Fears of Terrorized Suburbs to Court White Voters," *New York Times*, July 29, 2020.

18. John Stauffer, *The Black Hearts of Men: Radical Abolitionists and the Transformation of Race* (Cambridge, MA: Harvard University Press, 2002), 1–2.

19. Mark Twain, *The Adventures of Huckleberry Finn* (London, UK: Penguin, 2003), 71.

Chapter 1

1. Silvio A. Bedini, *The Life of Benjamin Banneker: The Definitive Biography of the First Black Man of Science* (Rancho Cordova, CA: Landmark Enterprises, 1972), 44.

2. Cited in Thomas Jefferson, *The Papers of Thomas Jefferson*, Vol. 19, *January 1791 to March 1791*, ed. Charles T. Cullen (Princeton: Princeton University Press, 1986), 41.

3. Thomas Jefferson, *Notes on Virginia*, in *Thomas Jefferson: Writings*, ed. Merrill D. Peterson (New York: The Library of America, 1984), 267.

4. Ibid.

5. Thomas Jefferson, *Thomas Jefferson Writings*, *Notes on the State of Virginia* (New York: The Library of America, 1984), 266.

6. The citation for all quotations taken from Banneker's letter to Jefferson can be found here: From Benjamin Banneker to Thomas Jefferson, 19 August 1791, *Founders Online*, National Archives, https://founders.archives.gov/documents/Jefferson/01-22-02-0049. [Original source: *The Papers of Thomas Jefferson*, , vol. 22, *6 August 1791–31 December 1791*, ed. Charles T. Cullen (Princeton: Princeton University Press, 1986), 49–54.]

7. "Thomas Jefferson to John Adams, 12 October 1813," *Founders Online*, National Archives, https://founders.archives.gov/documents/Jefferson/03-06-02-0431. [Original Source: *The Papers of Thomas Jefferson, Retirement Series*, vol. 6, *11 March to 27 November 1813*, ed. J. Jefferson Looney (Princeton: Princeton University Press, 2009), 548–552.]

8. Thomas Jefferson, *Notes on Virginia*, in *Thomas Jefferson: Writings* (New York: The Library of America, 1984), 267.

9. The italics are mine.

10. See the *New England Quarterly*: https://newenglandquarterly.wordpress.com/2013/08/27/colonial-almanacs/.

11. Angela G. Ray, "'In My Own Hand Writing': Jefferson Addresses the Slaveholder of Monticello," *Rhetoric and Public Affairs* 1, no. 3 (Fall 1998): 399.

12. Jefferson, *Notes*.

13. Annette Gordon-Reed, *Thomas Jefferson and Sally Hemings: An American Controversy* (Charlottesville: University of Virginia Press, 1997), 139.

14. The citation for all quotations taken from Banneker's letter to Jefferson can be found here: "From Thomas Jefferson to Benjamin Banneker, 30 August 1791," *Founders Online*, National Archives, https://founders.archives.gov/documents/Jefferson/01-22-02-0091. [Original source: *The Papers of Thomas Jefferson*, vol. 22, *6 August 1791–31 December 1791*, ed. Charles T. Cullen (Princeton: Princeton University Press, 1986), 98–99.]

15. See Renee C. Romano and Claire Bond Potter's (eds.), *Historians on Hamilton: How a Blockbuster Musical Is Restaging America's Past* (New Brunswick, NJ: Rutgers University Press, 2018), 287.

16. William Loughton Smith, *The Pretensions of Thomas Jefferson to the Presidency Examined; and the Charges against John Adams Refuted*, 1796, 10, https://archive.org/details/pretensionsofthooosmitrich/page/10.

17. Quoted in *The Papers of Thomas Jefferson*, vol. 22, *August 1791 to December 1791*, ed. Charles T. Cullen (Princeton: Princeton University Press, 1986), 54.

18. Marie Jean de Caritat, "Reflections on Negro Slavery," in *The French Revolution and Human Rights: A Brief Documentary History*, ed. and trans. Lynn Hunt (Boston: Bedford, 1996), 55–57.

19. "From Thomas Jefferson to Condorcet, 30 August 1791," *Founders Online*, National Archives, https://founders.archives.gov/documents/Jefferson/01-22-02-0091. [Original source: *The Papers of Thomas Jefferson*, vol. 22, *6 August 1791–31 December 1791*, ed. Charles T. Cullen (Princeton: Princeton University Press, 1986), 98–99.]

20. "From Thomas Jefferson to Benjamin Banneker, 30 August 1791," *Founders Online*, National Archives, https://founders.archives.gov/documents/Jefferson/01-22-02-0091. [Original source: *The Papers of Thomas Jefferson*, vol. 22, *6 August 1791–31 December 1791*, ed. Charles T. Cullen (Princeton: Princeton University Press, 1986), 97–98.]

21. William F. Buckley Jr., "Why the South Must Prevail," *National Review*, August 24, 1957.

22. Thomas Jefferson, *Jefferson: Writings* (New York: The Library of America, 1984), 1202.

23. Ibid.

24. "From Thomas Jefferson to Joel Barlow, 8 October 1809," *Founders Online*, National Archives, https://founders.archives.gov/documents/Jefferson/03-01-02-0461. [Original source: *The Papers of Thomas Jefferson*, vol. 1, *4 March 1809–15 November 1809*, ed. Charles T. Cullen (Princeton: Princeton University Press, 1986), 588–590.]

25. Ibid.

26. Ibid.

27. See Silvio A. Bedini, *The Life of Benjamin Banneker: The Definitive Biography of the First Black Man of Science* (Rancho Cordova, CA: Landmark Enterprises, 1972), 158.
28. Ibid., 177.
29. Ibid., 182.
30. Ibid., 188.
31. Ibid., 190.
32. Quoted in Angela G. Ray, "'In My Own Hand Writing': Jefferson Addresses the Slaveholder of Monticello," *Rhetoric and Public Affairs* 1, no. 3 (Fall 1998): 387.
33. "From Thomas Jefferson to Brissot de Warville, 11 February 1788," *Founders Online*, National Archives, https://founders.archives.gov/documents/Jefferson/01-12-02-0612. [Original source: *The Papers of Thomas Jefferson*, vol. 12, *7 August 1787–31 March 1788*, ed. Julian P. Boyd (Princeton: Princeton University Press, 1955), 557–577.]

Chapter 2

1. David W. Blight, *Frederick Douglass: Prophet of Freedom* (New York: Simon & Schuster, 2018), 437.
2. Eric Foner, *Reconstruction: America's Unfinished Revolution, 1863–1877* (New York: Perennial Classics, 2002), 6.
3. Blight, *Frederick Douglass*, 436.
4. See John Stauffer, Zoe Trodd, and Celeste-Marie Bernier, *Picturing Frederick Douglass: An Illustrated Biography of the Nineteenth Century's Most Photographed American* (New York: W. W. Norton & Co., 2015).
5. Blight, *Frederick Douglass*, 138.
6. Ibid., 139.
7. See Harold Holzer, *Lincoln at Cooper Union: The Speech that Made Abraham Lincoln President* (New York: Simon & Schuster Paperbacks, 2004), 113.
8. David W. Blight, "City Intelligence: Hon. Abraham Lincoln in New York," *New York Times*, February 25, 1860.
9. David W. Blight, "New Estimate Raises Civil War Death Toll," *New York Times*, April 2, 2012.
10. David W. Blight, "Fred. Douglass on the Proclamation," *New York Times*, February 7, 1863.
11. Louis P. Masur, *Lincoln's Hundred Days: The Emancipation Proclamation and the War for the Union* (Cambridge: Harvard University Press, 2012), 220.
12. Frederick Douglass *The Portable Frederick Douglass*, ed. John Stauffer and Henry Louis Gates Jr. (New York: Penguin Books, 2016), 458. Note that the italics are in the original.
13. Ibid., 460.

14. Ronald C. White Jr., *A. Lincoln: A Biography* (New York: Random House, 2010), 510.
15. Ibid., 511.
16. Blight, *Frederick Douglass*, 402.
17. My account of Douglass's meetings in Washington on August 10, 1863, are taken from Douglass's August 12, 1863, letter to his friend George Stearns, unless otherwise noted. Frederick Douglass, *Frederick Douglass Papers*, Series 3, *Correspondence*, vol. 2, Douglass letter to Major George L. Stearns, August 12, 1863 (New Haven: Yale University Press, 2018), 416–420.
18. Blight, *Frederick Douglass*, 407.
19. Blight, *Frederick Douglass*, 408.
20. William S. McFeely, *Frederick Douglass* (New York: W. W. Norton & Co., 1991), 229.
21. Frederick Douglass, *Frederick Douglass Papers*, Series 3, *Correspondence*. vol. 2: Douglass letter to Major George L. Stearns, August 12, 1863 John R. Kaufman McKivigan (New Haven: Yale University Press, 2018), 418.
22. Ibid.
23. James Oakes, *The Radical and the Republican: Frederick Douglass, Abraham Lincoln, and the Triumph of Antislavery Politics* (New York: W.W. Norton & Co., 2007), 213.
24. Frederick Douglass, *Selected Speeches and Writings*, ed. Philip Foner and Yuval Taylor (Chicago: Lawrence Hill Books, 2000), 551.
25. "Frederick Douglass letter to William Lloyd Garrison, September 17, 1864." In Douglass, *Selected Speeches and Writings*, 569.
26. See Sidney M. Milkis and Daniel J. Tichenor, *Rivalry and Reform: Presidents, Social Movements, and the Transformation of American Politics* (Chicago: University of Chicago Press, 2019).
27. My account and quotations are taken from Frederick Douglass, *The Complete Works of Frederick Douglass* (New York: Madison and Adams Press, 2018).
28. Blight, *Frederick Douglass*, 438.
29. Russell Freedman, *Abraham Lincoln and Frederick Douglass: The Story Behind an American Friendship* (New York: Clarion Books, 2012), 92.
30. "Frederick Douglass letter to Abraham Lincoln, August 29, 1864," Abraham Lincoln Papers, Series 1, *General Correspondence. 1833 to 1916: Frederick Douglass to Abraham Lincoln, Plan for helping slaves escape from rebel states. 1864.* Manuscript/mixed material. https://www.loc.gov/item/mal3565200/.
31. White, Jr., *A. Lincoln: A Biography*, 638.
32. Frederick Douglass, *The Frederick Douglass Papers*, Series 2: *Autobiographical Writings*, Vol. 3, *Life and Times of Frederick Douglass* (New Haven: Yale University Press, 2012), 281.

33. Ronald C. White, Jr., *Lincoln's Greatest Speech: The Second Inaugural* (New York: Simon & Schuster, 2002), 162.

34. Thomas Jefferson, *Writings* (New York: Library of America, 1984), 289.

35. Douglass, *Narrative of the Life of Frederick Douglass*, 101.

36. Douglass, *Life and Times*, 441.

37. Blight, *Frederick Douglass*, 458.

38. All quotations that reference Douglass's recollections of his experience at the Inaugural Address and reception are from *The Life and Times of Frederick Douglass* unless otherwise stated. See Frederick Douglass, *The Life and Times of Frederick Douglass: 1817–1882*, ed. John Bright (London: Christian Age Office, 1882), 319.

39. Ibid., 320.

40. For Douglass's account of Douglass at the second inaugural address, see Frederick Douglass, *The Frederick Douglass Papers*, Series 2, *Autobiographical Writings*, Vol. 3, *Life and Times of Frederick Douglass* (New Haven: Yale University Press, 2012), 285–287.

41. An online version of the letter can be found here: http://www.digitalhist ory.uh.edu/exhibits/douglass_exhibit/transcript.html. Accessed December 27, 2021.

42. James Oakes, *The Radical and the Republican: Frederick Douglass, Abraham Lincoln, and the Triumph of antislavery Politics* (New York: W. W. Norton & Co., 2007), 255.

43. My coverage of Douglass's oration is taken from the address found online here: https://edan.si.edu/transcription/pdf_files/12955. Accessed December 27, 2021.

44. Blight, *Frederick Douglass*, 462.

Chapter 3

1. Harold Bloom (ed.), *W. E. B. Du Bois* (New York: Chelsea House, 2001), 7.

2. David Levering Lewis, 1993. *W. E. B. Du Bois: Biography of a Race, 1868–1919* (New York: Henry Holt and Company, 1993), 80.

3. The invitation is housed at the University of Massachusetts–Amherst Special Collections Library (W. E. B. Du Bois Papers), and can be viewed online. "William James Letter to W. E. B. Du Bois, February 9, 1891," http://credo.library.umass.edu/view/pageturn/mums312-b003-i123/#page/1/mode/1up.

4. Bloom, *W. E. B. Du Bois*, 8.

5. W. E. B. Du Bois, *The Souls of Black Folk* (New York: W. W. Norton & Co., 1999), 3.

6. Christopher Ingraham, "Three-Quarters of Whites Don't Have Any Non-white Friends," *Washington Post*, August 25, 2014.

7. W. E. B. Du Bois, *The Souls of Black Folk* (New York: W. W. Norton & Co., 1999), 70.

8. W. E. B. Du Bois, *Dusk of Dawn* (Oxford: Oxford University Press, 2007), 19.

9. Ibid., 17.

10. W. E. B. Du Bois, Philosophy IV notebook, ca. 1889, W. E. B. Du Bois Papers (MS 312), Special Collections and University Archives, University of Massachusetts Amherst Libraries.

11. Du Bois, *Dusk of Dawn*, 20.

12. Dorothy Herrmann, *Helen Keller: A Life* (Chicago: University of Chicago Press, 1998), 363.

13. Robert D. Richardson, *William James in the Maelstrom of American Modernism* (New York: Mariner Books, 2006), 321.

14. Kim Townsend, *Manhood at Harvard: William James and Others* (New York: W. W. Norton & Company, 1996), 148.

15. Ibid., 17.

16. Richardson, *William James in the Maelstrom*, 189.

17. Alford A. Young, Jr., Jerry G. Watts, Manning Marable, Charles Lemert, and Elizabeth Higginbotham, *Souls of W. E. B. Du Bois* (New York: Routledge, 2006), 15.

18. See Peele's *Get Out* (2017) and *Us* (2019).

19. William James, "The Hidden Self," *Scribner's* (March, 1890): 361–373.

20. Du Bois, *Souls*, 11.

21. Martin Raitiere, *The Complicity of Friends, How George Eliot, G. H. Lewes, and John Hughlings-Jackson Encoded Herbert Spencer's Secret* (Lewisburg, PA: Bucknell University, Press, 2012), 185.

22. Dickson D. Bruce, Jr. "W. E. B. Du Bois and the Idea of Double Consciousness." *American Literature* 64, no. 2 (1992): 299–309.

23. James, "The Hidden Self," 369.

24. Ibid., 371.

25. Bruce, "W. E. B. Du Bois," 300.

26. Alexander Livingston, *Damn Great Empires! William James and the Politics of Pragmatism* (Oxford: Oxford University Press, 2016), 145.

27. W. E. B. Du Bois, "Strivings of the Negro People," *The Atlantic* (August 1897): 194-198. https://www.theatlantic.com/magazine/archive/1897/08/strivings-of-the-negro-people/305446/.

28. Ibid.

29. Kwame Anthony Appiah, *Lines of Descent: W. E. B. Du Bois and the Emergence of Modern Identity* (Cambridge, MA: Harvard University Press, 2014), 54–57.

30. Kenneth Barkin, "W. E. B. Du Bois and the German, 1892-1894." *The Journal of African American History* 96, no. 1 (2011): 2.

31. Kenneth Barkin, "W. E. B. Du Bois' Love Affair with Imperial Germany." *German Studies Review*, vol. 28, no. 2, 2005, pp. 286. *JSTOR*, www.jstor.org/stable/30038150. Accessed 30 May 2020.

32. Ibid., 289.

33. Hamilton Beck, "W. E. B. Du Bois as a Study Abroad Student in Germany, 1892–1894," *Frontiers: The Interdisciplinary Journal of Study Abroad* 2, no. 1 (Fall 1996): 45–63.

34. David Levering Lewis, *W. E. B. Du Bois: The Fight for Equality and the American Century, 1919–1963* (New York: Henry Holt, 2000), 97.

35. John Pettegrew, *Brutes in Suits: Male Sensibility in America, 1890–1920* (Baltimore: Johns Hopkins University Press, 2007), 240–241.

36. Lewis, *W. E. B. Du Bois*, 14.

37. See Eddie S. Glaude Jr., "Tragedy and Moral Experience," in *Pragmatism and the Problem of Race*, ed. Bill E. Lawson and Donald F. Koch (Bloomington: Indiana University Press, 2004), 115.

38. Richardson, *William James in the Maelstrom*, 70.

39. William James, *The Letters of William James*, Vol. 1 (Boston: The Atlantic Monthly Press, 1920), 67.

40. Robert Lowell, "For the Union Dead," See https://www.poetryfoundat ion.org/poems/57035/for-the-union-dead.

41. See Harvey Cormier, "William James on Nation and Race," in *Pragmatism, Nation, and Race: Community in the Age of Empire*, ed. Chad Kauzer and Eduardo Mendieta (Bloomington: Indiana University Press, 2009), 143.

42. See Maria DeGuzmán, "Consolidating Anglo-American Imperial Identity Around the Spanish-American War (1898)," in *Race and the Production of Modern American Nationalism*, ed. Reynolds J. Scott-Childress (New York: Routledge, 1999), 111.

43. See Louis Menand, *The Metaphysical Club* (New York: Farrar, Straus, & Giroux) 2001.

44. Du Bois, *Dusk of Dawn*, 127.

45. Trygve Thronveit, *William James and the Quest for an Ethical Republic* (New York: Palgrave Macmillan, 2014), 130.

46. Gerald E. Myers, *William James: His Life and Thought* (New Haven: Yale University Press, 1986), 596.

47. I'm quoting the letter from Appiah's *Lines of Descent*, 169.

48. Quote on W. E. B. Du Bois from Henry James, *The American Scene*, 1953. W. E. B. Du Bois Papers (MS 312). Special Collections and University Archives, University of Massachusetts Amherst Libraries.

49. Menand, *The Metaphysical Club*, 115.

50. See Eugene Taylor, "Transcending the Veil: William James and W. E. B. Du Bois, 1888–1910," unpublished manuscript, Harvard Divinity School, 1979.

51. Taylor, "Transcending the Veil," 8.

52. Francis L. Broderick, "The Academic Training of W. E. B. Du Bois," *Journal of Negro Education* 27, no. 1 (Winter 1958): 15.

53. Taylor, "Transcending the Veil," 22.

54. Menand, *The Metaphysical Club*, 394.

55. "William James letter to Sarah Wyman Whitman, June 8, 1903," in James, *The Correspondence of William James*, 261.
56. Herbert Aptheker, ed., *The Correspondence of W. E. B. Du Bois*, Vol. 1, *Selections, 1877–1934* (Amherst: University of Massachusetts Press, 1973), 133.
57. "William James Dies," *New York Times*, August 27, 1910.
58. Du Bois, *Souls*, 1999, 3.

Chapter 4

1.   See Ira Katznelson, *Fear Itself: The New Deal and the Origins of Our Time* (New York: Liveright Publishing, 2013), 176.
2.   Kevin McMahon, *Reconsidering Roosevelt on Race: How the Presidency Paved the Path to Brown* (Chicago: University of Chicago Press, 2004), 176.
3.   Jill Watts, *The Black Cabinet: The Untold Story of African Americans and Politics during the Age of Roosevelt* (New York: Grove Press, 2020).
4.   Mary McLeod Bethune, letter to Eleanor Roosevelt, January 27, 1942. Franklin D. Roosevelt Presidential Library, Selected Digitized Correspondence of Eleanor Roosevelt, 1933–1945.
5.   Patricia Bell-Scott, *The Firebrand and the First Lady: Pauli Murray, Eleanor Roosevelt, and the Struggle for Social Justice* (New York: Knopf, 2016), 7.
6.   Ibid.
7.   Ashley N. Robertson, *Mary McLeod Bethune in Florida: Bringing Social Justice to the Sunshine State* (Charleston: The History Press, 2015), 18.
8.   Rebecca Tuuri, *Strategic Sisterhood: The National Council of Negro Women in the Black Freedom Struggle* (Chapel Hill: University of North Carolina Press, 2018), 15.
9.   Robert Dallek, *Franklin Roosevelt: A Political Life* (New York: Penguin Books, 2017), 215.
10. See Dallek, 214–217. Mitchell Lerner's excellent article in *Presidential Studies Quarterly* likewise provides compelling evidence toward this theory of Johnson's subsequent leadership on race. See Mitchell Lerner, "'To Be Shot At by the Whites and Dodged by the Negroes': Lyndon Johnson and the Texas NYA," *Presidential Studies Quarterly* 39, no. 2 (2009): 245–274, www.jstor.org/stable/41427359, accessed April 20, 2020.
11. Ilene Cooper, *Eleanor Roosevelt: Fighter for Justice: Her Impact on the Civil Rights Movement, the White House, and the World* (New York: Harry N. Abrams, 2018), 102.
12. Eleanor Roosevelt, "Some of My Best Friends Are Negro," *Ebony*, November 1960, 73.
13. Doris Kearns Goodwin, *No Ordinary Time: Franklin and Eleanor Roosevelt: The Home Front in World War II* (New York: Simon & Schuster, 1994), 162.
14. Blanche Wiesen Cook, *Eleanor Roosevelt: The War Years and After*, Volume 3, *1939–1962* (New York: Penguin Books, 2016), 2.

15. Eleanor Roosevelt, *The Autobiography of Eleanor Roosevelt* (New York: Harper Perennial, 1989), 31.

16. Joyce A. Hanson, *Mary McLeod Bethune and Black Women's Political Activism* (Columbia: University of Missouri Press, 2003), 34.

17. Audrey Thomas McCluskey and Elaine M. Smith (eds.), *Mary McLeod Bethune: Building a Better World; Essays and Selected Documents* (Bloomington: Indiana University Press, 2001), 12, 14.

18. MMB letter to ER, July 10, 1941. File 100, Eleanor Roosevelt Papers, Franklin D. Roosevelt Library, Hyde Park, NY. As included in McCluskey and Smith, 240–241.

19. Katznelson, *Fear Itself*, 186.

20. Gary Younge, *The Speech: The Story Behind Dr. Martin Luther King, Jr.'s Dream* (Chicago: Haymarket Books, 2013), 59.

21. Mary McLeod Bethune, letter to Eleanor Roosevelt, February 18, 1943. Franklin D. Roosevelt Presidential Library, Selected Digitized Correspondence of Eleanor Roosevelt, 1933–1945.

22. Hanson, *Mary McLeod Bethune*, 158.

23. Memo from Marvin McIntyre to Aubrey Williams, December 10, 1938. McIntyre's comments were penciled in on this memo. Cited in Hanson, 158.

24. William E. Leuchtenburg: *Franklin D. Roosevelt and the New Deal, 1932–1940* (New York: Harper & Row, 1963), 187.

25. Christopher E. Linsin, "Something More than a Creed: Mary McLeod Bethune's Aim of Integrated Autonomy as Director of Negro Affairs." *The Florida Historical Quarterly* 76, no. 1 (1997): 20–41, www.jstor.org/stable/30148938, 29.

26. Mary McLeod Bethune, letter to FDR, November 27, 1939. Mary McLeod Bethune Papers, Mary McLeod Bethune Foundation. Bethune-Cookman College, Daytona, Florida. Cited in McCluskey and Smith, *Mary McLeod Bethune*, 237.

27. B. Joyce Ross, "Mary McLeod Bethune and the National Youth Administration: A Case Study of Power Relationships in the Black Cabinet of Franklin D. Roosevelt." *Journal of Negro History* 60, no. 1 (1975): 1–28, www.jstor.org/stable/2716791, accessed April 24, 2020.

28. See Jill Watts, *The Black Cabinet*.

29. Charles P. Henry, *Ralph Bunche: Model Negro or American Other?* (New York: New York University Press, 2004), 130.

30. Watts, *The Black Cabinet*, 188.

31. Bell-Scott, *Firebrand*, 25.

32. John Egerton, *Speak Now Against the Day: The Generation before the Civil Rights Movement in the South* (New York: Alfred A. Knopf, 1994), 292.

33. Bell-Scott, *Firebrand*, 25.

34. The case is covered extensively in Bell-Scott, 67–71.

35. Richard B. Sherman, *The Case of Odell Waller and Virginia Justice, 1940–1942* (Knoxville: University of Tennessee Press, 1992), 161.

36. A. Phillip Randolph, letter to Mary McLeod Bethune, June 22, 1942. Franklin D. Roosevelt Presidential Library, Selected Digitized Correspondence of Eleanor Roosevelt, 1933–1945.

37. Bell-Scott, *Firebrand*, 73–74.

38. Ibid., 73.

39. Ibid., 90–91.

40. Dallek, *Franklin Roosevelt*, 472.

41. Mary McLeod Bethune, letter to Franklin D. Roosevelt, June 4, 1940. Cited in McCluskey and Smith, *Mary McLeod Bethune*, 173.

42. Ibid., 174.

43. Eleanor Roosevelt, letter to Mary McLeod Bethune, April 10, 1942. Franklin D. Roosevelt Presidential Library, Selected Digitized Correspondence of Eleanor Roosevelt, 1933–1945. The proposal and its heading can be found attached to Eleanor's response.

44. See Christopher E. Linsin for a discussion of Bethune's political ideology contextualized within black political thought. Christopher E. Linsin, "Something More than a Creed: Mary McLeod Bethune's Aim of Integrated Autonomy as Director of Negro Affairs." *Florida Historical Quarterly* 76, no. 1 (1997): 20–41, www.jstor.org/stable/30148938, accessed April 26, 2020.

45. Mary McLeod Bethune, letter to Miss Malvina Thompson, August 29, 1942. Franklin D. Roosevelt Presidential Library, Selected Digitized Correspondence of Eleanor Roosevelt, 1933–1945.

46. Ibid.

47. Bell-Scott, *Firebrand*, 80.

48. Ibid., 80–81.

49. Walter W. Harris, letter to Mary McLeod Bethune, June 17, 1944. Franklin D. Roosevelt Presidential Library, Selected Digitized Correspondence of Eleanor Roosevelt, 1933–1945.

50. An Act for the Relief of Mrs. Yoneko Nakazawa, January 26, 1948, United States Statutes at Large, 1948, Vol. 62, Part 2. (Washington, DC: US Government Printing Office, 1949), 1301.

51. Eleanor Roosevelt, Memorandum to the President, July 21, 1943. Franklin D. Roosevelt Presidential Library, Selected Digitized Correspondence of Eleanor Roosevelt, 1933–1945.

52. Mary McLeod Bethune, letter to Eleanor Roosevelt, July 6, 1943. Franklin D. Roosevelt Presidential Library, Selected Digitized Correspondence of Eleanor Roosevelt, 1933–1945.

53. Hanson, *Mary McLeod Bethune*, 209.

54. Malvina Thompson, letter to Mary McLeod Bethune, November 8, 1943. Franklin D. Roosevelt Presidential Library, Selected Digitized Correspondence of Eleanor Roosevelt, 1933–1945.

55. Eleanor Roosevelt, letter to Mary McLeod Bethune, December 20, 1943. Franklin D. Roosevelt Presidential Library, Selected Digitized Correspondence of Eleanor Roosevelt, 1933-1945.

56. Mary McLeod Bethune, letter to Eleanor Roosevelt, October 9, 1944. Franklin D. Roosevelt Presidential Library, Selected Digitized Correspondence of Eleanor Roosevelt, 1933–1945.

57. Robertson, *Mary McLeod Bethune in Florida*, 43.

58. Tuuri, *Strategic Sisterhood*, 179.

59. McCluskey and Smith, *Mary McLeod Bethune*, 251.

60. Hanson, *Mary McLeod Bethune*, 187.

61. Eleanor Roosevelt, "My Day," May 3, 1952. *The Eleanor Roosevelt Papers Digital Edition* (2017), accessed 27 April 2020, https://www2.gwu.edu/~erpapers/myday/displaydoc.cfm?_y=1952&_f=md002212.

62. "Seek Aid for Negro Girls," *New York Times*, January 23, 1915.

63. "Mrs. Bethune's Daytona School a 'Civilizer,'" *New York Times*, March 5, 1916.

64. Ibid.

65. "Mary Bethune, 79, Educator, Is Dead," *New York Times*, May 19, 1955.

66. McCluskey and Smith, *Mary McLeod Bethune*, 14–15.

67. Eleanor Roosevelt, "My Day," May 20, 1955. *The Eleanor Roosevelt Papers Digital Edition* (2017), accessed 27 April 2020, https://www2.gwu.edu/~erpapers/myday/displaydocedits.cfm?_y=1955&_f=md003174.

Chapter 5

1. Ralph Ellison, letter to Stanley Hyman, July 15, 1942, in Stanley Edgar Hyman Papers, Box 6, Folder 30, Manuscript/Mixed Material, Library of Congress, Washington, DC.

2. Arnold Rampersad, *Ralph Ellison: A Biography* (New York: Alfred A. Knopf, 2007), 156.

3. Rampersad, 93. Ruth Franklin, *Shirley Jackson: A Rather Haunted Life* (New York: W. W. Norton & Co., 2016), 84–89.

4. Ralph Ellison, letter to Stanley Hyman, August 16, 1948, in Stanley Edgar Hyman Papers, Box 6, Folder 30, Manuscript/Mixed Material, Library of Congress, Washington, DC.

5. Franklin, *Shirley Jackson*, 181.

6. Ibid., 139.

7. Elliot E. Cohen, letter to Stanley Hyman, June 1, 1949, in Stanley Edgar Hyman Papers, Box 6, Folder 3, Manuscript/Mixed Material, Library of Congress, Washington, DC. See also Norman Podheretz's letter to Hyman, May 1, 1956 (on the problem of Jewish identity), in Stanley Edgar Hyman Papers, Box 6, Folder 3, Manuscript/Mixed Material, Library of Congress, Washington, DC.

8. Bryan Crable, *Ralph Ellison and Kenneth Burke: At the Roots of the Racial Divide* (Charlottesville: University of Virginia Press, 2012), 51.

9. Ralph Ellison, letter to Stanley Hyman, July 15, 1942, in Stanley Edgar Hyman Papers, Box 6, Folder 30, Manuscript/Mixed Material. Library of Congress, Washington, DC.

10. Norman Podhoretz, letter to Stanley Hyman, March 3, 1958, in Stanley Edgar Hyman Papers, Box 6, Folder 3, Manuscript/Mixed Material, Library of Congress, Washington, DC.
11. Rampersad, *Ralph Ellison*, 96–97.
12. Crable, *Ralph Ellison and Kenneth Burke*, 52.
13. Rampersad, *Ralph Ellison*, 156.
14. Letter to Kenneth Burke, November 23, 1945, in John F. Callahan (ed.), *The Selected Letters of Ralph Ellison* (New York: Random House, 2019), 204.
15. Letter to Stanley Hyman, August 13, 1948, in Callahan, 259.
16. Rampersad, *Ralph Ellison*, 164.
17. Franklin, *Shirley Jackson*, 316.
18. Rampersad, *Ralph Ellison*, 233.
19. Ralph Ellison, letter to Stanley Hyman, September 16, 1946, in Stanley Edgar Hyman Papers, Box 6, Folder 30, Manuscript/Mixed Material, Library of Congress, Washington, DC.
20. Franklin, *Shirley Jackson*, 159.
21. Letter to Stanley Hyman, September 18, 1945, in Callahan, *Selected Letters*, 201.
22. Crable, *Ralph Ellison and Kenneth Burke*, 60.
23. Rampersad, *Ralph Ellison*, 233–234.
24. Ralph Ellison, letter to Stanley Hyman, in Callahan, *Selected Letters*, 225.
25. Ibid., 226.
26. Franklin, *Shirley Jackson*, 221–222.
27. "The Literary Roots of Apocalypse Now," *New York Times*, October 21, 1979.
28. Franklin, *Shirley Jackson*, 224.
29. Ralph Ellison, letter to Stanley Hyman, August 13, 1948, in Callahan, 261.
30. Ralph Ellison, *Invisible Man* (New York: Vintage, 1995), 20.
31. Franklin, *Shirley Jackson*, 222–223.
32. For my discussion of "The Lottery," see Shirley Jackson, *The Lottery and Other Stories* (New York: Farrar, Strauss and Giroux, 2005), 291–302.
33. Franklin, *Shirley Jackson*, 236.
34. Ibid., 249.
35. Ralph Ellison, letter to Stanley Hyman, March 10, 1961, in Callahan, 596.
36. Ralph Ellison, letter to Stanley Hyman, February 21, 1949, in Stanley Edgar Hyman Papers, Box 6, Folder 30, Manuscript/Mixed Material. Library of Congress, Washington, DC.
37. Ralph Ellison, letter to Albert Murray, June 6, 1951, in Callahan, 292.
38. Rampersad, *Ralph Ellison*, 258.
39. Ibid., 403.
40. See F. B. Eyes, Digital Archive: FBI Files on African American Authors and Literary Institutions Obtained through the Freedom of Information Act. http://omeka.wustl.edu/omeka/files/original/31681825a4cd67ee1d980 566dd5fc7ad.pdf.

41. Rampersad, *Ralph Ellison*, 419.

42. Ibid., 367.

43. Ralph Ellison, letter to Stanley Hyman, September 16, 1945, in Callahan, 202.

44. Marjorie Nicholson, invitation to Mrs. Jackson, July 24, 1959, in Stanley Edgar Hyman Papers, Box 6, Folder 1, Manuscript/Mixed Material, Library of Congress, Washington, DC.

45. Franklin, *Shirley Jackson*, 297.

46. Shirley Jackson, dietary notes, meals, October 7–10 (undated). Shirley Jackson Papers, Box 51, Miscellany, 1938–1966. Library of Congress, Washington, DC.

47. Stanley Edgar Hyman, "Richard Wright Reappraised," *The Atlantic Monthly*, March 1970.

48. My discussion of Ellison's last letter to Hyman is referenced here. Ralph Ellison, letter to Stanley Hyman, May 29, 1970, in Callahan, 676–684.

49. Ibid., 477.

50. "Ralph Ellison, The Art of Fiction, No. 8," *Paris Review* 8 (Spring 1955). https://www.theparisreview.org/interviews/5053/the-art-of-fiction-no-8-ralph-ellison

Chapter 6

1. My discussion and quotations from this letter are referenced here. James Baldwin Papers, James Baldwin letter to Marlon Brando, undated. Schomburg Center for Research in Black Culture. New York Public Library Archives and Manuscripts. Correspondence, Box 3a, Folder 8.

2. See David Leeming, *James Baldwin: A Biography* (New York: Arcade Publishing, 2015), 238, 241; and James Campbell, *Talking at the Gates: A Life of James Baldwin* (Berkeley: University of California Press, 1991), 126, 151, 155, 253.

3. William J. Maxwell, *James Baldwin: The FBI File* (New York: Arcade Publishing, 2017), 323.

4. Dramatic Workshop Repertory Information Book, New School Archives and Special Collections, New School for Social Research, New School Development and Public Relations Office Records, NS.03.02.02, Box 1.

5. See Nico Chilla, "The Centennial: A Fact Check," *The New School Free Press*, February 21, 2019.

6. See James Baldwin, "Marlon Brando," in Roddy McDowall's *Double Exposure* (New York: William Morrow and Company, Inc., 1990), 216.

7. *Hector's* was later memorialized in Jack Kerouac's *On the Road*.

8. Marlon Brando (with Robert Lindsey), *Brando: Songs My Mother Taught Me* (New York: Random House, 1994), 63.

9. Susan L. Mizruchi, *Brando's Smile: His Life, Thought, and Work* (New York: W. W. Norton & Company, 2014), 35.

10. Leeming, *James Baldwin*, 46.

11. Darwin Porter, *Brando Unzipped: Bad Boy, Megastar, Sexual Outlaw* (New York: Blood Moon Productions, 2006), 11. Porter's first meeting

account places Hector's Cafeteria in the Village at 4th Street and Seventh Avenue.

12. See David Marchese, "Quincy Jones: The Music Legend on the Secret Michael Jackson, His Relationship with the Trumps, and the Problem with Modern Pop" (online interview), *Vulture*, In Conversation, February 7, 2018, https://www.vulture.com/2018/02/quincy-jones-in-conversation.html.

13. Quoted in Lawrie Balfour, *The Evidence of Things Not Said: James Baldwin and the Promise of American Democracy* (Ithaca, NY: Cornell University Press, 2001), 51.

14. Ibid., 52.

15. See Grissom's online blog: http://jamesgrissom.blogspot.com/2015/01/marlon-brando-on-james-baldwin-what-was.html.

16. Mizruchi, *Brando's Smile*, 35.

17. For treatment of Baldwin's father, see Leeming, *James Baldwin* , 1–8.

18. Brando, *Songs My Mother Taught Me*, 7.

19. William Mann, *The Contender: The Story of Marlon Brando* (New York: HarperCollins, 2019), 167.

20. Quoted in Douglas Field (ed.), *A Historical Guide to James Baldwin* (Oxford: Oxford University Press, 2009), 31.

21. Leeming, *James Baldwin*, 44.

22. McDowall, *Double Exposure*, 216.

23. Porter, *Brando Unzipped*, 10.

24. Mann, *The Contender*, 167.

25. Brando, *Songs My Mother Taught Me*, 64, 65.

26. Mizruchi, *Brando's Smile*, 331.

27. Ibid.

28. W. J. Weatherby, *James Baldwin: Artist on Fire: A Portrait* (New York: Donald I. Fine, Inc., 1989), 94.

29. See Campbell, *Talking at the Gates*, 80.

30. Weatherby, *James Baldwin*, 96.

31. Ibid., 97.

32. James Baldwin, *No Name in the Street* (New York: Vintage International, 2000), 141–142.

33. James Baldwin, *Another Country* (New York: The Dial Press, 1962).

34. Baldwin, *No Name in the Street*, 141.

35. David Margolick, *The Promise and the Dream: The Untold Story of Martin Luther King, Jr. and Robert F. Kennedy* (New York: Rosetta Books, 2018), 181.

36. Ibid., 140.

37. As David Leeming has written, Baldwin "suspected the question of Rustin's alleged homosexuality may have had something to do" with efforts to oust Rustin from any involvement with the March on Washington. See Leeming, *James Baldwin*, 228.

38. Campbell, *Talking at the Gates*, 175.
39. Ibid.
40. Weatherby, *James Baldwin*, 230.
41. Leeming, *James Baldwin*, 228.
42. Malcolm X, *Malcolm X Speaks: Selected Speeches and Statements*, ed. George Breitman (New York: Grove Press, 1965), 16.
43. There remains some debate about how Heston came on board. See Emilie Raymond, *Stars for Freedom: Hollywood, Black Celebrities, and the Civil Rights Movement* (Seattle: University of Washington Press, 2015), 125.
44. Mann, *The Contender*, 478.
45. Margolick, *The Promise and the Dream*, 144.
46. Brando, *Songs My Mother Taught Me*, 298.
47. Sarah Lyall, "David Schoenbrun Is Dead at 73," *New York Times*, May 24, 1988.
48. https://www.archives.gov/research/foreign-policy/related-records/rg-306.
49. Joel Whitney, *Finks: How the CIA Tricked the World's Best Writers* (New York: OR Books, 2016), 109.
50. Ibid..
51. My discussion of the Hollywood Round Table is taken from this official National Archives online document: https://www.youtube.com/watch?v=1u27coFlGXg.
52. Poitier and Belafonte's parents were born in the Bahamas and Jamaica, respectively. Poitier retained his Bahamian citizenship, although he was born in Miami while his parents were visiting the United States.
53. Gary Younge, *The Speech: The Story Behind Dr. Martin Luther King, Jr.'s Dream* (Chicago: Haymarket Books, 2013).
54. Mizruchi, *Brando's Smile*, 334.
55. Brando, *Songs My Mother Taught Me*, 295.
56. Whitney, *Finks*, 126.
57. "Hollywood Roundtable," *The Unwritten Record* (blog), September 21, 2012, National Archives, https://unwritten-record.blogs.archives.gov/2012/09/21/hollywood-roundtable/.
58. Campbell, *Talking at the Gates*, 253.
59. Leeming, *James Baldwin*, 298.
60. Mizruchi, *Brando's Smile*, 336.
61. Ibid., 335–336.
62. Mann, *The Contender*, 9.
63. McDowall, *Double Exposure*, 216.

Chapter 7

1. Helaine Silverman and D. Fairchild Ruggles (eds.), *Cultural Heritage and Human Rights* (New York: Springer, 2007), 108.
2. Mark Bailey, *Of All the Gin Joints: Stumbling through Hollywood History* (Chapel Hill, NC: Algonquin Books, 2014), 191.

3. See https://www.knkx.org/post/how-marilyn-monroe-changed-ella-fitz
geralds-life; http://www.openculture.com/2017/10/how-marilyn-monroe-
helped-break-ella-fitzgerald-into-the-big-time-1955.html#:~:text=How%20
Marilyn%20Monroe%20Helped%20Break,Into%20the%20Big%20T
ime%20(1955)&text=%22She%20personally%20called%20the%20ow
ner,%2C%20front%20table%2C%20every%20night; https://immortal-
beauties.com/2019/05/17/ella-fitzgerald-was-actually-launched-by-mari
lyn-monroe/; https://worldofwonder.net/that-time-marilyn-monroe-came-
to-the-rescue-of-ella-fitzgerald/#:~:text=In%201947%2C%20Ella%20Fit
zgerald%20joined,the%20venues%20on%20the%20tour; and https://www.
iloveoldschoolmusic.com/many-never-knew-marilyn-monroe-surprisin
gly-risked-whole-career-ella-fitzgerald/#:~:text=Many%20Never%20K
new%20Marilyn%20Monroe%20Surprisingly%20Risked%20Her%20Wh
ole%20Career%20For%20Ella%20Fitzgerald,-Posted%20On%20%3A%20J
uly&text=Via%20MuseyOn%2D%20The%20Mocambo%20nightclub,Fit
zgerald%20because%20she%20was%20Black, respectively.

4. See Gwendolyn Du Bois Shaw, *Seeing the Unspeakable: The Art of Kara
Walker* (Durham, NC: Duke University Press, 2004), 93–97.

5. The photo is even the basis for a new illustrated children's book by Vivian
Kirkfield, *Making Their Voices Heard: The Inspiring Friendship of Ella
Fitzgerald and Marilyn Monroe* (New York: Little Bee Books, 2020).

6. https://www.gettyimages.com/photos/marilyn-monroe-ella-fitzgerald?fam
ily=editorial&phrase=marilyn%20monroe%20ella%20fitzgerald&sort=
mostpopular#license.

7. Stuart Nicholson, *Ella Fitzgerald: A Biography of the First Lady of Jazz*
(New York: Da Capo Press, 1993), 149.

8. Cited in Gary Vitacco-Robles, *The Life and Times of Marilyn Monroe*, vol.
1, *1926–1956* (Albany, GA: Bear Mountain Media, 2015), 419–420.

9. See April Vevea, *Marilyn Monroe: A Day in the Life* (Scotts Valley,
CA: CreateSpace Independent Publishing Platform, 2016).

10. https://www.julienslive.com/view-auctions/catalog/id/180/lot/
83136/?url=%2Fview-auctions%2Fcatalog%2Fid%2F180%2F%3Fp
age%3D1%26key%3Della%2Bfitzgerald%26cat%3D%26xclosed%3Dno.

11. Michelle Morgan, *Marilyn Monroe: Private and Undisclosed*
(New York: Carroll and Graf, 2007), 165.

12. Ibid.

13. Mark Geoffrey, interview with Paul Lisnek, April 27, 2018, https://wgnra
dio.com/wgn-plus/paul-lisnek-behind-the-curtain/paul-lisneks-behind-
the-curtain-up-and-coming-second-city-performers-talk-chill-vibes-in-a-
nuclear-war-a-new-definitive-bio-of-the-legendary-ella-fitzgerald-with-aut
hor-geoffrey-mark/.

14. Mark Geoffrey, *Ella: A Biography of the Legendary Ella Fitzgerald*
(New York: Ultimate Symbol, 2018), 190.

15. See Annette Gordon-Reed, *The Hemings of Monticello: An American
Family* (New York: W. W. Norton & Co.), 2009.

16. See Francis D. Cogliano, *Thomas Jefferson: Reputation and Legacy* (Charlottesville: University of Virginia Press, 2008), 171–173.

17. "The Election of 1800," *The Atlantic Monthly* 32 (1873): 27–28.

18. Margaret L. Hunter, *Race, Gender, and the Politics of Skin Tone* (New York: Routledge, 2005), 120.

19. Richard Dyer, *Heavenly Bodies: Film Stars and Society* (New York: Routledge, 2004), 40.

20. J. Randy Taraborrelli, *The Secret Life of Marilyn Monroe* (New York: Grand Central Publishing, 2009), 343.

21. Nicholson, *Ella Fitzgerald*, 4.

22. Ibid., 14–15.

23. Ibid., 21.

24. "Gillespie Gives Concert: Features Ella Fitzgerald with Band at Carnegie Hall," *New York Times*, September 30, 1947.

25. Sonny Rollins, quoted in Nicholson, *Ella Fitzgerald*, 92.

26. Ibid., 2.

27. Ibid., 36.

28. Margo Jefferson, "Ella in Wonderland," *New York Times*, December 29, 1996.

29. See Nicholson, *Ella Fitzgerald*, 47, 131.

30. Ibid., 50

31. Ibid., 57, 146.

32. Taraborrelli, *The Secret Life*, 323.

33. Ibid., 24.

34. Ibid., 323.

35. Lois Banner, *Marilyn: The Passion and the Paradox* (New York: Bloomsbury, 2012), 13.

36. Ibid., 254.

37. Ibid., 254.

38. Ibid., 255.

39. Never mind that Miller would face his own challenges as a purported communist sympathizer during the House Un-American Committee (HUAC) hearings of the 1950s (ibid., 255).

40. Taraborrelli, *The Secret Life*, 130.

41. Ralph Ellison, *Invisible Man* (New York: Vintage International, 1995), 186.

42. Banner, *Marilyn*, 256.

43. Taraborrelli, *The Secret Life*, 220.

44. Morgan, *Marilyn Monroe*, 164.

45. See Vivian Kirkfield, *Making Their Voices Heard: The Inspiring Friendship of Ella Fitzgerald and Marilyn Monroe* (New York: Little Bee Books, 2020) and Tamra B. Orr, *Famous Friends: True Tales of Friendship, Ella Fitzgerald and Marilyn Monroe* (Kennett Square, PA: Purple Toad Publishing, 2020).

46. "Marilyn and Ella: The Meeting of the Misfits," *Independent*, February 13, 2008. https://www.independent.co.uk/arts-entertainment/theatre-dance/features/marilyn-and-ella-the-meeting-of-the-misfits-781442.html.

47. "Talent Topics," *Billboard*, March 12, 1955, 24.

48. "Ella Fitzgerald a Big Hit," *Jet*, April 7, 1955.

49. Taraborrelli, *The Secret Life*, 313. Taraborrelli's only reference to Monroe attending a Fitzgerald performance is for a San Francisco appearance Ella made in 1960, 357.

50. Nicholson, *Ella Fitzgerald*, 149.

51. Ibid.

52. Ibid.

53. See Judith Butler, *Bodies that Matter: On the Discursive Limits of Sex* (New York: Routledge, 2011), 128.

54. Banner, *Marilyn*, 227.

55. Taraborrelli, *The Secret Life*, 470.

56. Nicholson, *Ella Fitzgerald*, 243.

Chapter 8

1. Author's telephone interview with Dr. Clarence B. Jones, August 7, 2020, 11:30 a.m. (52 minutes).

2. Edward K. Kaplan, *Abraham Joshua Heschel: Mind, Heart, Soul* (Lincoln: University of Nebraska Press, 2019), 318.

3. Taylor Branch, *Pillar of Fire: America in the King Years, 1963–1965* (New York: Simon & Schuster, 1998), 21.

4. Author's telephone interview with Rev. Richard Fernandez, August 12, 2020, 9:00 a.m. (55 minutes).

5. Abraham Heschel, *Abraham Joshua Heschel: Essential Writings*, ed. Susannah Heschel (New York: Orbis Books, 2019), 65–75.

6. Branch, *Pillar of Fire*, 31.

7. Lewis Baldwin, *The Voice of Conscience: The Church in the Mind of Martin Luther King, Jr.* (Oxford: Oxford University Press, 2010), 179.

8. Leo Strauss, "Jerusalem and Athens: Some Introductory Reflections," *Commentary*, June 1967, https://www.commentarymagazine.com/articles/leo-strauss/jerusalem-and-athens-some-introductory-reflections/.

9. Kaplan, *Abraham Joshua Heschel: Mind, Heart, Soul*, 3.

10. Heschel, *Abraham Joshua Heschel: Essential Writings*, 19.

11. Quoted in Kaplan, *Abraham Joshua Heschel: Mind, Heart, Soul*, 10.

12. Abraham Joshua Heschel, *God in Search of Man: A Philosophy of Judaism* (New York: Farrar, Straus and Giroux, 1983), 369.

13. Ibid., 345.

14. Robert D. McFadden, "Rabbi Abraham Joshua Heschel Dead," *New York Times*, December 24, 1972.

15. As recounted by Dr. Susannah Heschel: "Following in my father's footsteps: Selma 40 years later," https://blogs.library.duke.edu/rub

enstein/2015/01/14/jewish-voices-selma-montgomery-march/#:~:text=
%E2%80%9CFor%20many%20of%20us%20the,words%2C%20our%20ma
rch%20was%20worship.

16.   Taylor Branch, *Parting the Waters: America in the King Years, 1954–1963*
        (New York: Simon & Schuster, 1988), 27.

17.   See Stephen Oates, *Let the Trumpet Sound: A Life of Martin Luther King,
        Jr.* (New York: Harper Perennial, 1994), 16.

18.   E. Franklin Frazier, *Black Bourgeoisie: The Rise of a New Middle Class in
        the United States* (Glencoe, IL: The Free Press, 1957).

19.   In order, the letters are: Lucius M. Tobin to Charles E. Batten, February
        25, 1948; Benjamin E. Mays to Charles E. Batten, February 28, 1948; and
        George D. Kelsey to Charles E. Batten, March 12, 1948, in *The Papers
        of Martin Luther King, Jr.*, Vol. 1, *Called to Service, January 1929–June
        1951*, ed. Clayborne Carson, Ralph E. Luker and Penny A. Russell
        (Berkeley: University of California Press, 1992), 151, 152, 155.

20.   Branch, *Parting the Waters*, 90.

21.   James H. Cone, *Malcolm & Martin & America: A Dream or a Nightmare*
        (New York: Orbis Books, 1991), 33.

22.   Author's telephone interview with Rev. Richard Fernandez, August 12,
        2020, 9:00 a.m. (55 minutes).

23.   Branch, *Parting the Waters*, 142.

24.   W. E. B. Du Bois, *The Souls of Black Folk* (Oxford: Oxford University
        Press, 2007), 39.

25.   Ibid.

26.   The Martin Luther King, Jr. Research and Education Institute, Stanford
        University. MIA Mass Meeting at Holt Street Baptist Church. For text,
        see https://kinginstitute.stanford.edu/king-papers/documents/mia-mass-
        meeting-holt-street-baptist-church.

27.   Heschel, *Abraham Joshua Heschel: Essential Writings*, 66.

28.   Kaplan, *Abraham Joshua Heschel: Mind, Heart, Soul*, 242.

29.   Ibid., 136. Agudat Israel's role in organizing the protest: author's email
        exchange with Dr. Susannah Heschel, September 2, 2020.

30.   John F. Kennedy Presidential Library and Museum, transcript of
        Commencement Address at American University, Washington, DC, June
        10, 1963, https://www.jfklibrary.org/archives/other-resources/john-f-kenn
        edy-speeches/american-university-19630610.

31.   Ibid.

32.   John F. Kennedy Presidential Library and Museum, transcript of
        Televised Address to the Nation on Civil Rights, June 11, 1963, https://
        www.jfklibrary.org/learn/about-jfk/historic-speeches/televised-address-to-
        the-nation-on-civil-rights.

33.   Heschel, *Abraham Joshua Heschel: Essential Writings*, 64–65.

34.   Susannah Heschel notes that Andrew Young offered one possible reason
        to her: the goal was to invite the heads of major organizations—hence

they invited the head of the American Jewish Congress, Rabbi Joachim Prinz, to represent the Jewish community. Author's email exchange with Dr. Heschel, September 2, 2020.

35. Author's telephone interview with Dr. Clarence B. Jones, August 7, 2020 (52 minutes).

36. Susannah Heschel, "Two Friends, Two Prophets: Abraham Joshua Heschel and Martin Luther King, Jr., *Plough Quarterly*, May 9, 2018. https://www.plough.com/en/topics/community/leadership/two-friends-two-prophets.

37. Branch, *Pillar of Fire*, 143–144.

38. Telephone conversation, President Lyndon Johnson, Martin Luther King Jr., November 25, 1963, 9:20 p.m. Lyndon Baines Johnson Presidential Library, https://millercenter.org/the-presidency/educational-resources/lbj-and-mlk

39. Sidney M. Milkis and Daniel J. Tichenor, *Rivalry and Reform: Presidents, Social Movements, and the Transformation of American Politics* (Chicago: University of Chicago Press, 2019), 157.

40. Susannah Heschel, "Two Friends, Two Prophets."

41. Kaplan, *Abraham Joshua Heschel: Mind, Heart, Soul*, 242–243.

42. Ibid., 243.

43. Taylor Branch, *At Canaan's Edge: America in the King Years, 1965–1968* (New York: Simon & Schuster, 2006), 140, 145.

44. Edward K. Kaplan, *Spiritual Radical: Abraham Joshua Heschel in America, 1940–1972* (New Haven: Yale University Press, 2007), 222.

45. Author's telephone interview with Dr. Clarence B. Jones, Friday, August 7, 2020, 11:30 a.m. (52 minutes).

46. Clarence Jones and Stuart Connelly, *Behind the Dream: The Making of the Speech That Transformed a Nation* (New York: Palgrave, 2012), 108–109.

47. Author's telephone interview with Dr. Clarence B. Jones, August 7, 2020, 11:30 a.m. (52 minutes).

48. Ibid.

49. National Archives, Vietnam War U.S. Military Fatal Casualty Statistics, https://www.archives.gov/research/military/vietnam-war/casualty-statistics. Accessed December 27, 2021.

50. Fernandez's memory is impressive. The total deaths suffered in Vietnam by Philadelphia's Thomas Alva Edison High School is 64. Author's telephone interview with Rev. Richard Fernandez, August 12, 2020, 9:00 a.m. (55 minutes). "This Philly High School Lost 64 Grads in Vietnam," *Philadelphia Inquirer*, November 9, 2018, https://www.inquirer.com/philly/columnists/ronnie_polaneczky/veterans-day-edison-high-school-vietnam-war-killed-in-action-20181109.html.

51. Branch, *At Canaan's Edge*, 577.

52. Ibid., 586.

53. Kaplan, *Abraham Joshua Heschel: Mind, Heart, Soul*, 295. The actual line in *The Prophets* is "Above all, the prophets remind us of the moral state of a people: Few are guilty, but all are responsible"; Abraham Joshua Heschel, *The Prophets* (New York: HarperCollins, 1962), 19.

54. Author's telephone interview with Rev. Richard Fernandez, August 12, 2020, 9:00 a.m. (55 minutes).

55. Heschel, *Abraham Joshua Heschel: Essential Writings*, 36.

56. Author's telephone interview with Dr. Clarence B. Jones, August 7, 2020, 11:30 a.m. (52 minutes).

57. Paul Harvey and Philip Goff (eds.), *The Columbia University Documentary History of Religion in America Since 1945* (New York: Columbia University Press, 2006)274.

58. Branch, *At Canaan's Edge*, 586.

59. Ibid., 603.

60. Author's telephone interview with Dr. Clarence B. Jones, August 7, 2020, 11:30 a.m. (52 minutes).

61. Author's telephone interview with Rev. Richard Fernandez, August 12, 2020, 9:00 a.m. (55 minutes).

62. Ibid.

63. Ibid.

64. Martin Luther King Jr., *A Time to Break Silence: The Essential Works of Martin Luther King, Jr. for Students* (Boston: Beacon Press, 1994), 80.

65. Ibid., 82.

66. Author's telephone interview with Dr. Clarence B. Jones, August 7, 2020, 11:30 a.m. (52 minutes).

67. King, *A Time to Break Silence*, 92–93.

68. The Martin Luther King, Jr. Research and Education Institute, Stanford University, "Beyond Vietnam." For text, see https://kinginstitute.stanford.edu/king-papers/documents/beyond-vietnam.

69. Kaplan, *Abraham Joshua Heschel: Mind, Heart, Soul*, 303.

70. Branch, *At Canaan's Edge*, 621.

71. Susannah Heschel, "The Challenge of the Selma Photograph." For more on Tepper, see Clive Webb, *Fight against Fear: Southern Jews and Black Civil Rights* (Athens: University of Georgia, 2001), 117, https://www.truah.org/wp-content/uploads/2019/11/Challenge-of-Selma-photo.pdf.

72. James Baldwin, "Negroes Are Anti-Semitic Because They're Anti-White," *New York Times*, April 9, 1967.

73. Author's telephone interview with Rev. Richard Fernandez, August 12, 2020, 9:00 a.m. (55 minutes).

Chapter 9

1. "Observer," *New York Times*, November 16, 1963. https://timesmachine.nytimes.com/timesmachine/1963/11/16/issue.html

2. *Angela Davis: An Autobiography* (New York: International Publishers, 1988), 79.

3. Ibid., 130.
4. Condoleezza Rice, *Extraordinary, Ordinary People: A Memoir of Family* (New York: Crown Publishing, 2010), 93–94.
5. Davis, *Autobiography*, 124.
6. Ibid., 134–135.
7. "Angela Davis on Protest, 1968, and Her Old Teacher, Herbert Marcuse," *Literary Hub*, April 3, 2019, https://lithub.com/angela-davis-on-protest-1968-and-her-old-teacher-herbert-marcuse/.
8. Charles L. Sanders, "The Radicalization of Angela Davis," *Ebony* (July, 1971): 114–118.
9. Davis, *Autobiography*, 144–145.
10. Davis met Carmichael at a London conference where both he and Marcuse spoke. Davis was hopeful that Carmichael would begin to broaden his views of white people upon his return from a scheduled trip to Cuba; ibid., 150–151. See also Joseph Peniel, *Stokely: A Life* (New York: Basic Civitas Books, 2014), 198.
11. Joy James, *Shadowboxing: Representations of Black Feminist Politics* (New York: Palgrave, 2002), 108.
12. Jane Kramer, "Road Warrior," *The New Yorker*, October 15, 2015.
13. Gloria Steinem, *Gloria Steinem: My Life on the Road* (New York: Random House, 2016), 10–11.
14. Jane Kramer, "Road Warrior," *The New Yorker*, October 15, 2015.
15. Patricia Cronin Marcello, *Gloria Steinem: A Biography* (Westport, CT: Greenwood Press, 2004), 33.
16. Carolyn G. Heilbrun, *Education of a Woman: The Life of Gloria Steinem* (New York: Ballantine Books, 1995), 148.
17. Ibid.
18. Steinem, *My Life on the Road*, 31.
19. Ibid., 36.
20. Steinem, *My Life on the Road*, dedication.
21. Gloria Steinem, "A Bunny's Tale: Show's First Exposé for Intelligent People," *Show*, May, 1963, https://manoff703.files.wordpress.com/2014/10/show-a-bunnys-tale-part-one-may-19632.pdf.
22. Ibid.
23. Jane Kramer, "Road Warrior," *The New Yorker*, October 15, 2015.
24. Gloria Steinem, "After Black Power, Women's Liberation," *New York*, April 1969, https://jwa.org/sites/default/files/jwa067a.pdf.
25. Ibid.
26. Kimberlé Crenshaw, "Demarginalizing the Intersection of Race and Sex: A Black Feminist Critique of Antidiscrimination Doctrine, Feminist Theory and Antiracist Politics," *University of Chicago Legal Forum* 1989, no. 1, Article 8, https://chicagounbound.uchicago.edu/cgi/viewcontent.cgi?article=1052&context=uclf.
27. Jane Kramer, "Road Warrior," *The New Yorker*, October 15, 2015.

28. Marcello, *Gloria Steinem: A Biography*, 122.
29. Bettina Aptheker, *The Morning Breaks: Trial of Angela Davis* (Ithaca: Cornell University Press, 1999), 63.
30. Ibid.
31. Young Americans such as Alice Walker, who would later befriend both Davis and Steinem, were in attendance. Walker did not recall meeting either at Helsinki. See Deborah G. Plant, *Alice Walker: A Woman for Our Times* (Santa Barbara: Praeger, 2017), 29.
32. Joni Krekola and Simo Mikkonen, "Backlash of the Free World: The US Presence at the World Youth Festival in Helsinki, 1962," *Scandinavian Journal of History* 36, no. 2 (2011): 230–255, DOI: https://doi.org/10.1080/03468755.2011.565566.
33. "CIA Subsidized Federal Trips," *New York Times*, February 21, 1967.
34. Robert G. Kaiser, "Work of CIA with Youths at Festivals Is Defended," *Washington Post*, February 18, 1967.
35. James, *Shadowboxing*, 90.
36. Earl Caldwell, "Angela Davis Found Not Guilty by White Jury on All Charges," *New York Times*, June 5, 1972.
37. James, *Shadowboxing*, 91.
38. Kum-Kum Bhavnani and Angela Y. Davis, "Complexity, Activism, Optimism: An Interview with Angela Y. Davis," *Feminist Review* 31 (Spring, 1989: The Past before Us: Twenty Years of Feminism): 66–81, https://doi.org/10.2307/1395091.
39. Steinem, *My Life on the Road*, 47.
40. National Portrait Gallery, Smithsonian Institution, Washington, DC, https://npg.si.edu/object/npg_NPG.2005.121.
41. https://www.prnewswire.com/news-releases/re-enacted-portrait-of-gloria-steinem-and-dorothy-pitman-hughes-in-iconic-1971-pose-of-female-empowerment-and-equal-rights-taken-by-daniel-bagan-accepted-into-smithsonian-national-portrait-gallery-collection-300537740.html.
42. Violet Zhang (Sally Nixon, illustrator), *Bosom Buddies: A Celebration of Female Friendships throughout History* (San Francisco: Chronicle Books, 2018), 88–89.
43. Barbara Winslow, *Shirley Chisholm: Catalyst for Change* (New York: Westview Press, 2014), 116.
44. Ibid., 115.
45. Ibid.
46. Beth Potier, "Abolish Prisons, Says Angela Davis, " *Harvard Gazette*, March 13, 2003, https://news.harvard.edu/gazette/story/2003/03/abolish-prisons-says-angela-davis/.
47. Steinem, *My Life on the Road*, 235.
48. See, for example, Peter Noel, "Mumia's Last Stand," *Village Voice*, November 9, 1999, https://www.villagevoice.com/1999/11/09/mumias-last-stand/.

49. Lily Workneh, "Angela Davis and Gloria Steinem on the Power of Revolutionary Movements," *Huffington Post*, June 3, 2016, https://www. huffpost.com/entry/angela-davis-gloria-steinem-power-of-revolutionary-movements_n_57511492e4b0eb20fa0d900c?guccounter=1&guce_referrer=aHR0cHM6Ly93d3cuZ29vZ2xlLmNvbS88&guce_referrer_sig=AQAA AFVcbPmsVYRoF52SEzS-_5CM6VezbQMK87xD_61XJ2yVHRkW8iM C9II9vlIuJXYw9g6hOQfyZO7YqoQSk26r77mZW7EWV61iaY81Ckc-K0aaY7Zd4hMqOB06UVRvSZbxfKU5V8sXNYOpbCRT9-NIlshTxi5Ry E4XgMlDSD4zYAJW.

50. Rosanna Ryan, "US Election: Activist Angela Davis Warns Donald Trump Paving Way for Fascist Movement," ABC Radio National, October 20, 2016.

51. Gloria Steinem, "Feminists and the Clinton Question," *New York Times*, March 22, 1998.

52. "Amid Division, "A March in Washington Seeks to Bring Women Together," *New York Times*, November 18, 2016.

53. Jane Junn, "Hiding in Plain Sight: White Women Vote Republican," *Politics of Color*, November 13, 2016, http://politicsofcolor.com/white-women-vote-republican/.

54. Amanda Hess, "How a Fractious Women's Movement Came to Lead the Left," *New York Times*, February 7, 2017.

55. Ibid.

56. Jia Tolentino, "The Somehow Controversial Women's March on Washington," *New Yorker*, January 18, 2017.

57. Laurie Collier Hillstrom, *The #Me Too Movement* (Santa Barbara: ABC-CLIO, 2019), 47.

58. All quotations and references to the Women's March on Washington are cited from ABC News' streaming of the event and *Elle* magazine's transcription, https://www.youtube.com/watch?v=rp1FyjB8WXQ; https://www.elle.com/culture/career-politics/a42337/angela-davis-womens-march-speech-full-transcript/.

59. Roy S. Johnson, "Dr. Angela Davis to Accept Once-Rescinded Fred L. Shuttlesworth Award," Birmingham Real-Time News, August 29, 2019, https://www.al.com/news/birmingham/2019/08/dr-angela-davis-to-accept-once-rescinded-fred-l-shuttleworth-award.html

60. Quoted in Stacey Tisdale, "Gloria Steinem on Black Women: 'They Invented the Feminist Movement,'" *Black Enterprise*, March 19, 2015, https://www.blackenterprise.com/be-womens-history-month-feminist-icon-gloria-steinem-talks-black-women-feminism/.

Chapter 10

1. See Stokely Carmichael and Charles V. Hamilton, *Black Power: The Politics of Liberation in America* (New York: Random House, 1967). Citation fromStokely Carmichael and Charles V. Hamilton, "'The Myths

of Coalition' from *Black Power: The Politics of Liberation in America*," *Race/Ethnicity: Multidisciplinary Global Contexts* 1, no. 2 (2008): 171–188, accessed July 19, 2021, http://www.jstor.org/stable/25594984.

2. Peter Carlson, "Vernon Jordan, the Quicker Fixer-Upper," *Washington Post*, January 24, 1998.

3. Jill Abramson, "For Jordan, Lewinsky Matter Tests a Friendship," *New York Times*, February 22, 1998.

4. Pew Research Center, "Public Opinion on Race Relations, 1990–2016," https://www.pewresearch.org/interactives/public-opinion-on-race-relations-1990-2016/.

5. Elisabeth Bumiller, *Condoleezza Rice: An American Life* (New York: Random House, 2009), 127.

6. Laura Kipnis, "Condi's Freudian Slip," *Slate*, April 26, 2004. https://slate.com/culture/2004/04/condi-s-alleged-freudian-slip.html. Accessed December 27, 2021.

7. Jodi Kantor, "Obama's Friends Form Strategy to Stay Close," *New York Times*, December 13, 2008.

8. Evan Osnos, *Joe Biden: The Life, the Run, and What Matters Now* (New York: Scribner, 2020), 1–2.

9. Joe Biden, *Promises to Keep* (New York: Random House, 2007), 79.

10. Osnos, *Joe Biden*, 31.

11. Sarah Jones, "Joe Biden Should Retire the Phrase, 'Dignity of Work,'" *Intelligencer*, May 1, 2019, https://nymag.com/intelligencer/2019/05/joe-biden-should-retire-the-phrase-dignity-of-work.html.

12. Osnos, *Joe Biden*, 35.

13. Massimo Faggioli, *Joe Biden and Catholicism in the United States* (New London: Bayard, Inc., 2021), 126.

14. Steven Levingston, *Barack and Joe: The Making of an Extraordinary Partnership* (New York: Hachette Books, 2019), 18.

15. Osnos, *Joe Biden*, 47.

16. Arendt's paper was "Home to Roost," read on May 20, 1975, at Boston's Faneuil Hall; see Osnos, 43–44.

17. National Health Statistics Report, 2013, Center for Disease Control (CDC), https://www.cdc.gov/nchs/data/nhsr/nhsr071.pdf.

18. See the text of the June 15, 2008, address at https://www.politico.com/story/2008/06/text-of-obamas-fatherhood-speech-011094.

19. See an annotated version of the Report here: https://www.theatlantic.com/politics/archive/2015/09/the-moynihan-report-an-annotated-edition/404632/. See also "Moynihan's Anti-Feminism," in *Jacobin* magazine: https://www.jacobinmag.com/2015/07/moynihans-report-fiftieth-anniversary-black-family/.

20. Barack Obama, *Dreams from My Father* (New York: Broadway Paperbacks, 2004), 8–9.

21. David Garrow, *Rising Star: The Making of Barack Obama* (New York: HarperCollins, 2017).

22.   Carlos Lozada, "Before Michelle, Obama Asked Another Woman to Marry Him. Then Politics Got in the Way," *Washington Post*, May 2, 2017, https://www.washingtonpost.com/news/book-party/wp/2017/05/02/before-michelle-barack-obama-asked-another-woman-to-marry-him-then-politics-got-in-the-way/.

23.   Obama, *Dreams*, 5.

24.   Obama, *Dreams*, 12.

25.   Levingston, *Barack and Joe*, 231.

26.   Michael Fletcher, "The Speech on Race That Saved Obama's Candidacy," *Washington Post*, April 22, 2016.

27.   John M. Broder, "The Great Seal of Obamaland?," *New York Times*, June 20, 2008.

28.   Levingston, *Barack and Joe*, 183–184.

29.   See Christopher S. Parker and Matt A. Barreto, *Change They Can't Believe In: The Tea Party and Reactionary Politics in America* (Princeton: Princeton University Press, 2013).

30.   Levingston, *Barack and Joe*, 40.

31.   Ibid., 40.

32.   Ibid., 24.

33.   Barack Obama, *A Promised Land* (New York: Crown, 2020), 434.

34.   Levingston, *Barack and Joe*, 194.

35.   Osnos, *Joe Biden*, 72.

36.   Donna M. Owens, "Jim Clyburn Changed Everything for Joe Biden's Campaign," *Washington Post*, April 1, 2020.

37.   Levingston, *Barack and Joe*, 254.

38.   Leonard Greene, "Trump Called for Death Penalty after Central Park Jogger Attack," *Daily News*, July 19, 2018.

39.   Caitlin O'Kane, "Trump Says He's the 'Least Racist Person in the Room.' Biden Says He's 'One of the Most Racist Presidents,'" CBS News, October 23, 2020, https://www.cbsnews.com/news/trump-biden-racism-debate/.

40.   Linda Qiu, "Trump's False Claim that 'Nobody Has Ever Done' More for the Black Community than He Has," *New York Times*, June 5, 2020.

41.   Nick Corasaniti, "'Look at My African-American over Here,' Trump Says at Rally," *New York Times*, June 3, 2016.

42.   Kathleen Parker, "Trump Can't Fake Love of 'the Blacks,'" *Washington Post*, August 30, 2016.

43.   "Joe Biden Writes about 'Restoring the Soul of Our Nation,'" NPR, Morning Edition, December 31, 2019, https://www.npr.org/2019/12/31/792545353/joe-biden-writes-about-restoring-the-soul-of-our-nation.

44.   Alex Thompson, "'The President Was Not Encouraging': What Obama Really Thought about Biden," Politico, August 14, 2020, https://www.politico.com/news/magazine/2020/08/14/obama-biden-relationship-393570.

45. See Marc Hetherington, "The Election: The More Things Change," in
     The Elections of 2020, ed. Michael Nelson (Charlottesville: University of
     Virginia Press, 2021), 75.

46. Andrew L. Yarrow, "Biden Has White Men to Thank For Putting Him in
     the White House," *USA Today*, November 29, 2020, https://www.usato
     day.com/story/opinion/2020/11/29/how-biden-needs-handle-his-new-
     voter-base-white-males-column/6347523002/.

REFERENCES

Allen, Danielle S. *Talking to Strangers: Anxieties of Citizenship Since Brown v. Board of Education.* Chicago: University of Chicago Press, 2004.

Appiah, Kwame Anthony. *Lines of Descent: W. E. B. Du Bois and the Emergence of Modern Identity.* Cambridge: Harvard University Press, 2014.

Aptheker, Bettina. *The Morning Breaks: Trial of Angela Davis.* Ithaca: Cornell University Press, 1999.

Aptheker, Herbert, ed. *The Correspondence of W. E. B. Du Bois.* Vol. 1: *Selections, 1877–1934.* Amherst: University of Massachusetts Press. 1973.

Bailey, Mark. *Of All the Gin Joints: Stumbling through Hollywood History.* Chapel Hill, NC: Algonquin Books, 2014.

Baldwin, Lewis. *The Voice of Conscience: The Church in the Mind of Martin Luther King, Jr.* Oxford: Oxford University Press, 2010.

Balfour, Lawrie. *The Evidence of Things Not Said: James Baldwin and the Promise of American Democracy.* Ithaca: Cornell University Press, 2001.

Banner, Lois. *Marilyn: The Passion and the Paradox.* New York: Bloomsbury, 2012.

Bedini, Silvio A. *The Life of Benjamin Banneker: The Definitive Biography of the First Black Man of Science.* Rancho Cordova, CA: Landmark Enterprises, 1972.

Bell-Scott, Patricia. *The Firebrand and the First Lady: Pauli Murray, Eleanor Roosevelt, and the Struggle for Social Justice.* New York: Knopf, 2016.

Benhabib, Seyla, ed. *Democracy and Difference: Contesting the Boundaries of the Political.* Princeton: Princeton University Press, 1996.

Biden, Joe. *Promises to Keep.* New York: Random House, 2007.

Blight, David W. *Frederick Douglass: Prophet of Freedom*. New York: Simon & Schuster, 2018.

Bloom, Harold, ed. *W. E. B. Du Bois*. New York: Chelsea House, 2001.

Branch, Taylor. *At Canaan's Edge: America in the King Years, 1965–1968*. New York: Simon & Schuster, 2006.Branch, Taylor. *Parting the Waters: America in the King Years, 1954–1963*. New York: Simon & Schuster, 1988.

Branch, Taylor. *Pillar of Fire: America in the King Years, 1963–1965*. New York: Simon & Schuster, 1998.

Brando, Marlon. *Brando: Songs My Mother Taught Me*. New York: Random House, 1994.

Bright, John (ed.). *The Life and Times of Frederick Douglass: 1817–1882*. London: Christian Age Office, *1882*.

Butler, Judith. *Bodies That Matter: On the Discursive Limits of Sex*. New York: Routledge, 2011.

Callahan, John F., ed. *The Selected Letters of Ralph Ellison*. New York: Random House, 2019.

Campbell, James. *Talking at the Gates: A Life of James Baldwin*. Berkeley: University of California Press, 1991.

Carmichael, Stokely, and Charles V. Hamilton. *Black Power: The Politics of Liberation in America*. New York: Random House, 1967.

Carson, Clayborne, Luker, Ralph E., and Penny A. Russell, eds. *The Papers of Martin Luther King, Jr.*, Vol. 1, *Called to Service, January 1929–June 1951*. Berkeley: University of California Press, 1992.

Cooper, Ilene. *Eleanor Roosevelt: Fighter for Justice: Her Impact on the Civil Rights Movement, the White House, and the World*. New York: Harry N. Abrams, 2018.

Crable, Bryan. *Ellison and Kenneth Burke: At the Roots of the Racial Divide*. Charlottesville: University of Virginia Press, 2012.

Dallek, Robert. *Franklin Roosevelt: A Political Life*. New York: Penguin Books, 2017.

Davis, Angela. *Angela Davis: An Autobiography*. New York: International Publishers, 1988.

Douglass, Frederick. *Frederick Douglass Papers*, Series 2: *Autobiographical Writings*. Vol. 3: *Life and Times of Frederick Douglass*. New Haven: Yale University Press, 2012.

Douglass, Frederick. *Frederick Douglass Papers*. Series 3: Correspondence. Vol. 2: *Douglass letter to Major George L. Stearns, August 12, 1863*. New Haven: Yale University Press, 2018.

Douglass, Frederick. *The Portable Frederick Douglass*, ed. John Stauffer and Henry Louis Gates, Jr. New York: Penguin Books, 2016.

Du Bois, W. E. B. *Dusk of Dawn*. Oxford: Oxford University Press, 2007.

Du Bois, W. E. B. *The Souls of Black Folk*. New York: W. W. Norton & Co., 1999.

Du Bois, W. E. B. *The Souls of Black Folk*. Oxford: Oxford University Press, 2007.

Du Bois, W. E. B. *The Souls of Black Folk*. Oxford: Oxford University Press, 2007.

Dyer, Richard. *Heavenly Bodies: Film Stars and Society*. New York: Routledge, 2004.

Egerton, John. *Speak Now against the Day: The Generation Before the Civil Rights Movement in the South*. New York: Alfred A. Knopf, 1994.

Ellison, Ralph. *Invisible Man*. New York: Vintage Books, 1995. Ellison, Ralph. *Invisible Man*. New York: Vintage International, 1995.

Faggioli, Massimo. *Joe Biden and Catholicism in the United States*. New London: Bayard, Inc., 2021.

Field, Douglas, ed. *A Historical Guide to James Baldwin*. Oxford: Oxford University Press, 2009.

Foner, Eric. *Reconstruction: America's Unfinished Revolution, 1863–1877*. New York: Perennial Classics, 2002.

Foner, Philip, and Yuval Taylor, eds. *Selected Speeches and Writings*. Chicago: Lawrence Hill Books, 2000.

Franklin, Ruth. *Shirley Jackson: A Rather Haunted Life*. New York: W. W. Norton & Co., 2016.

Frazier, E. Franklin. *Black Bourgeoisie: The Rise of a New Middle Class in the United States*. Glencoe, IL: The Free Press, 1957.

Garrow, David. *Rising Star: The Making of Barack Obama*. New York: HarperCollins, 2017.

Geoffrey, Mark. *Ella: A Biography of the Legendary Ella Fitzgerald*. New York: Ultimate Symbol, 2018.

Gilroy, Paul. *Postcolonial Melancholia*. New York: Columbia University Press, 2005.

Goodwin, Doris Kearns. *No Ordinary Time: Franklin and Eleanor Roosevelt: The Home Front in World War II*. New York: Simon & Schuster, 1994.

Gordon-Reed, Annette. *The Hemings of Monticello: An American Family*. New York: W. W. Norton & Co., 2009.

Gordon-Reed, Annette. *Thomas Jefferson and Sally Hemings: An American Controversy*. Charlottesville: University of Virginia Press, 1997.

Hanson, Joyce A. *Mary McLeod Bethune and Black Women's Political Activism*. Columbia: University of Missouri Press, 2003.

Harvey, Paul, and Philip Goff, eds. *The Columbia University Documentary History of Religion in America Since 1945*. New York: Columbia University Press, 2006.

Heilbrun, Carolyn G. *Education of a Woman: The Life of Gloria Steinem*. New York: Ballantine Books, 1995.

Henry, Charles P. *Ralph Bunche: Model Negro or American Other?* New York: New York University Press, 2004.

Herrmann, Dorothy. *Helen Keller: A Life*. Chicago: University of Chicago Press, 1998.

Heschel, Abraham. *Abraham Joshua Heschel: Essential Writings*, ed. Susannah Heschel. New York: Orbis Books, 2019.

Heschel, Abraham. *God in Search of Man: A Philosophy of Judaism.*
    New York: Farrar, Straus and Giroux, 1983.

Heschel, Abraham. *The Prophets.* New York: HarperCollins, 1962.

Holzer, Harold. *Lincoln at Cooper Union: The Speech that Made Abraham
    Lincoln President.* New York: Simon & Schuster Paperbacks, 2004.

Hunt, Lynn (ed.). The French Revolution and Human Rights: A Brief
    Documentary History. Boston: Bedford, 1996.

Hunter, Margaret L. *Race, Gender, and the Politics of Skin Tone.*
    New York: Routledge, 2005.

Jackson, Shirley. *The Lottery and Other Stories.* New York: Farrar, Strauss and
    Giroux, 2005.

James H. Cone, James H. *Malcolm & Martin & America: A Dream or a
    Nightmare.* New York: Orbis Books, 1991.

James, Joy. *Shadowboxing: Representations of Black Feminist Politics.*
    New York: Palgrave, 2002.

James, William. *The Correspondence of William James.* Vol. 10: *March
    1902--1905,* ed. Ignas K. Skrupskelis and Elizabeth M. Berkeley.
    Charlottesville: University Press of Virginia, 2002.

James, William. *The Letters of William James.* Vol. 1. Boston: The Atlantic
    Monthly Press, 1920.

Jefferson, Thomas. "Notes on Virginia." In *Thomas Jefferson: Writings,* ed.
    Merrill D. Peterson. New York: The Library of America, 1984.

Jefferson, Thomas. *The Papers of Thomas Jefferson,* ed. Charles T. Cullen. *Vol.
    19: January 1791 to March 1791.* Princeton: Princeton University Press, 1986.

Jefferson, Thomas. *Writings.* New York: Library of America, 1984.

Jones, Clarence, and Stuart Connelly. *Behind the Dream: The Making of the
    Speech That Transformed a Nation.* New York: Palgrave, 2012.

Joseph, Peniel. *Stokely: A Life.* New York: Basic Civitas Books, 2014.

Kaplan, Edward K. *Abraham Joshua Heschel: Mind, Heart, Soul.*
    Lincoln: University of Nebraska Press, 2019.

Kaplan, Edward K. *Spiritual Radical: Abraham Joshua Heschel in America, 1940–
    1972.* New Haven: Yale University Press, 2007.

Katznelson, Ira. *Fear Itself: The New Deal and the Origins of Our Time.* Liveright
    Publishing: New York, 2013.

Kauzer, Chad, and Eduardo Mendieta. *Pragmatism, Nation, and
    Race: Community in the Age of Empire.* Bloomington: Indiana University
    Press, 2009.

Kerouac, Jack. *On the Road.* New York: Penguin, 1999.

King, Martin Luther, Jr. *A Time to Break Silence: The Essential Works of Martin
    Luther King, Jr. for Students.* Boston: Beacon Press, 1994.

Kirkfield, Vivian. *Making Their Voices Heard: The Inspiring Friendship of Ella
    Fitzgerald and Marilyn Monroe.* New York: Little Bee Books, 2020.

Lawson, Bill E., and Donald F. Koch, eds., *Pragmatism and the Problem of Race.*
    Bloomington: Indiana University Press, 2004.

Leeming, David. *James Baldwin: A Biography*. New York: Arcade Publishing, 2015.

Levingston, Steven. *Barack and Joe: The Making of an Extraordinary Partnership*. New York: Hachette Books, 2019.

Lewis, David Levering. *W. E .B. Du Bois: The Fight for Equality and the American Century, 1919–1963*. New York: Henry Holt, 2000.

Lewis, David Levering. *W. E. B. Du Bois: Biography of a Race, 1868–1919*. New York: Henry Holt and Company, 1993.

Livingston, Alexander. *Damn Great Empires! William James and the Politics of Pragmatism*. Oxford: Oxford University Press, 2016.

Mann, William. *The Contender: The Story of Marlon Brando*. New York: HarperCollins, 2019.

Marcello Patricia Cronin. *Gloria Steinem: A Biography*. Westport, CT: Greenwood Press, 2004.

Margolick, David. *The Promise and the Dream: The Untold Story of Martin Luther King, Jr. and Robert F. Kennedy*. New York: Rosetta Books, 2018.

McCluskey, Audrey Thomas, and Elaine M. Smith, eds. *Mary McLeod Bethune: Building a Better World, Essays and Selected Documents*. Bloomington: Indiana University Press, 2001.

McDowall, Roddy. *Double Exposure*. New York: William Morrow and Company, Inc., 1990.

McFeely, William S. *Frederick Douglass*. New York: W. W. Norton & Co., 1991.

McWilliams, Wilson Carey. *The Idea of Fraternity in America*. Berkeley: University of California Press, 1973.

Menand, Louis. *The Metaphysical Club*. New York: Farrar, Straus, & Giroux, 2001.

Milkis, Sidney M., and Daniel J. Tichenor. *Rivalry and Reform: Presidents, Social Movements, and the Transformation of American Politics*. Chicago: University of Chicago Press, 2019.

Mizruchi, Susan L. *Brando's Smile: His Life, Thought, and Work*. New York: W. W. Norton & Company, 2014.

Morgan, Michelle. *Marilyn Monroe: Private and Undisclosed*. New York: Carroll and Graf, 2007.

Myers, Gerald E. *William James: His Life and Thought*. New Haven: Yale University Press, 1986.

Nelson, Michael, ed. *The Elections of 2020*. Charlottesville: University of Virginia Press, 2021.

Oakes, James. *The Radical and the Republican: Frederick Douglass, Abraham Lincoln, and the Triumph of Antislavery Politics*. New York: W. W. Norton & Co., 2007.

Oates, Stephen. *Let the Trumpet Sound: A Life of Martin Luther King, Jr*. New York: Harper Perennial, 1994.

Obama, Barack. *A Promised Land*. New York: Crown, 2020.

Obama, Barack. *Dreams from My Father*. New York: Broadway Paperbacks, 2004.

Orr, Tamra B. *Famous Friends: True Tales of Friendship, Ella Fitzgerald and Marilyn Monroe*. Kennett Square, PA: Purple Toad Publishing, 2020.

Osnos, Evan. *Joe Biden: The Life, the Run, and What Matters Now*. New York: Scribner, 2020.

Parker, Christopher S., and Matt A. Barreto. *Change They Can't Believe In: The Tea Party and Reactionary Politics in America*. Princeton: Princeton University Press, 2013.

Pettegrew, John. *Brutes in Suits: Male Sensibility in America, 1890–1920*. Baltimore: Johns Hopkins University Press, 2007.

Plant, Deborah G. *Alice Walker: A Woman for Our Times*. Santa Barbara: Praeger, 2017.

Porter, Darwin. *Brando Unzipped: Bad Boy, Megastar, Sexual Outlaw*. New York: Blood Moon Productions, 2006.

Raitiere, Martin. *The Complicity of Friends, How George Eliot, G. H. Lewes, and John Hughlings-Jackson Encoded Herbert Spencer's Secret*. Lewisburg, PA Bucknell University Press, 2012.

Rampersad, Arnold. *Ralph Ellison: A Biography*. New York: Alfred A. Knopf, 2007.

Raymond, Emilie. *Stars for Freedom: Hollywood, Black Celebrities, and the Civil Rights Movement*. Seattle: University of Washington Press, 2015.

Richardson, Robert D. *William James in the Maelstrom of American Modernism*. New York: Mariner Books, 2006.

Robertson, Ashley N. *Mary McLeod Bethune in Florida: Bringing Social Justice to the Sunshine State*. Charleston: The History Press, 2015.

Romano, Renee C., and Claire Bond Potter, eds. *Historians on Hamilton: How a Blockbuster Musical Is Restaging America's Past*. New Brunswick, NJ: Rutgers University Press, 2018.

Roosevelt, Eleanor. *The Autobiography of Eleanor Roosevelt*. New York: Harper Perennial, 1989.

Scott-Childress, Reynolds J. *Race and the Production of Modern American Nationalism*. New York: Routledge, 1999.

Shaw, Gwendolyn Du Bois. *Seeing the Unspeakable: The Art of Kara Walker*. Durham: Duke University Press, 2004.

Sherman, Richard B. *The Case of Odell Waller and Virginia Justice, 1940–1942*. Knoxville: University of Tennessee Press, 1992.

Silverman, Helaine, and D. Fairchild Ruggles, eds. *Cultural Heritage and Human Rights*. New York: Springer, 2007.

Smith, William Loughton. The Pretensions of Thomas Jefferson to the Presidency *Examined; and the Charges against John Adams, Refuted*. Surry Hills, Australia: Wentworth Press, 2016.

Stauffer, John, Zoe Trodd, and Celeste-Marie Bernier. *Picturing Frederick Douglass: An Illustrated Biography of the Nineteenth Century's Most Photographed American*. New York: W. W. Norton & Co., 2015.

Stauffer, John. *The Black Hearts of Men: Radical Abolitionists and the Transformation of Race*. Cambridge, MA: Harvard University Press, 2002.

Steinem, Gloria. *Gloria Steinem: My Life on the Road.* New York: Random House, 2016.

Taraborrelli, J. Randy. *The Secret Life of Marilyn Monroe.* New York: Grand Central Publishing, 2009.

Taylor, Eugene. "Transcending the Veil: William James and W. E. B. Du Bois, 1888–1910." Unpublished manuscript, Harvard Divinity School, 1979.

Thronveit, Trygve. *William James and the Quest for an Ethical Republic.* New York: Palgrave Macmillan, 2014.

Townsend, Kim, *Manhood at Harvard: William James and Others.* New York: W. W. Norton & Company, 1996.

Tuuri, Rebecca. *Strategic Sisterhood: The National Council of Negro Women in the Black Freedom Struggle.* Chapel Hill: University of North Carolina Press, 2018.

Twain, Mark. *The Adventures of Huckleberry Finn,* London, UK: Penguin, 2003.

Vevea, April. *Marilyn Monroe: A Day in the Life.* Scotts Valley, CA: CreateSpace Independent Publishing Platform, 2016.

Vitacco-Robles, Gary. *The Life and Times of Marilyn Monroe.* Vol. 1: *1926–1956.* Albany, GA: Bear Mountain Media, 2015.

Watts, Jill. *The Black Cabinet: The Untold Story of African Americans and Politics During the Age of Roosevelt.* New York: Grove Press, 2020.

Webb, Clive. *Fight against Fear: Southern Jews and Black Civil Rights.* Athens: University of Georgia, 2001.

White, Ronald C., Jr. A. *Lincoln: A Biography.* New York: Random House, 2010.

White, Ronald C., Jr. *Lincoln's Greatest Speech: The Second Inaugural.* New York: Simon & Schuster, 2002.

Whitney, Joel. *Finks: How the CIA Tricked the World's Best Writers.* New York: OR Books, 2016.

Wiesen Cook, Blanche. *Eleanor Roosevelt: The War Years and After.* Vol. 3: *1939–1962.* New York: Penguin Books, 2016.

Winslow, Barbara. *Shirley Chisholm: Catalyst for Change.* New York: Westview Press, 2014.

X, Malcolm. *Malcolm X Speaks: Selected Speeches and Statements,* ed. George Breitman. New York: Grove Press, 1965.

Young, Alford A., Jr., Jerry G. Watts, Manning Marable, Charles Lemert, and Elizabeth Higginbotham. *Souls of W. E. B. Du Bois.* New York: Routledge, 2006.

Younge, Gary. *The Speech: The Story Behind Dr. Martin Luther King, Jr.'s Dream.* Chicago: Haymarket Books, 2013.

INDEX

———≈◆◈◆≈———

For the benefit of digital users, indexed terms that span two pages (e.g., 52–53) may, on occasion, appear on only one of those pages.